大院君의 革新政治

THE RULE OF THE TAEWŎN'GUN

1864-1873

RESTORATION IN YI KOREA

Ching Young Choe

Harvard East Asian Monographs

HARVARD EAST ASIAN MONOGRAPHS

45

THE RULE OF THE TAEWŎN'GUN, 1864-1873

RESTORATION IN YI KOREA

THE RULE OF THE TAEWŎN'GUN, 1864-1873

Restoration in Yi Korea

by

Ching Young Choe

Published by
East Asian Research Center
Harvard University

Distributed by
Harvard University Press
Cambridge, Mass.
1972

Copyright, 1972, by
The President and Fellows of
Harvard College

The East Asian Research Center at Harvard University
administers research projects designed to further
scholarly understanding of China, Japan, Korea,
Vietnam, and adjacent areas. These studies have been
assisted by grants from the Ford Foundation.

Library of Congress No. 73-183975
SBN 674-78030-2

I dedicate this book to the memory of my parents.

I dedicate this book to the memory of my parents.

CONTENTS

TABLES

MAPS

FOREWORD

Dr. Ching Young Choe spent six years as a graduate student at Harvard;
and during the six years that remained to him after he received his doctorate,
he was able to develop his thesis into this book for publication. Setting out
to study the decade 1864-1873, before Japan's opening of Korea in 1876, he
first analyzed the old institutions of land holding, taxation, and military
service, their traditional evils and the consequent ideas of reform, and the
rise of social unrest evidenced in the Tonghak movement of the early 1860s.
In this context Dr. Choe then studied the conservative reform program of the
vigorous and embattled regent known to history as the Taewŏn'gun, whose
efforts to suppress rebellion, ward off foreign contact, and revive the old
order show such fascinating parallels to the Ch'ing dynasty "Restoration" in
contemporary China. This doughty figure shook up the central administration bureaucrats, pressured the academic literati, fought off French and
American expeditionary forces, and did his best to check the onward march
of Western-inspired "progress." In Dr. Choe's book the Taewŏn'gun now
takes his place as one of those bitter-end supporters of a great tradition who
in their own minds defy the trends of modern history while actually making
history anew. At the same time this study gives us an over-view of Korea's
institutions, social conditions, and thought on the eve of her opening to
modern contact.

Ching Young Choe was born in a small village in the district of
Yŏngch'ŏn (North Kyŏngsang province) on December 27, 1927. His family
belonged to the old landed aristocracy of South Korea and at the age of four
Ching Young began to study Chinese and the Chinese classics. From 1940 to
1945 he attended the Middle School in Yamaguchi, Japan. After receiving
the diploma of a high-school teacher in 1946, he taught English and
mathematics in Kyŏngju until 1948, when he entered Chungang University
in Seoul. His studies of English literature were interrupted by the Korean
War, during which he served as an interpreter to the United Nations forces.

In January 1952 he was admitted to the University of Denver, where
he received a B.A. in international relations in the summer of 1954. To
support himself he held various jobs outside the university. In the fall of the

same year he was admitted to Harvard. Scholarships from the Harvard-Yenching Institute facilitated his studies, which reflected the wide scope of his interests: Chinese and Japanese history, Russian studies, economics and anthropology. In June 1956 he received the M.A. degree in Regional Studies —East Asia. Always deeply concerned with the fate of his country, he then turned to Korean history and finished his Ph.D. in June 1960. From 1956 to 1958 he taught Korean at Harvard. In the academic year 1960-1961 he was engaged in compiling a Korean history syllabus for the American Council of Learned Societies. The following year he was a research fellow of the East Asian Research Center.

In October 1962 he received a fellowship from the Alexander von Humboldt Stiftung and went to Bonn, Germany, where he continued his studies of Korea's social and economic history. At the same time he taught Korean language and history at the University of Bonn. His article "Kim Yuk (1580-1658) and the Taedongbŏp Reform" was published in the *Journal of Asian Studies* (vol. 23, no. 1; November 1963). In the fall of 1965 he was called to Marburg/Lahn where he was responsible for the Korean section of the Staatsbibliothek, Preussischer Kulturbesitz. Serious illness was destroying his health, however, and after many months of suffering Ching Young Choe died in Zurich on July 8, 1966. The present volume is thus not only a study of value in itself but also a memorial to a gifted and promising young scholar. It has been made possible by the devoted and scholarly care with which Dr. Martina Deuchler, herself a specialist in the history of traditional Korea and a Harvard Ph.D. of 1967, has aided the editorial process. Dr. Deuchler has also contributed a brief Epilogue such as Dr. Choe himself might have added in summing up his work.

East Asian Research Center

ACKNOWLEDGMENTS

This book has developed out of my doctoral dissertation (1960) at Harvard University. I am greatly indebted to my two advisers, Professors Benjamin I. Schwartz and Edwin O. Reischauer, for their encouragement and assistance in preparing my thesis. I am also grateful to Professor Edward W. Wagner, whose criticism and editorial assistance contributed considerably to its final version. No words are adequate to express my gratitude to the Harvard-Yenching Institute. Without its financial assistance, neither my studies at Harvard nor my thesis could have been completed.

For their help in revising my dissertation for publication, I wish to thank a number of people. Professor John K. Fairbank kindly encouraged this revision and saw it through to publication. The East Asian Research Center and the Harvard-Yenching Institute gave me generous grants which enabled me to undertake this work during the academic year 1961-1962. Mrs. Elizabeth M. Matheson, the chief editor of the East Asian Research Center, carefully guided this revision through the various editorial stages. I owe to Mrs. Susan Leites an especially great debt. With her editorial skills and her untiring attention, she has brought this manuscript to its final state. Finally, I want to thank Miss Martina Deuchler whose candid criticism and generous offering of time have helped me to bring this book to completion. Of course, the responsibility for all errors and shortcomings lies with me.

Marburg/Lahn (Germany)
September 23, 1965

Ching Young Choe

KOREAN WEIGHTS AND MEASURES

kyŏl   A land measure; although the size of one *kyŏl* varied according to time, region, and the quality of the land, an average *kyŏl* at this time was approximately equal to 2.5 acres.

tu   A measure of capacity used in Korea until 1894; one *tu* of rice probably equaled 5.2 lbs. The actual capacity, however, differed greatly with the time, place, and the individual. For calculations of the size of the *tu,* see Pak Si-hyŏng, *Chŏsŏn t'oji chedo sa,* II, 402-404.

sŏk   One *sŏk* equaled 15 *tu,* hence, approximately 78 lbs.

p'il   A cloth measure; one *p'il* equaled 35 *ch'ŏk,* and was the equivalent worth of 8 *tu* of rice.

ch'ŏk   One *ch'ŏk* was about one foot long by .7 foot wide, i.e., .7 sq. ft.

tong   One *tong* equaled 50 *p'il.*

KOREAN DATES

Dates are by year, month, and day of the king's reign. Hence Ch'ŏlchong 4.3.21 means the 21st day of the 3rd month of the 4th reign year of King Ch'ŏlchong. Since a Korean king's first year on the throne was not counted as his first reign year, this first year is here indicated by 0 as in Ch'ŏlchong 0.4.5. Intercalary months are indicated by +. When a king's name does not precede a Korean date in this book, the reference is to King Kojong's reign.

INTRODUCTION

The decade 1864-1873 is known in Korean history as the era of the Taewŏn'gun. During these years the Taewŏn'gun (1821-1898), whose full title was Hŭngsŏn Taewŏn'gun[1] or Grand Prince Hŭngsŏn and whose personal name was Yi Ha-ŭng, ruled as de facto regent for his son, King Kojong (r. 1864-1907). His "regency" left a lasting imprint on Korea; he was the first and only ruler of the Yi dynasty (1392-1910) to attempt to introduce wide-ranging reforms into Korea and at the same time preserve the ancient order of Korean society. This order was threatened from two directions. From within, social unrest had slowly fermented during centuries of maladministration and reached its climax in rebellion in 1862-1863. From without, the West and Japan tried to break into Korea's age-old seclusion. When he assumed power in 1864, he faced diverse and complex problems, some as old as the dynasty, others of relatively recent origin. This monograph considers the Taewŏn'gun's regency and especially the Taewŏn'gun's attempts to meet the diverse threats to Korean society and the dynasty.

The Taewŏn'gun came to power from a humble and rather unconventional background. He was the fourth son of Yi Ch'ae-jung, who was given the name Yi Ku and the title Prince Namyŏn by royal decree in 1816. Yi was appointed to succeed the important but long-discontinued line of the house of Prince Ŭnsin, a half-brother of King Chŏngjo (r. 1777-1800). Thus the standing of the Taewŏn'gun within the dynastic clan derived from "adoption" rather than from blood. When King Ch'ŏlchong (r. 1849-1864) died heirless, the Taewŏn'gun's house was the closest to the royal main line. This was a decisive factor in the selection of Kojong as successor to the vacant throne.

The Taewŏn'gun was a direct descendant of Grand Prince Inp'yŏng (Yi Myo, 1622-1658), a son of King Injo (r. 1623-1649). The grand prince had received his early education from Yun Sŏn-do (1587-1671), one of the early leaders of a political faction known as the Namin or "Southerners." Consequently many of his descendants, possibly the Taewŏn'gun himself, were associated with the Namin. By marriage the Taewŏn'gun was related to a Min family belonging to the Noron or Old Doctrine faction.

In his youth the Taewŏn'gun seems to have been intensively schooled in Confucianism and the Chinese classics. In addition to his traditional education, he had acquired repute in calligraphy and painting, for which he was greatly indebted to Kim Chŏng-hŭi (1786-1856), a great nineteenth-century master of calligraphy and a follower of the Sirhak, or Practical Learning School. His early career in the government was hardly spectacular; he held some minor posts, which were mostly honorary and ceremonial. His title and his connection with the royal house apparently were of little help to him. The fact that at times he was poor and was humiliated by the rich in-laws of the royal house seems to have contributed to the development of an attitude toward men of lowly birth that was unconventional for his time.

The political organization of Yi Korea, like that of Koryŏ (918-1392), was in principle modeled after the ancient Chinese political system. It was characterized by a high degree of centralization aimed at bringing the land under the tightest possible control to provide "wise and ideal" rule for "ignorant" subjects. The smooth working of such a system required a high degree of functional efficiency in the central government. If the authority of the central government failed to reach the lower political units, which required constant supervision and guidance, the result was apt to be maladministration, irresponsibility, and corruption at the local level. The Yi government was highly centralized but inefficient. For example, the existence of several government offices for the performance of similar or identical duties unavoidably created confusion in the governmental process. Moreover, the peculiar system of official tenure added to the inefficiency of the government. Officials were not allowed to stay in one post long enough to become familiar with their duties. This practice may have evolved because the number of officials at any given time far outnumbered the actual number of administrative posts. Needless to say, this practice tempted officials at all levels to reap the highest profits during their short terms in office.

The government's chief weakness, however, was its susceptibility to multiple pressures. One of the most significant was factional strife. Factionalism arose over petty ritual and private matters, rarely over national affairs. Yet, factional strife weakened the dynasty, hampered the functioning of the entire government, and spread its harmful effects far beyond the capital into every segment of local government and upper-class *(yangban)* society.

Although factionalism began to wane late in the eighteenth century, the government found itself in new difficulties as nepotism began to permeate all levels of government and paralyze the administration. This problem arose largely because of the growing influence of royal in-laws. This, in turn, was the result of having a weakened dynastic line. Nepotism crept not only into the appointment of officials, but also into the entire civil service structure.

Although vitality and progress were hardly characteristic features of the Yi economy, there is some evidence that the economy did develop to some small degree even prior to the "modern" period which followed the opening of the country in the late 1870s and the early 1880s. Early in the eighteenth century the barter economy began to decline and a money economy and the exchange market (periodical trading fairs) began to assume greater importance.

The absence of true political feudalism and the early development of political centralism may have contributed to the basically static nature of the economy, but the traditional economic policy, influenced by the teachings of Confucianism, was chiefly to blame. The yangban were completely disengaged from production; trade was tightly controlled to prevent excessive profit-making; merchants were relegated to the lowest level of the social structure. There was virtually no foreign trade, except for a small amount of private trading with China and limited government trade through the tribute missions. Trade with Japan was kept equally minimal. All commercial activities with foreign lands were strictly supervised by the government, and in certain areas the circulation of money was sometimes prohibited.

Weak trade affected adversely the general development of industry by depressing the production of commodities for the market. The predominance of home production by primitive methods, primarily weaving and food-processing for domestic consumption, also impeded industrialization. Industry, too, was subject to close government surveillance. Any innovation in technology was suppressed; specialization in manufacture was hardly known; and the mining of raw materials was kept to a minimum.

Agriculture fared no better than industry and commerce. To be sure, farming had been considered the foundation of the nation for centuries and

one of the main duties of local magistrates had been the promotion of agriculture, but in reality, the government's performance fell far short of this
ideal. The land system made the peasants into virtual serfs of the yangban.
The imposition of ever-increasing duties and taxes, and finally the grain-loan
system, exacerbated the life of the peasants. Exploitation by local magistrates,
clerks, yangban landlords, the Confucian academies *(sŏwŏn)*, and the princely
houses and government agencies eventually brought the peasantry to near
bankruptcy. Naturally an impoverished agricultural class was another major
reason for Korea's backwardness in industry and commerce.

These political and economic ills were complemented by the archaic
class structure of Korean society, discrimination against certain groups because of their birthplace or the circumstances of birth (illegitimacy), and the
misuse of the *sŏwŏn*.

There is little doubt that the Taewŏn'gun understood these problems.
He undertook ambitious reforms to try and combat them. His approach, however, did not reach beyond the traditional aims of reform. Moreover, Korea's
peculiar status in the Far East strongly influenced her response to foreign
challenge during the decade of his regency.

Chapter I

SOCIAL AND ECONOMIC CONDITIONS
IN YI KOREA BEFORE 1860

The Land Tenure System

The Yi land tenure system can be traced back to the Koryŏ dynasty.
During the political and economic turmoil of the latter part of the Koryŏ
most of the land had fallen into the hands of a small group of powerful
officials. To combat this trend, Yi Sŏng-gye, the founder of the Yi dynasty,
and his supporters introduced a far-reaching land reform law in 1391 called
kwajŏn pŏp or the "law of rank land."[1] This system was continued by its
initiator in 1392. The aim was to turn over all the land in the country to the
state and redistribute it to those people and institutions whose services were
particularly important to the maintenance of the dynasty and the state.
Under the new system, the land was divided into categories according to the
nature of its recipient. The most important categories were: *kwajŏn* or "rank
land," *kongsinjŏn* or "merit-subject land," and *kunjŏn* or "military land."

In principle *kwajŏn* was allotted to ranked persons residing in the capital, whether or not they held office. The recipients obtained this land, which
was classified according to eighteen grades *(kwa)* ranging from 10 to 150
kyŏl, mainly on the basis of their rank *(p'um). Kwajŏn* was normally allotted
only for the lifetime of the recipient and in theory was subject to revision if
the recipient's rank changed. Recipients of *kwajŏn* who were also merit-
subjects[2] received varying portions of *kongsinjŏn* in addition to *kwajŏn.*
Kongsinjŏn could be inherited. *Kunjŏn* was allotted principally to the titled
yangban and aspirants to military positions in return for their services in the
capital, for example as royal guards. The allottments ranged from five to ten
kyŏl, depending upon the amount of land the recipients already owned,[3] and
were, in principle, valid only as long as the grantees performed their services.

For allotment purposes the country was divided into three regions:
Kyŏnggi, the five provinces (Hwanghae, Kangwŏn, Ch'ungch'ŏng, Chŏlla, and
Kyŏngsang), and the two northern provinces of P'yŏngan and Hamgyŏng.
According to figures given in 1391, Kyŏnggi, which was at that time much

larger than it is today, contained in all 131,755 *kyŏl* of cultivated land and 8,387 *kyŏl* of wasteland. This land was primarily reserved for *kwajŏn,* but *kongsinjŏn* was also given from it. In the five provinces which had a total of 491,343 *kyŏl* of cultivated land and 166,643 *kyŏl* of wasteland a large part of the land was reserved for *kunjŏn;* other portions were granted to various departments and agencies of the central government, the royal house and a number of its housekeeping offices, local governments, government establishments such as inns, postal stations, and ferry stations, and to government artisans and Buddhist temples. The rest was owned and administered by the state and used for cultivating "provisions for the military" *(kunjajŏn)* and for paying the salaries that officials received in addition to *kwajŏn.* The land in the two northern provinces was primarily reserved for *kunjajŏn,* but before long, local authorities, public institutions and their personnel, and a limited number of the local populace began to receive shares from it.[4]

The categories of land mentioned above were cultivated by slaves, tenant farmers *(chŏnho),* who were commoners, or the recipients themselves (for instance, in the case of guards of the royal tombs). In principal the peasants' tillage rights were inviolable, and they became in most cases more or less attached to the land.*

Most of the individuals and institutions that owned land collected rent *(chŏnjo)* from those who cultivated their land. The state collected rent on those lands it administered directly, for instance, on *kunjajŏn.* This land rent was a major source of state revenue. The rent on paddy land was thirty *tu*[5] of half-cleaned rice per *kyŏl,* and on dry land, thirty *tu* of miscellaneous grains. Thus, the rent ideally averaged ten per cent of the yield in a normal year. The land tax *(chŏnse)* exacted two *tu* of cleaned rice per *kyŏl* on paddy land and two *tu* of soybeans on dry fields. Originally recipients of land grants paid the tax to the state; later, the tax was customarily levied against the tenants. Certain fields, such as those owned by the royal house, government departments and agencies, local governments and some public institutions, and *kongsinjŏn* were entirely exempt from this tax.

The land tenure system was founded on the principle of state ownership, yet almost from the beginning it was characterized by private ownership. In theory land was granted to individuals for life, except in the case of merit-subjects and members of the royal house; in reality, land tenure became

---

*Editor's note: The author's statement about the peasants' almost serf-like attachment to the land may be too strong in the light of more recent research.

1. KOREA DURING THE YI DYNASTY

TUMEN RIVER

YALU RIVER

HAMGYŎNG

P'YŎNGAN

TAEDONG RIVER

SEA OF JAPAN

PYŎNGYANG

HWANGHAE

KANGWŎN

KANGHWA Is.

SEOUL

HAN RIVER

YELLOW SEA

KYŎNGGI

CHUNGCH'ŎNG

KYŎNGSANG

CHŎLLA

PUSAN

TSUSHIMA

CHEJU ISLAND

hereditary almost from the outset. The system was originally introduced to break up large landholdings, yet powerful individuals continued to encroach on public fields. The increasing alienation of state holdings, legitimate or illegitimate, and the increase in the amount of "rent-exempt" and "tax-exempt" land resulted ultimately in the collapse of state finances and the breakdown of the land tenure system.

Only a decade after the inception of the Yi dynasty, arable land at the disposal of the state became scarce. By 1402 Kyǒnggi, which was the best surveyed region of the country, had increased its registered arable land acreage to 149,300 kyǒl.[6] This included 84,100 kyǒl of kwajǒn, 31,240 kyǒl[7] of kongsinjǒn, 4,680 kyǒl of temple land, and probably 22,000 kyǒl[8] of kunjǒn, but did not include "special award land" (pyǒlsajǒn),[9] which certain officials received in addition to regular land grants. The rest belonged to various government and public institutions. The largest reserve for land grants to incoming officials, whose numbers increased rapidly, was the 22,000 kyǒl of kunjǒn administered by the state. Inevitably, the land shortage in Kyǒnggi affected the other provinces. At the beginning of the fifteenth century vast areas in northern Korea were still frontier land. In 1404 the total of registered arable land only amounted to 9,919 kyǒl.[10] In the five provinces the land was poorly surveyed and the registers were incomplete; they had together but a total of 772,624 kyǒl registered in 1404.[11] In 1395 the government had directed that land grants to minor merit-subjects be granted in the home provinces of the recipients.[12] In 1417 one third of the kwajǒn and perhaps portions of kongsinjǒn and pyǒlsajǒn which had been allotted in Kyǒnggi were replaced by areas in Kyǒngsang, Chǒlla, and Ch'ungch'ǒng.[13] This ruling opened the way for yangban officials to overrun the land in the richest regions of the country.[14] The officials conspired with local authorities to annex wasteland and fields whose deeds of ownership were uncertain, and began to carve out big estates for themselves.

The reintroduction of the tunjǒn (colonies) system in all magistracies in 1424[15] and additional land grants such as the hyanggyojǒn (school fields) to local governments further reduced government landholdings. This process caused state revenue to dwindle and made grants of kunjǒn almost impossible. Finally, in an attempt to curb the reduction of state-owned land, the government carried out a series of land and tax reforms, including the confiscation

of some 29,000 *kyŏl* of temple land in 1406 and the abolition or reduction
of land grants to many government and public institutions.

The most important change in the land tenure system took place in 1444.
Land was reclassified according to quality. A *kyŏl* remained the basic land
unit, but it was determined by its yield rather than its size. Each *kyŏl* was to
produce a fixed amount, hence, a *kyŏl* of poor land was larger than one that was
more productive.

Table 1: CLASSIFICATION OF LAND BY QUALITY

Grade	Area in *kyŏl*	Approximate size in *mu*	Approximate size in *p'yŏng*	Approximate size in acres
1	1	38	2758	2.25
2	2	44	3245	2.65
3	1	54	3934	3.2
4	1	69	5009	4.1
5	1	95	6897	5.64
6	1	152	11,035	9.0

See: *MHBG*, 141:11b-12b; *Sejong sillok*, 106:22. The rate of conversion between
kyŏl and *p'yŏng* is based upon later land surveys undertaken by Japanese
authorities. See *Tochi seido chizei seido chōsa hōkokusho* (Report on the
findings about the land and tax systems; Keijo, 1920), pp. 710-711.

In a normal year the maximum rent on each field was fixed at twenty *tu* of
grain per *kyŏl*, or five per cent of the total yield. The maximum varied, however, depending on the harvest. There were nine different categories of crop-
year. In the poorest crop years the rent would only be four *tu* per *kyŏl*. Yet,
the rate of the land tax which individual and institutional recipients paid to
the state generally remained at two *tu* per *kyŏl*. [16]

The reclassification of land was made in an effort to increase the number
of taxable *kyŏl*, and consequently, increase state revenue, but the unfortunate
result was that poor land was overrated and partly cultivated wasteland was
inaccurately registered as good farm land. The problem of diminishing
government holdings was not alleviated by the new land tax system, which
was not fully introduced into the eight provinces until almost the end of the
fifteenth century, because the number of persons entitled to grants of land
increased sharply. Between 1453 and 1506 the government granted some

30,000 *kyŏl* to nearly 360 new merit-subjects (exclusive of several thousand minor merit-subjects).[17] Between 1400 and 1567 over seventy princes were born;[18] all these princes and their respective descendants were entitled to grants of tax-exempt land in amounts ranging from 180 to 300 *kyŏl*. [19] Numerous princesses were also entitled to similar grants. In these years recipients of *pyŏlsajŏn* also increased, and the *tunjŏn* of both state and local governments expanded[20] until their holdings probably exceeded 40,000 *kyŏl*.

Between 1394 and 1466 nearly 1,500 Koreans passed the higher civil service examinations *(munkwa)*[21] and approximately the same number were granted the military degree *(mukwa)*. These new yangban degree-holders numbered altogether something like 3,000. All of them and a considerable number of descendants of merit-subjects and of high-ranking officials were, in principle, entitled to allotments of land upon starting their government careers, but the majority of them never appeared to have received their *kwajŏn*. In short, the *kwajŏn* system was totally unworkable. In 1466 the "rank-land" system was abolished and replaced by a "office-land" *(chikchŏn)* system, which only granted land to those who were currently in office.[22] This system also failed.[23]

After the Hideyoshi invasions, 1592-1598, the emergence of notorious "palace estates" *(kungbangjŏn)*[24] belonging to the royal families, and the growth of *amun tunjŏn* (colonies of various central government offices and military outfits in the vicinity of the capital) intensified the alienation of public land.[25] The *kungbangjŏn,* sometimes called *chin,* started with a moderate amount of land from the state, but grew rapidly by taking advantage of their tax-exempt status. By 1662, in Hwanghae alone there were over 92 palace estates, comprising one half of the land in that province.[26]

The high rent[27] extorted by the *kungbangjŏn* and the *tunjŏn* and the heavy military tax exacted by the government accounted for the transformation of the Korean peasants into virtual serfs. From the beginning of the eighteenth century this transformation was accelerated by the introduction of money. The estates and the wealthy began to lend money or grain to destitute peasants, taking their tillage rights as security. When the peasants were unable to repay, they forfeited their land. With the loss of their sole source of income, they had no alternative but to give themselves up to their creditors and become their slaves. Furthermore, whenever laborers were needed on the estates, stewards were sent to recruit peasant labor with promises of protection.[28] The expansion of the estates and colonies inevitably increased the amount of tax-exempt land and further decreased government revenue. By 1807 tax-exempt lands comprised 204, 635 *kyŏl* or 14.1 per cent of the total 1,456,592 *kyŏl* of registered arable land in the country. Another 411, 250 *kyŏl* (28.2 per cent) were listed as semi-permanently unavailable for taxation. Only 840,714 *kyŏl* (57.7 per cent) of the total amount could actually be taxed.[29] Thus, financing the government became a crucial problem in the Yi dynasty.

The Grain-loan System

The grain-loan system, customarily known as *chojŏk* (the selling and buying of grain) or *hwanja* (the gathering and distributing of grain), was one of the most important relief measures of the Yi dynasty. At the beginning of the dynasty grain-loan was largely handled through two granary systems: the *ŭich'ang* ("beneficiary granary") and the *sangp'yŏngch'ang* ("stabilization granary"). The *ŭich'ang* system, an ancient institution of Han and T'ang China, was first introduced into Korea in the early part of the Koryŏ period and was continued after the inception of the Yi dynasty.[30] Under this system, the government set up granaries throughout the country and loaned small quantities of grain to destitute peasants during the farming season or in times of famine. The grain had to be repaid with a small interest after the harvest or in years of good harvest. The *sangp'yŏngch'ang,* a copy of the Chinese *ch'ang-p'ing-ts'ang* or "ever-normal granary" system, which had also been in use on and off during the Koryŏ was not re-established until 1458.[31] Although the original function of this system was to control the price of grain, its actual function differed little from that of the *ŭich'ang.* At the outset both systems had been instrumental in relieving hungry farmers during the planting season, but from the beginning of the sixteenth century, they gradually began to lose their importance. As a result of the decrease in land revenue and the government's growing financial difficulties, the grain-loan was often operated for profit. Its administration was later taken over by the Chinhyulch'ŏng, the Office of Relief Affairs,[32] which was first created during

Chungjong's reign (1506-1544). The Hideyoshi invasions drastically changed this system.

The Japanese invasions devastated Korea. The sources of government revenue were squeezed dry, official expenses could not be met, officials could not be paid. In these circumstances the grain-loan system turned into an instrument of official usury. Various government agencies and military establishments set up special "funds" with whatever grain was available, hoping to loan the grain to the peasants and use the interest on the loans to finance specific governmental or military projects. The loans, however, were administered by various local governments on a purely speculative basis.[33] In principle the authorities were not allowed to lend more than a prescribed amount of the grain in storage at one time, usually one half, the rest to be reserved for emergencies such as droughts and famines.[34] Since more loans meant more profit, however, this rule was seldom observed. The official rate of interest on grain was normally set at ten per cent, but actual rates soared much higher. Even when harvests were good, when the peasants did not need to borrow, they were forced to borrow grain that was often wet and mixed with chaff and pebbles. Grain was also frequently moved from one area to another in search of profitable markets.

The system became increasingly intolerable after the end of the eighteenth century. The peasants began to refuse to liquidate their debts or to borrow more grain. After 1807 the amount of grain loaned declined sharply;[35] the government began to lose another of its important sources of revenue.

Table 2: GRAIN OUTSTANDING TO PEASANTS

Year	Amount in sŏk
pre-1725	416,900(max.)
1769	7,161,261
1797	9,269,600
1807	9,995,599
1862	2,311,690

When it was no longer profitable to loan grain, the officials resorted to extorting grain from the peasants. Many peasants abandoned their homes and villages to escape punishment. In the end the government had to cancel the peasants' debts.[36]

Thus the grain-loan system, instead of relieving the peasants' misery, only added to the already unbearable economic burdens and contributed decisively to the popular uprisings of 1862-1863.

The Military Service System[37]

During the Yi dynasty, as during the Koryŏ, universal military service prevailed. In principle all males between the ages of sixteen and sixty were subject to military duty; in practice, however, yangban and men of lowly birth, such as artisans and slaves, were exempt, leaving only the peasants to serve.

The adult male peasant population was divided into the "regulars" *(chŏngjŏng)* and the "reserves" or "attendants" *(pongjok or poin).* In exchange for active military service each regular was assigned a number of reserves. The number ranged from two to four, depending upon conditions such as the amount of land cultivated by the regular.[38] The most common arrangement was the "three-man" group—one regular and two reserves. While the regular went on active duty, usually two months out of the year, the reserves stayed at home to work their partner's land and support him financially during his tour of duty.[39]

This system worked reasonably well until the latter part of the fifteenth century, when the reserves were obliged to discharge their obligations to the regulars by paying the *pop'o* ("reserve-cloth"), generally two *p'il* of cloth a year.[40] Shortly afterwards, a similar payment was required of the regulars who were relieved from active duty or were permitted to hire substitutes. This payment was usually collected from the regular and his reserves,[41] and eventually led to the decay of the regular-reserve system. Owing to the difficulties of financing the military and the long period of peace in Korea, soldiers were released from active duty in growing numbers so as to increase the collection of the impost. Hence, military service came to mean little more than paying a tax which became one of the heaviest burdens.[42]

The dissolution of the military system, however, was not completed until 1598. From that time, the military garrisons, in particular those around the capital, were almost entirely manned by hired professional soldiers.[43]

Men of military age were not assigned to actual military service, but to pay taxes, which were usually much higher than two *p'il* of cloth per capita.[44] With this new development, the military tax, which was popularly known as *yangyŏk* (commoner's duty) became literally the "evil of evils." Those who possessed influence or economic means managed to avoid payment through bribery; others gave false reports about their sex or genealogy; others entered Buddhist temples or sought the protection of powerful yangban by becoming their slaves or servants; some joined local Confucian shrines *(hyanggyo)* and *sŏwŏn* or entered local government service; some castrated themselves, and others simply disappeared.[45] This "evasion movement" naturally shifted the main tax burden onto the weak and poor left behind in the villages. In numerous cases taxes were even assessed on the dead and on children.[46] Memorials in the official chronicles and folk tales written after the inception of the military tax bear ample witness to those dreadful conditions.

After 1672 a few officials began to search for ways to reduce the military tax and thus improve the lot of the peasant. However, factional strife subjected the government to upheavals too frequent to allow for any reformist sentiments to materialize. It was not until 1750 that the *kyunyŏkpŏp* ("law of equalizing labor") was enacted, reducing the long-standing tax of two *p'il* per capita to one *p'il.*

With a population of military age estimated at 500,000 men, the tax reduction of one *p'il* per capita meant a loss of 500,000 *p'il,* or over 1,000,000 *yang* to the government. This decrease in revenue necessitated a cut of about 500,000 *yang* in the budget for central and provincial offices and garrisons. To cover the deficit of about 400,000 *yang* for the maintenance of military establishments, the government levied a total of some 100,000 *yang* on salt, fishing grounds, trade junks (most of them operated by princely houses and various government agencies), unregistered lands (most of which were in the hands of local authorities), and on well-to-do commoner adults who had previously evaded payment of the military tax. These wealthy commoners who now paid the tax were given an empty honorary title, *sŏnmu kun'gwan* ("selected military officer"). The remaining 300,000 *yang* was levied on the country exclusive of the two northern provinces. The new surtax on land, the *kyŏlmi* (levy of grain on land) or *kyŏlchŏn* (levy of money on land), was two *tu* of rice or five *chŏn* in cash (0.5 *yang*) per *kyŏl* of land.[47]

The reduction of the military tax was indeed a relief to many of the peasants. Of the 1,340,000 households officially recorded on February 27, 1752,[48] about 100,000 households, comprising nearly 500,000 males, were subject to the tax. The average income of a household of five males did not exceed twenty sŏk of cleaned rice. Under the old tax rate a household with five adult males tilling an average of one kyŏl or less of land[49] would have had to pay sixteen sŏk and 6 tu of grain. This covered the military tax of ten p'il of cloth (one p'il was then equivalent to eight tu of rice); a long-standing surtax on land, the taedongmi, which exacted twelve tu of rice per kyŏl; the land tax of four tu of rice per kyŏl; and the rent, which comprised roughly half the total yield. Thus, after a year's toil, the household was only left with three sŏk and nine tu of grain, hardly enough to subsist on. Obviously, even the two sŏk and ten tu additional income effected by the new tax system gave great relief to the destitute peasants.

The new system, however, could not solve the basic economic problems of the country. Too many households were exempt from the military tax. Furthermore, government curtailing of expenditures owing to lack of funds forced various government agencies and military establishments to loan out their grain holdings to compensate for their reduced share of government revenue.[50] No doubt this largely explains why the amount of grain loaned to peasants increased sharply toward the last quarter of the eighteenth century. Thus, the new tax system merely contributed to the growth of the grain-loan system. The deterioration of the latter around 1840 and the occurrence of natural calamities accelerated the general breakdown of the national economy.

Table 3: FREQUENCY OF NATURAL DISASTERS[a]

Period	Number of Great "Disaster" Years	Number Left Without Food*	Deaths by Epidemic Diseases
1752-1781	6	1,691,397	23,179
1782-1811	15	23,334,229	128,000
1812-1840	15	21,674,066	10,500

Table 3: FREQUENCY OF NATURAL DISASTERS[a] (contd.)

MAJOR FLOODS[a]

Period	Frequency	Houses Lost or Damaged
1751-1780	2	200
1781-1810	6	23,559
1811-1840	17	57,634
1841-1860	12	65,352

* These numbers are inaccurate because many persons were reported as facing starvation on two or more occasions.

a See: *Yŏngjo sillok, Chŏngjo sillok, Sunjo sillok, Hŏnjong sillok, Ch'ŏlchong sillok,* and Moritani Katsumi,"Kyūrai no Chōsen nōgyō shakai ni tsuite no kenkyū no tame ni" (Toward a study of the agrarian society in old Korea), in *Chōsen shakai keizai shi kenkyū* (Studies of the socio-economic history of Korea; Tokyo, 1933), pp. 414-454.

Between 1752 and 1840 the total number of those reported to have been without food is rather astonishing when compared with the total population of the country (estimated at 6,708,572 in 1838). Between 1782 and 1840 the country suffered a great famine or an epidemic on an average of once every two years, drastically increasing the number of the starving. The *Sillok* abundantly document the flight of hungry people who abandoned their land in the south and flocked to the capital.

Moreover, as the following table shows, central government revenue began to decrease after 1843, reaching its lowest point in 1861:

Table 4: ANNUAL BALANCES OF THE CENTRAL GOVERNMENT

Year	Gold cash by *yang*	Silver cash by *yang*	Copper cash by *yang*	Grain by *sŏk*	Cloth by *tong*
1781	358	431,555	1,281,896	464,230	6,232
1808	256	432,551	1,316,742	504,514	11,651
1842	145	236,973	1,108,790	287,052	3,800
1846	136	203,936	632,736	319,966	4,144
1852	103	195,394	349,042	253,084	3,454
1861	99	216,152	273,457	173,148	2,599

Statistics compiled from the *Chŏngjo sillok,* 13:7; *Hŏnjong sillok,* 10:1; and *CS,* ser. 6, vol. 1, p. 281; vol. 3, pp. 165, 370, 623.

12

Even this depleted treasury had to finance at least a token amount of relief for the victims of famine, flood, and epidemics. Such were the socio-economic conditions of Korea on the eve of the peasant uprisings of 1862-1863.

Chapter II

REFORMIST THOUGHT IN YI KOREA

As the fabric of Korean society slowly disintegrated, there were some who voiced their deep concern at the fate of the country and the welfare of her people. At the beginning of the seventeenth century there emerged a small group of progressive thinkers who might be called social reformers. Although most of them belonged to the privileged class, they were bitter critics of their fellow yangban. They were painfully aware of the pressing national problems and spent much of their time and energy in search of basic answers to these problems. The group is commonly known in Korean historiography as the Sirhakp'a, or the School of Practical Learning.

The origin and growth of the Sirhakp'a may be attributed to: the devastation of the country after the Japanese and Manchu invasions; the influence of the Tung-lin movement of the late Ming dynasty which emphasized the *shih-hsüeh,* the "learning of practical matters";[1] the anti-Chu Hsi school of philosophy during the Ch'ing which used a similar slogan, *shih-shih-ch'iu-shih* (Seek truth through the verification of things);[2] and the contrast between the prosperity of early Ch'ing China and the poverty and misery of Korea.

Yu Hyŏng-wŏn (1622-1673), Yi Ik (1681-1763), Hong Tae-yong (1731-1783), Pak Chi-wŏn (1737-1805), Pak Che-ga (1750-1805),[3] and Chŏng Yag-yong (1762-1836) were some of the reformers. Only Chŏng had received the *munkwa.* All except Pak Che-ga came from prominent families; Pak had an "illegitimate" ancestry. Yi Ik and Chŏng were related by marriage and both belonged to the Namin faction; Pak Chi-wŏn and Pak Che-ga had a master-disciple relationship. Hong and the two Paks had visited Peking.

There is evidence that the Taewŏn'gun had something to do with the Sirhakp'a. Kim Chŏng-hŭi (1786-1856), who taught the Taewŏn'gun calligraphy and the art of painting orchids,[4] was a member of the Sirhakp'a. He wrote the first Korean discourse on the concept of *silsa kusi (shih-shih-ch'iu-shih)* of the *Han-shu,* which became one of the slogans of the school.[5] Pak Kyu-su (1807-1876), a grandson of Pak Chi-wŏn and a faithful follower of the Sirhakp'a, was also a close associate of the Taewŏn'gun,[6] and one of his students, Kim Yun-sik, who was active in foreign affairs in the last days of the Yi dynasty, was the official author of the Taewŏn'gun's epitaph.[7] Two other students of the Sirhakp'a, Yi Ik and An Chŏng-bok (1712-1791), were posthumously honored by the Taewŏn'gun in 1867.[8] Thus it is evident that the Taewŏn'gun was exposed to and probably influenced by the ideas on social reform advocated by the Sirhakp'a.

Land Tenure

All the reformers were equally concerned about the concentration of land in the hands of a few powerful families. However, they proposed different means to remedy the inequality. Yu Hyŏng-wŏn wanted to introduce a new land system which nevertheless recognized the basic principle of the original Yi system.[9] He proposed to replace the old complicated land measure with a new uniform unit called the *kyŏng* (one *kyŏng* would equal roughly 10,000 square paces, or some six acres); to allot a minimum of one *kyŏng* to each adult farmer over twenty years of age; to reduce land grants to degree-holders and members of the royal family, for example, only twelve *kyŏng* to sons of kings; to abolish special awards such as *kongsinjŏn,* which he thought were a major cause of the disintegration of the land system; to establish a land tax as low as one-fortieth of the annual yield per *kyŏng,* and to abolish land grants to government offices, other public institutions (with a few exceptions, such as schools), and *tunjŏn.*[10] Each feature of Yu's plan reflected a realistic grasp of the defects inherent in the Yi land system.

In contrast to Yu's wholesale reform program, Yi Ik's program was more moderate. He thought that the government should control further alienation of peasant land and work for the gradual equalization of landholdings. According to his plan, adult males of all social classes would designate a fixed amount of land out of their individual holdings as a "permanent plot," which, although he did not specifically say so, he probably intended the government to give to landless farmers. The government would keep registers of the permanent plots to prevent unauthorized sales, but would allow additional holdings to be disposed of freely. The government would also encourage those farmers who had only permanent plots to buy additional land little by little so that eventually, rich and poor would have equal landholdings.[11] Yi thought that his reform program would have the important side-effect of making yangban landowners do their own farming, for his system would make every peasant a petty landowner, and the yangban would be forced to till his own fields. In anticipation of the yangban using slave labor Yi also advocated the emancipation of slaves.[12]

Yi's ideas were more or less followed by Pak Chi-wŏn, who did not offer any detailed reform program. Pak thought that the root of the peasants' cultural backwardness lay in their abject poverty. He believed that the peasants' general inertia stemmed from not owning any personal property. He advocated that the government break up the large landholdings in the hands of the minority and create small holdings for the peasants, so that pride in ownership might change their attitude toward life.[13]

Chŏng Yag-yong's approach to the land tenure problem was much more radical and original than those of the others. Chŏng called his proposed land system the *yŏjŏn,*[14] or "communal land" system. According to his plan, all individual rice fields were to be transferred to communal farms or villages comprising approximately thirty households each. All able-bodied villagers, male and female, and children over a certain age, were to participate in farming—adults engaging in heavy work and children in lighter work, such as weeding and picking up loose grain. An elected village elder would keep a working record on each villager. At the harvest the grain would be brought to the elder's office, where taxes and the elder's salary were first deducted before the grain was divided among the villagers commensurable with the total number of hours which each had contributed to its production.

Under this system, the principle of "no work, no food" was to be strictly observed. The yangban literati who had no experience in farming would have to work all the harder to be treated on an equal basis with the experienced farmers. If they were totally incapable of working the land, they would have to be assigned to other occupations, such as trade or handicrafts, according to the principle: "Let those who can farm have land, and those who cannot farm have no land." Chŏng believed this system would enable each man to produce and to contribute to the enrichment of the country.

Chŏng contrasted his reform program with earlier proposals made by Yu Hyŏng-wŏn and Yi Ik. He asserted that Yu's "well-field" system was outdated because the increase in population made the *kyunjŏn* (equalization of land) system of the T'ang and Yi dynasties impractical. The *hanjŏn* (limited landholdings) system favored by Yi Ik and Pak Chi-wŏn was not realistic, for people might buy or sell land under false names, and non-farmers would still be able to acquire land.

Grain-loan and Military Service

The man who offered the most concrete and practical solution to the problems of the grain-loan system and the military tax was again Yu Hyŏng-wŏn.[15] He compared the harmful effects of the grain-loan system with those of Wang An-shih's *ch'ing-miao-ch'ien* system. Nevertheless, he conceded that there was some "little and temporary" benefit in the system in spite of its "great and lasting harm."

Yu thought that the existing system should be abolished and replaced by the old "stabilization granary" system. His plan was to set up a granary in each town and city in the country using loan-grain for capital. The main function of these granaries would be to control prices. When there was surplus grain on the market for a low price the granaries would buy it up at 150 per cent of the market price to protect the interests of the farmers. Then, when grain was scarce and prices went up, the granaries would sell their grain at a lower price. Yu also planned to bring back the village granary *(sach'ang)* as a subsidiary of the stabilization granary. The *sach'ang's* function was purely relief. Yu asserted that the village granary system had failed in the past because of government interference. He believed that the people might voluntarily establish village granaries on the principle of the stabilization granaries if they had government sympathy and support and the encouragement of local magistrates. These granaries would be managed exclusively by honest retired officials and village elders.[16]

Yu's proposal for military service or military tax reform was conjunctive with his program for land reform. Yu envisaged the establishment of a true military system consisting of infantry, cavalry, navy, and slave militia *(sogogun)* units, with conscription based upon the size of landholdings. He had proposed in his land reform program that each adult peasant receive a "permanent plot" of one *kyŏng* of land. On that basis, a family that owned one *kyŏng* of land would only send one adult to fulfill military service, even though there might be several adult males in the family. Four adult males living in one village and owning between them four *kyŏng* of land would form a basic military unit. The four would take turns doing active duty as under the original Yi system. While the one was on active duty the three others would drill at home and pay twelve *tu* of rice or two *p'il* of cloth per man to support the fourth man. No other tax would be imposed on those in the military service pool,[17] since the impost paid by each reserve constituted a land tax on his one *kyŏng*. Yu's program did not allow soldiers to have substitutes and did not give exemptions from active duty because Yu believed that such practices led to the disintegration of the system. His plan was undoubtedly an improvement on the Yi military service system for it would shorten military service by four years; a man would not be eligible for service until he was twenty, whereas he was eligible to serve at sixteen under the old system.

The Civil Service Examination System

The Yi civil service examination system was more or less a modified version of the system during the Koryŏ, which was largely based on the civil service examination system of T'ang China. The objective of the examination system was the selection of qualified men for government service. Although the examination system played an important role in the formation of Yi bureaucracy and in the promotion of education and culture in Korea, it was seriously defective, and much criticized. Yu Hyŏng-wŏn was one of the chief critics of the system. He felt one of the chief defects of the system was the excessive emphasis on style in poetry and essay composition and on memorization of the classics without regard for content. He challenged the efficacy of the system as a whole in recruiting men of talent and virtue for government service, and attacked in particular the special examinations that had been held with increasing frequency by successive Yi kings. He recalled the popular saying: "Even the blind can pass and babies can compete," which suggested that many of the successful candidates in these examinations, mostly the sons of Seoul yangban, passed only because of favoritism.[18]

Yu proposed replacing the examination system with training schools for civil servants. Since the existing schools in Seoul did not function properly and did not serve his purposes, he wanted to introduce a new educational system based on that of T'ang China. This system of education would comprise four levels: (1) district schools, one in each district and four in the capital, (2) provincial schools, one in each province and one in the capital, (3) a university *(t'aehak)* in the capital, and (4) a *chinsa* academy *(chinsawŏn),* roughly equivalent to a modern graduate school.

The enrollment in district schools would vary between twenty and a hundred. All children over the age of thirteen were eligible to compete for admission. Once admitted, the students were each entitled to two *kyŏng* of land. In these schools they would study almost all of the Confucian classics and their commentaries and compose essays on practical subjects. The curriculum did not include poetry or prose. At the end of the third year in the district school, the students would be subjected to a comprehensive examination administered by a committee consisting of the provincial governor and the regular instructors. A number of successful students from each district school would be recommended for the provincial schools on the basis of "virtue and talent." The unsuccessful students would be assigned to military duty.

The curriculum of the provincial schools would include Korean history in addition to the Confucian classics. There would be occasional conferences between visiting lecturers (such as governors and ranking provincial officials) and students to discuss such subjects as human nature, ethics, history, government, customs, and the art of healing. Yu felt that all these subjects would be invaluable to the students in their future roles as government servants.

At the end of the first academic year in provincial school a special committee would select 150 students from various provincial schools to enter the university. At the end of the first academic year in the university, thirty-five students would be recommended to the government for their "virtue, talent, scholarship, personality, and knowledge of administration." These students would then take a final oral examination in the palace before a body of leading government officials. This examination would cover selected Confucian classics, Korean history, and statute law. Those who passed would receive the *chinsa* degree and admittance to the *chinsawŏn.* After another year of study and apprenticeship, they would be formally appointed to various posts on the basis of individual merit.[19]

Clearly, Yu's aim was to create the truly virtuous civil servant of the Confucian ideal, but one also well versed in Korean history and institutions. Under the traditional examination system a candidate's personal integrity and his knowledge of the country's history and institutions were neglected. Yu asserted that such a system could only produce incompetent civil servants, susceptible to corruption. His system, on the other hand, would test students periodically on their understanding of the true meaning of the classics, and check their integrity and their ability to carry out their duties as civil servants.

Yi Ik's criticism of the traditional examination system focussed chiefly on the discriminatory policy against northerners and against children of concubines and commoners. He pointed out that the examinations—and consequently, government positions—were nothing but the "exclusive property" of a few powerful families. In a society that maintained such a policy all but the "august class" would refrain from taking an active part in national affairs and would harbor resentment against the state.[20] He asserted, however, ironically, that the examination system created internal strife among the proud families and laid the foundations for factional strife. Yi also condemned the system for creating and perpetuating a yangban class that considered manual work beneath them. This ever-increasing class constituted a growing burden on the peasantry, thus hastening the ruin of the agricultural economy.[21]

Yi Ik did not offer any original solutions for the defects. However, he did suggest that the recommendations of qualified individuals, irrespective of their social origins,[22] be given greater weight. Yi's criticisms of the system were largely seconded by Hong Tae-yong and Pak Che-ga. Hong championed the proposal that civil servants be selected according to their talents rather than their social standing.[23] Pak's main concern was the monopoly of examination degrees and government posts by influential families at the expense of other yangban. According to Pak, nearly 100,000 men of varying ages took the examinations each year, but only ten per cent of those who passed were able to find worthwhile positions. The rest, who had studied until their "hair turned grey," were left without portfolio. If it was difficult for degree-holders without influence to obtain office, it was more difficult for the yangban without influence to pass the examinations. Pak related how, when the examination books were collected and brought to the readers, those books written by the sons of powerful families were chosen first, regardless of achievement. Even brilliant candidates were rejected unless they had backing in high places.[24]

Although Pak felt that the system should be abolished, he suggested only a mild reform program whereby a number of degrees might be reserved for the scions of powerful families and the rest left to the commoners on a strictly competitive basis.

Government Organization

Yu Hyŏng-wŏn was most outspoken against the traditional structure of the Yi government. He felt that the Yi system was weak, basically because it lacked simplicity and efficiency.[25] He suggested that redundant and minor offices be abolished or incorporated into already existing departments so as to relieve the great economic strain on the government. Those offices that he considered dispensable included leading offices such as the Board of Defense (Pibyŏnsa), the Council of Merit-Subjects, the Censorate, the Council of the Royal Lectures, the Bureau of the Royal Kinsmen (Tollyŏngbu), the Special Tribunal, the Metropolitan Police Headquarters, and several councils responsible for the affairs of the royal family. Yu gave specific reasons for the abolition of each office in addition to that of economy. He argued, for instance, that the Censorate's duty to remonstrate to the throne was in fact performed by the state councillors and other government officials. Moreover, as he pointed out, the Censorate did more harm than good. He also demanded the abolition of the Bureau of the Royal Household on the grounds that its existence violated the Confucian principle of kingly virtue; he argued that "there is no property in the domain that is not the king's property."[26]

Yu was also much concerned that many offices lacked clearly defined spheres of responsibility, creating much confusion and inefficiency in the government. He attributed the problem mainly to the excessive practice of concurrent appointment. Yu asserted that officials should be appointed to one office at a time.[27] Finally, he blamed the insufficient salaries of officials and other government employees (clerks, for example) for the graft and corruption; he believed that both evils could be prevented if the salary scale were raised by means of governmental reorganization.[28]

Poverty and Wealth

Apart from their criticisms of specific institutions, the Sirhak reformers spoke out against the extreme poverty in Korea. Some saw the basic root of such poverty in the collapse of Korea's agricultural economy; others traced it to the government's rigorous suppression of industry, commerce, and foreign trade. Naturally, the remedies they suggested also differed, ranging from the protection and promotion of agriculture at all costs to the development of natural resources. Yi Ik thought that the fundamental means of enriching the people lay in promoting agriculture, enforcing austerity, and checking the exploitation of the people by officials. He believed that progress in agriculture could only be achieved by suppressing trade, which was taking farmers away from the land.[29]

Pak Chi-wŏn, on the other hand, believed that the exploitation of natural resources such as gold, marine products, salt, and fruit, and the development of foreign trade and commerce would enrich the country. He felt that better roads and improved means of transportation were essential for the development of natural resources and commerce.[30] He suggested introducing carts like those used by the Manchus. It is believed that his famous biography of an imaginary character called Hŏ Saeng was written to stimulate trade. The story is that of a man with a great vision living in Seoul who turned his back on the civil service examinations and decided to become a trader-colonist. Through his trading activities, Hŏ accumulated a great fortune, over a million *yang* in silver cash, but it was too much for his homeland to absorb. Consequently, he founded an island colony to which he sent many outlaws and unemployed, giving them the money that he had earned from his enterprises.[31] Many of Pak Chi-wŏn's social criticisms and ideas for reform were vividly expressed in his realistic short stories.

Pak Chi-wŏn's views on the development of trade and natural resources were largely shared by Pak Che-ga. The latter believed that the fundamental cause of Korea's poverty was the excessive and irrational emphasis on frugality, a traditional concept which he thought restricted the use of the country's natural resources.[32] He believed that the exploitation of natural resources would lead to the development of industry, commerce, and foreign trade. Moreover, if the country produced more iron and more smelters, more agricultural tools would be manufactured.[33] An ardent advocate of foreign trade, Pak said:

> Our country is small and her people are poor. Even if we cultivate all the land we have, work diligently, use all the wise and talented people, promote commerce and industry, and make the best use of our domestic resources, it is still not enough . . . If we trade with far lands, our wealth will increase and hundreds of industries will rise . . . Previously, Japan did not trade with China. She had to buy Chinese goods through us. Therefore, we could make a profit . . . However, the Japanese knew that this was unprofitable for them. Thus, they now trade directly with China . . . and all kinds of goods under the sun pour into the port of Nagasaki. How can there be in the world a country which does not wish to be rich and strong? How can we leave the arts of acquiring wealth and strength to other people?[34]

Chŏng Yag-yong argued that greater wealth would come about with advanced technology in farming, weaving, shipbuilding, and transportation: "When farming technology improves, more and better grain will be produced with less land and labor . . . When weaving technology develops, more and finer cloth can be produced with fewer materials and with greater speed . . . Upon attaining mastery of all technologies, a nation will become rich and her armies will become strong."[35]

How were such improvements to be achieved in a society where technological learning was traditionally ignored if not entirely suppressed? Chŏng rejected the traditional attitude as absurd; he asserted that learning about technology was a function of human nature, and that all human beings possessed "innate wisdom and wit which could be used to learn technology for their benefit." He compared human wisdom and ideas to birds' claws and the horns and teeth of animals, which served to secure food and protection. The basic function of human wisdom and ideas was also to be used to secure man's daily necessities and the protection of human society through learning and developing technology.[36]

Chŏng proposed a "communal" or village system as a means of developing technology. According to this system, every one in the village would work together for the advancement of technology to benefit all. Chŏng maintained, "There is always a limit on human wisdom and ideas . . . even a sage cannot accomplish more than the concentrated efforts of a hundred men." Thus he believed that if every member of a community used his limited wisdom and ideas for the common objective of the advancement of technology, it would be possible to make unlimited progress.[37]

Several of these reformers had freed themselves in many respects from their Confucian heritage and Korea's past. They conceived of a fundamental reform of Yi Korea. They argued for the promotion of industry and foreign trade, clamored for the abolition of the irrational class system, and envisaged the creation of a kind of agricultural commune where even the august yangban would be put to work. The originality of their ideas is all the more impressive when one considers that long after their time Korea was still clinging to her traditional past.

Chapter III

SOCIAL UNREST ON THE EVE OF THE
TAEWŎN'GUN'S RISE TO POWER

During the last two years of Ch'ŏlchong's reign (1849-1864) Korea witnessed spontaneous uprisings of a discontented populace. Only Hwanghae, P'yŏngan and Kangwŏn were free of serious disturbances. The revolts involved more than 100,000 people in nearly twenty-one major districts, taken together comparable in size to one large province. The peasants were the major component of the rebel groups, but it was not uncommon for prominent local yangban and former government officials to participate or even to lead the uprisings. Although these uprisings were of no immediate threat to the dynasty, they were significant in two ways: they were the first major popular uprisings in the entire history of the Yi dynasty, and they served as a prelude to the Tonghak rebellion three decades later. Also, the government's response to these uprisings revealed a great deal about the Yi dynasty on the eve of the Taewŏn'gun's rise to power.

Causes of the Peasant Uprisings

Although contemporary opinion on the causes of official abuse and plunder varied, most observers concluded that the root of the problem was the grain-loan system, which all too easily permitted the magistrates to be dishonest.[1] Yet, instead of tackling the grain-loan system itself, the government merely urged officials to be honest and dispatched secret inspectors to check on magistrates and governors.

Between 1850 and 1862 nearly 450 provincial governors, magistrates, and military commanders were charged with corruption and were dismissed. However, they were often able to use their influence to gain reappointment. Even the powerful secret inspectors who charged them were not themselves entirely immune to personal corruption or political attacks, and often found themselves accused in turn by those in the government whose protégés they had victimized. Yu An, who incriminated eight magistrates when he was sent

to Kyŏnggi in April 1851, and Cho Un-gyŏng, who, as secret inspector to
Chŏlla in May 1851, censured ten magistrates and the military commander,
were both in turn disgraced because they were found to have accepted bribes,
a fact discovered by the vice-censor-general, Ch'ae Wŏn-muk.[2] Most of the
secret inspectors, however, were young men with great zeal and personal
integrity.

The dismissal of governors and magistrates en masse did not put semi-
institutionalized corruption to an end; instead, it caused conditions to degen-
erate further. Those who replaced the disgraced officials were usually chosen
from the descendants of merit-subjects or other eminent persons, and as a
rule they were impoverished.[3] Once they were sent down to a district as
powerful magistrates, they devoted their attention to the accumulation of as
much money and land as they might during their precarious tenure. Since
they had no previous experience in administration, they had to rely on local
clerks, who were masters of the arts of graft. Thus the collaboration between
magistrates and their clerks continued.

Although the immediate cause of the peasant uprisings was the abuses
commonly found in the disintegrating grain-loan, taxation and land systems,
there were other reasons why the uprisings broke out during that particular
time. They were, namely, the resurgence of the Taiping rebels and the Anglo-
French invasion of Tientsin and the rise of the Tonghak. Full accounts of the
two Chinese crises reached Korea in February of 1858 and in January of
1859 respectively. They greatly shocked the officialdom and the populace in
Seoul.[4] In the belief that the dangers then besetting China would soon engulf
Korea too, many began to flee southward. The news, greatly distorted,
quickly spread over the country. Some people actually thought the end of
the world was coming. On March 10, 1861, the king asked Left Councillor
Pak Hoe-su how popular unrest could be quelled.[5] By this time, however,
the disciples of Ch'oe Che-u, the founder of Tonghak, had taken advantage
of the prevalent restlessness and had begun to preach a new "way" of salvation.

The Rise of Tonghak (Eastern Learning)

It is as difficult to analyze the background of the Tonghak as it is to
explain the origin of any religious system. There is no discernible continuity

either in the rise of the Tonghak or in its development, and the traditional interpretation of its origin is obscured by mysticism. Contrary to popular belief, the founder of Tonghak, Ch'oe,[6] was not born with a messianic mission. Tonghak was a product of the time and the society in which it originated; it developed in an environment in which the underprivileged struggled to rise above their predetermined social status.

Ch'oe Che-u (1824-1864), whose pen name was Suun,[7] was born on October 18, 1824, in Kajŏngni, a small village near Kumi Mountain, west of Kyŏngju. His ancestry could be traced back to Ch'oe Ch'i-wŏn, the noted scholar of the Silla period. His father, Ch'oe Ok (or Ok-kŭm), was one of the many impoverished literati who taught the classics to the village children. Che-u was a *sŏja,* a son by a concubine. In Yi society this social stigma frustrated his aspirations from the outset. Ch'oe's formative years were not happy. When he was six his mother died; at thirteen he was forced to marry; when he was sixteen, his father died. Four years later a mysterious fire destroyed the entire family library, treasured for generations, and most of the household furniture. From that time young Ch'oe was haunted with a sense of guilt against his ancestors, particularly against his father. With this guilt and his filial sympathy for his father's failure in life,[8] Ch'oe could no longer endure the inane and hopeless life that he had been born into. He pledged to discover a "new way" by which he might regain his lost property and achieve the fame that his father had failed to win.[9]

With this new sense of mission, Ch'oe left his native village sometime in 1845 and ultimately arrived in Ulsan, the home town of his wife. There, secluded from all earthly distractions, he searched for truth in the ancient classics, especially those written by Taoists and Korean prophets. This period of study was fruitless and lasted until 1855, when he met a Buddhist monk who gave him a secret book.[10] This book taught Ch'oe that truth could be discovered only through prayer and meditation. Accordingly, he became absorbed in intense meditation and prayer at various Buddhist temples on Ch'ŏnsŏng Mountain near Yangsan in southern Kyŏngsang. His mysterious conduct, however, soon drew the attention of the local authorities, and he had to leave the mountain and return to his native village, where he arrived early in 1859.

The turning point in his life came soon after his return. News of the Western invasions in China spurred Ch'oe to transcend his narrow personal ambition to the greater one of dedication to the salvation of his people. He decided that religion was the paramount reason for the West's invasion of China. Furthermore, he believed that the same Western religion might bring about a foreign invasion of Korea. From that time Ch'oe became a furious enemy of "Western learning" (sŏhak), by which he meant Western religion, or Catholicism.[11] He felt a greater sense of urgency to receive a supernatural power or inspiration which alone, he felt, could save Korea from the impending crisis.

He asked himself why the Western nations were strong enough to bring the once invincible Middle Kingdom to its knees. He believed that the source of the West's strength lay in its possession of Ch'ŏnju (t'ien-chu, or God). Then he began to wonder if the Ch'ŏnju were necessarily the monopoly of the West, and concluded that that was surely not the case. He professed to believe that anyone could receive the mandate from the Ch'ŏnju, and he rejoiced at the possibility that he himself might receive a mandate to found an "Eastern learning" (tonghak) as a counterpart to sŏhak, so that his country could become strong too. Accordingly, he began to pray for a mandate. The official Tonghak account (actually Ch'oe's own account) shows that his fervent prayers were finally rewarded on May 25, 1860, with a visionary communication with the Ch'ŏnju.[12]

After the vision, Ch'oe considered himself destined to found a new Way, which would teach about the fundamental identity of man and ch'ŏn (heaven).[13] He believed that his religion, born after Confucianism and Buddhism had fulfilled their mission in the world,[14] would replace those teachings in accordance with what he called "the principle of the cycle of divine destiny."[15] He thought the birth of his Way would herald a new era for Korea, the return of the golden age of Yao and Shun, and the people would enjoy unending prosperity and tranquility.[16] In this new era, again in accordance with the principle of the cycle, "the poor and the lowly shall become rich and mighty and the rich and the mighty shall become poor and lowly."[17] For this reason, Ch'oe's message appealed greatly to the masses, bound in social and economic misery. He also held out the hope of relief from worldly distress in a song, which said that he was sent by the Ch'ŏnju to "safeguard the nation."[18]

Ch'oe's teachings did not make much of an impression in his native village, so he left on an evangelical mission to Chŏlla. By 1862 his teaching had spread over an area encompassing most of the rebellion-torn districts. This is borne out in the report of Chŏng Un-gu, who was sent to Kyŏngju to apprehend Ch'oe late in 1863. Chŏng said that in numerous districts between Choryŏng and Kyŏngju, in an area covering more than 400 *i,* there was not a single place where he did not hear about Tonghak: "There was not a shop-woman or a mountain boy who was not able to recite the scripture."[19] Thus, on the eve of the Taewŏn'gun's rise to power, Tonghak had become a social force which gave every indication of aiming at social revolution. In short, Tonghak provided a psychological impetus to the 1862-1863 uprisings.

Government Policy Toward Social Upheaval

News of the Chinju uprising, which occurred on March 18, 1862, first reached the capital on March 29. The government immediately dispatched Pak Kyu-su as special investigator *(anhaeksa)* to Chinju,[20] and promulgated several emergency decrees aimed at curbing some of the worst official abuses. On April 23, in accordance with a proposal made by Chief Councillor Kim Chwa-gŭn (1797-1869), King Ch'ŏlchong issued an edict reducing the number of district clerks and warning those magistrates who had embezzled more than 400 *yang* of public funds that they would be punished under the Ming penal code.[21] On May 13 the king promulgated another edict warning officials against further graft and ordering them to return whatever they had extorted.[22]

These emergency measures, however, did nothing to prevent the Chinju uprising from spreading to other regions. By May 19 three other districts had fallen to the rebels. Consequently, the government took more positive steps to extirpate what were considered to be the direct causes of the rebellions. On May 22 the king ordered the Pibyŏnsa to take necessary measures to avert illicit levies on markets and ports *(p'ogu)* and to suppress the illegal seizure of land.[23] On May 27 he requested the senior members of the Pibyŏnsa and a number of other ranking officials to recommend men of proven honesty and integrity to important posts, for example, as magistrates of the most ill-governed districts.[24] On June 6 the members of the royal house were specially warned against extorting from the peasants.[25]

The government also began to take direct action against the rebels. On June 10 the Pibyŏnsa decreed that leaders of the uprisings be killed on the spot as a warning to others.[26] More than twenty-eight leaders were beheaded.[27] On the other hand, magistrates and governors who were responsible for the rapid spread of the uprisings, which, by June 28, had broken out in sixteen other districts, were only lightly punished. Most of them were merely dismissed from their official posts, although in a few cases they were banished for a brief term.[28]

While these measures were being taken, the investigators who had been sent down to the troubled south began to report their findings to the government. One of the most disturbing reports was submitted on June 18 by Pak Kyu-su. He depicted the unfortunate conditions in the south and pointed out that the root of the current social unrest lay in the degeneration of the three systems.[29] He recommended that a special committee be created to study the deteriorated systems, with a view to their reform. Pak's proposal was promptly approved by the king on June 22.[30] On June 23 a joint conference was held by the minister of revenue with the senior members of the Pibyŏnsa and the Sŏnhyech'ŏng (Bureau of Tribute). This meeting resulted in the establishment of the Ijŏngch'ŏng (Committee for Reforms).[31] On the same day, Chŏng Wŏn-yong (1783-1873), Kim Hŭng-gŭn (1796-1870), Kim Chwa-gŭn, and Cho Tu-sun (1796-1870) were appointed co-chairmen of the committee. On June 24 fifteen other leading officials were added to the committee; by July 19 there were thirty-four members in all.[32]

At first the reform project showed considerable promise. To gather ideas, the king summoned all government officials and prominent scholars on July 8 and asked them to compose essays on "The Rectification of the Defects in the Three Systems." The essayists were given ten days to compose their ideas. The grand old man Chŏng Wŏn-yong was appointed reader of the essays. The king also ordered the government to circulate the title of the essay throughout the provinces, so that each locality could make known its specific problems. High-ranking officials were especially asked to offer the king their oral opinions on the reforms.[33]

While the essays were being read, the committee resolved to put an end to the age-old institution of abuse and graft perpetrated by clerks, magistrates, and yangban. Between July 31 and August 2, acting on the recommendation of the committee, the king promulgated half a dozen edicts to this effect.[34] Meanwhile, a general "reform plan" was drafted and, on September 23, submitted to the throne.[35] The plan called for the abolition of the grain-loan system and an increase in the land tax to make up for the loss of state revenue. Though it was apparent that the proposed reform would greatly relieve the burden on the people, it had first to be approved by the entire committee. On October 4 the four co-chairmen of the committee and twenty-seven of its senior members met before the throne for the final debate on the draft plan. The members of the committee were divided: the conservatives led by Chŏng Wŏn-yong opposed the abolition of the grain-loan system, largely on the sentimental ground that "it had been in existence for many years"; the others, led by Kim Hŭng-gŭn, Kim Chwa-gŭn, and Cho Tu-sun, supported the draft.[36]

The issue could not be decided by votes, but only by compromise. The king requested Chŏng to draft a new plan, and this was presented to the throne on October 10. The new draft contained nothing important, except one provision permitting the three southern provinces of Kyŏngsang, Chŏlla, and Ch'ungch'ŏng to make some minor reforms in the grain-loan system.[37] Since Chŏng was the dean of the official corps and the king's most trusted counselor, his plan was accepted. The committee, which was originally designed to be an arena for the mutual exchange of opinions on the reform policy, now became a "one-man committee" that ignored the wishes of the majority. Perhaps under the influence of Chŏng, the committee was dissolved on October 12.[38] Soon after, on December 10, Cho Tu-sun, who had supported the original draft, resigned from his post. At the same time, Chŏng was appointed chief councillor.[39] Cho's resignation may well have indicated his disapproval of Chŏng's unilateral action.

The original reform plan, however, was not forgotten by some in the government. When Chŏng left his post, Kim Chwa-gŭn became chief council-lor and Cho was reappointed left councillor on October 20, 1863; the question of the abolition of the grain-loan system was again brought up in official circles.[40] On January 12, 1864, a junior civil servant named Chŏng Sŏng-il presented a memorial in which he appealed for the abolition of the system. In response to this memorial, the king ordered the Ŭijŏngbu to deliberate on the matter.[41] Unfortunately, King Ch' ŏlchong died four days later, and all questions of reform were left in abeyance.

Chapter IV

THE TAEWŎN'GUN AND ECONOMIC RECONSTRUCTION

When King Ch'ŏlchong died on January 16, 1864, he left no heir and had named no successor. In circumstances such as these it was traditional for the widow of the deceased monarch to designate a new king. However, if the widow of a predecessor of the deceased monarch were still alive, this right was exercised by the senior widow. At the time of Ch'ŏlchong's death there were three surviving dowagers. Munjo's consort, Queen Sinjŏng (1809-1890), a P'ungyang Cho, was the oldest, and thus the "designation right" was vested in her.[1]

The formal designation of the heir was made immediately after the king's death was officially proclaimed. In her edict, Dowager Regent Cho (Queen Sinjŏng), who had received the royal seal from the dying king, announced that the second son of Yi Ha-ŭng, Yi Myŏng-bok, should reign as the twenty-sixth Yi king, and succeed Munjo's line.[2] Yi was chosen apparently because he was the only suitable surviving male member of the Yi clan and closest by blood to the royal house. That same day, January 16, Yi Myŏng-bok was temporarily appointed the Prince of Iksŏng. On January 17 his father was given the title of Taewŏn'gun or Grand Prince. On January 21 the new king was enthroned and Dowager Queen Sinjŏng began her regency.[3]

The new regent invited the Taewŏn'gun to assist the young king, who was but twelve years old. She virtually renounced her own right to the regency in spite of opposition from the Kim family headed by Kim Chwa-gŭn and Kim Hŭng-gŭn.[4] Thus the Taewŏn'gun ruled as de facto regent although Dowager Queen Sinjŏng remained titular regent until March 29, 1866.[5]

Partly because his son had succeeded circumstantially to the broken dynastic line, the Taewŏn'gun was preoccupied with the idea of restoration. Although he formulated no general program defining his ideas in terms of a restoration *(yusin),* he was aiming at a new beginning for the dynasty, a return to the time of King T'aejo and the golden age when true harmony reigned between the sovereign and his subjects. This harmony had long since been lost through the deterioration or the transformation of the original

institutions. Thus, the Taewŏn'gun pressed for *yusin* in an effort to revitalize
and fortify the dynastic line both symbolically and institutionally.

The Anti-Corruption Campaign

One of the most pressing tasks which the Taewŏn'gun undertook right
from the beginning of his regime was the eradication of the corruption of the
local governments. His targets were the "debted clerks" *(p'ori),* the magistrates, and the provincial officials who had misappropriated public funds
during Ch'ŏlchong's reign. Although he was not successful in recovering the
embezzled capital, this massive campaign, which was carried on until 1866,
revealed for the first time the incredible extent of corruption on local levels.

The most sensational case uncovered by the secret inspectors in charge
of the campaign was that of Sim I-t'aek, who served as magistrate of Ŭiju
from 1862 to 1863. Sim was reported to have amassed a fortune of some
273,700 *yang* during his tenure. He had speculated with and embezzled
public funds, offered bribes, sold local posts, levied illegal taxes, extorted
money from merchants and rich people, and sold islands in the Yalu.[6] These
findings, reported on February 3, 1864, actually opened the formal drive
against corruption.[7] Ch'ungch'ŏng, P'yŏngan, and Kyŏngsang were found to
have the most corrupt officials. In Ch'ungch'ŏng more than seventy-six clerks
had each embezzled more than 100 *sŏk* of grain; innumerable others had
embezzled amounts of less than 100 *sŏk.*[8] In P'yŏngan six clerks had each
swindled between 6,000 and 30,000 *yang,* and eight others between 1,000
and 2,000 *yang.*[9] In Kyŏngsang, in addition to a large number of minor
offenders, some forty clerks each misappropriated between 200 and 1,000
sŏk of public grain, and five former provincial naval commanders were convicted of having embezzled public funds.[10] The total number of major
offenders apprehended in the country between 1864 and 1866 was no less
than 156. The punishment meted out was unusually heavy. The clerks were
forced to dispose of all their possessions, and then, according to the serious-
ness of their offense, were either sent to the galleys or were decapitated.
Convicted officials were generally banished and their descendants barred
from government service.

The anti-corruption campaign was followed by measures designed to
prevent recurrences of malpractice in the local governments. Magistrates

were put under the frequent surveillance of secret inspectors, and edict after edict warned against maladministration. Officials who were suspected of maladministration or found guilty of tending toward corruption caused by their incompetence, were dismissed without warning. Between May 1867 and January 1869 some 120 magistrates, one governor, and one naval commander were removed from office on such charges. On the other hand, local administrators of proven integrity were rewarded with royal citations and gifts, promotions, extension of their normal tenure, and the appointment of their sons to government posts.[11] It was proposed that the number of local clerks be drastically reduced, and persistent warnings against transactions and speculations with public grain were issued.[12]

Powerful local landlords were mercilessly dealt with. These landlords, known as *t'oho,* had worked hand in glove with the clerks and were reported to have interfered in almost every field of local administration. They had encroached upon public land and openly evaded paying taxes. Their victims were the peasants, who were severely punished whenever they were unable to discharge their debts. The purge of the *t'oho* was formally announced in a special edict by the dowager regent on April 3, 1864. Secret inspectors were sent out, and although the success of this campaign cannot be readily assessed, a few records indicate that in 1867 alone some forty *t'oho* were apprehended in Ch'ungch'ŏng and Kyŏngsang and subsequently banished.[13]

Trenchant measures were also taken against corruption in the transportation of tax grain by sea. Those in charge of the transportation were found guilty of speculating with the grain. This had led to endless delays in delivery and to overloading, which frequently caused shipwrecks. Under the Taewŏn'gun, new ships which could be converted into warships were constructed to facilitate grain transportation, and loading and unloading was more strictly supervised.[14]

In the early part of 1873 an order was issued to scrutinize the government account books more closely. The government agencies in charge of receiving the various taxes were instructed to submit quarterly audits of their books instead of a general statement of the accounts at the end of each year.[15]

The Reform of the Three Systems

Any attempt to revitalize the Yi economy would have been futile without a drastic reform of the land system. Tax-exempt land, the largest part of
which was held by the royal house and palace estates, had to be reduced. A
large amount of cultivated land was missing from the land registers, whereas
land that had been left uncultivated for years was subject to taxation. The
land tax varied from region to region despite the fixed legal rate. Many public
lots were used by officials and powerful yangban for their own ends. The
settlement of many of these and related problems depended largely upon
reliable land surveys. The most recent surveys, however, dated from 1720,
and the archaic land registers were a source of graft and corruption in the
local governments. Throughout the decade of the Taewŏn'gun's rule, edicts
and memorials alike pointed out the urgent need for new land surveys.
Although provincial and district authorities were ordered to undertake
them,[16] available documents report their completion in only a few districts.[17]

Several measures were introduced to limit the landholdings of the
members of the royal house, which seemed to have totaled some 30,000
kyŏl,[18] and the related abuses. In February 1864 the dowager regent issued
an edict formally dismissing the stewards *(tojang)* of the palace estates,[19]
and turning over the collection of rents to the district authorities.[20] The
exemption of taxes on privately purchased land *(chabijŏn)* was gradually
made illegal. The law under which land granted to a princely house would be
returned to the state after the fourth generation of the grantee had passed
was reinforced, and the size of legal land grants was reduced.[21]

One of the major events in the economic history of Yi Korea was the
Taewŏn'gun's reform of the military tax system. Although the date of the
actual introduction of this reform cannot be obtained readily, there is
evidence that the ancient system of levying military tax on individual adults
was abolished during the early years of his regime and replaced by a system
of taxing villages.[22] In 1870, however, this system was superseded by the
establishment of the *hop'o,* or household tax system. This specified a
military tax of two *yang* on every household which was raised to three *yang*
in 1894. Yangban households that had enjoyed exemption from the military
tax in the past were not exempted. They were allowed, however, to fulfill

their dues in the name of their household slaves. This face-saving measure was apparently intended to stress the sharp social division between the yangban and the commoners. Nevertheless, commoners began to ridicule the yangban, saying that "we and they" were equal.[23]

After the uprisings of 1862-1863 the grain-loan system was practically, although not formally, abandoned. The Taewŏn'gun's policy toward grain-loan was two-fold. On the one hand he attempted to recover some of the grain that had been enbezzled by the clerks; on the other hand, he restored the grain-loan system through a number of reinvestments of money and grain. The first such reinvestment was made in 1866 with 300,000 yang which were especially appropriated for this purpose from the royal treasury. The money was distributed to Kyŏnggi (40,000 yang), Kyŏngsang (70,000 yang), Chŏlla (60,000 yang), Hwanghae (60,000 yang), Ch'ungch'ŏng (50,000 yang), and Kangwŏn (20,000 yang). The grain purchased with these funds was known as pyŏngin pyŏlbigok (the special grain of 1866), and was loaned out for profit. The profits were to be used primarily to finance the provincial and district governments.[24]

In 1867 a second major investment of 1,420,000 yang in newly minted cash was allocated to Kyŏngsang (600,000 yang), Chŏlla (400,000 yang), Ch'ungch'ŏng (300,000 yang), and Hwanghae (120,000 yang). The grain purchased with this money was called hojo pyŏlbi hyŏllok or the special grain of the Department of Revenue.[25]

In addition to these two major investments, three special loan-funds were established. One fund was especially designed to finance the defense of the island of Kanghwa. The capital grain for this fund amounted to 3,806 sŏk and was provided by the Taewŏn'gun's palace in 1870. The two other loan-funds, each in the amount of 15,000 yang, were set up to finance the military in Ch'ungch'ŏng and Hamgyŏng. Two-thirds of the capital designated for Hamgyŏng was also given by the Taewŏn'gun's palace.[26] Thus, the total of both investments and the loan-funds was some 586,000 sŏk of uncleaned rice by the end of 1870.[27]

The greater part of this grain seems to have been managed through the village granaries (sach'ang). The establishment of these village granaries was first proposed by Minister of Revenue Kim Pyŏng-guk on July 7, 1867, and soon approved by the government. The granaries, which were borrowed in name and principle from Chu Hsi's *she-ts'ang,* were instituted to prevent the defects of the old grain-loan system. Although the regulations pertaining to the amount of interest to be levied and the means of payment generally differed little from those of the old system, the actual management of the granaries was placed directly in the hands of the elders of the *myŏn* (the lowest administrative unit with limited autonomy) under the general supervision of the district and provincial governments. The influence of the clerks was thus decisively lessened.

A *myŏn* usually had one granary. Each village in the *myŏn* was held responsible as a whole for the repayment of the borrowed grain and the interest. Should a villager become insolvent or flee the village, the burden of paying his dues would be shared equally by all the villagers and no longer just by his kinsmen.[28]

The Introduction of New Taxes

Besides the reform of the three major economic institutions, the Taewŏn'gun introduced a number of new taxes, the proceeds of which were needed to finance his defense program. The much criticized gate tax *(munse),* which was levied on all commodities that passed through the seven main gates of Seoul, came into being in April 1867. The tax was collected by the military authorities and varied according to the quantity and the kind of commodity, ranging from one *p'un* (100 *p'un* equaled 1 *yang*) to two *p'un* of each load carried by one man.[29] Similar measures were enforced in two other localities. On May 2, 1867, the authorities of the recently restored garrison district of Ch'ŏngsŏkchin near the commercial town of Kaesŏng were authorized to collect a kind of toll tax on commodities being transported through the district. On November 20, 1868, the Yŏgakchuin was reestablished at the important commercial port of Kyŏlsŏng in Hwanghae. The Yŏgakchuin was an agency commissioned by the government to engage in the storage and brokerage business for merchants arriving at the port. The revenue from both the tax and the commission was used for the maintenance of the military.[30]

The *p'oryangmi* (lit., "artillery or rifle rice") was a surtax on land that was introduced on July 12, 1871, in response to a proposal by Kim Pyŏng-hak, then the chief councillor of state. This tax exacted one *tu* of rice on each *kyŏl* of land in six of the eight provinces (Hamgyŏng and P'yŏngan were excluded); the yield per year was calculated at some 50,000 *sŏk* of rice, an amount enough to maintain a permanent rifle contingent of 3,000 to 4,000 men for the defense of the island of Kanghwa. The important provision was that the tax was to be paid by the landlords and not by the tenants.[31]

Aside from the above-mentioned taxes, the Taewŏn'gun also imposed taxes on the fishing and salt-manufacturing industries to bolster the military budget.[32] Both industries had been government monopolies during the early Yi dynasty. After the Hideyoshi invasion they had fallen into the hands of princely houses and influential yangban. In 1751, in connection with the reform of the military tax, some measures were introduced to bring them back under the direct control of the central government; the results were limited. Heavy taxes had virtually ruined these industries, and to a large extent they remained under the control of princely houses, powerful local yangban, and merchant speculators.[33] The Taewŏn'gun confiscated the privately owned fishing grounds and means of salt production and turned them over to the management of the local governments.

During this period the export tax on ginseng was raised from fourteen *yang* per *kŭn* (approximately 1.3 lbs.) to fifteen *yang*. The export quota of ginseng was increased at one time from between 8,000 and 12,000 *kŭn* to 30,000 *kŭn*, and a new levy of two *yang* per *kŭn* was imposed on domestic consumption.[34] Traditionally the ginseng trade was conducted by commissioned Ŭiju merchants and interpreters of the Bureau of Interpreters. However, the Ŭiju merchants had been gradually forced out of their commission by Seoul merchants who were backed by influential political friends. The Taewŏn'gun restored the privilege of the Ŭiju merchants and increased the number of licensed merchants from thirty to forty.[35] Ginseng smuggling was energetically suppressed.

The Taewŏn'gun's Monetary Venture

Ever since the reigns of King Injo (r. 1623-1649) and King Sukchong (r. 1675-1720)[36] the Korean economy had suffered from an insufficient supply of cash. It had been traditional for the government not to mint coins unless there was an acute financial crisis, for minting was costly owing to an insufficient supply of copper.[37] The last major mintings of the famous *sangp'yŏng t'ongbo* were in 1852 and 1858.[38] In the face of an unprecedented financial crisis, the Taewŏn'gun was compelled to resume minting operations. However, since copper was scarce, he introduced a new coin and imported Chinese coins. His actions may have been prompted by a variety of factors: the traditional fiscal practices, the financial collapse at the end of Ch'ŏlchong's reign, the increasing military expenditures, the restoration of the grain-loan system, large-scale public works, and his difficulties with Japan.

The new coin was slightly larger and heavier than the *sangp'yŏng t'ongbo* and had the denomination of *tangbaekchŏn* (lit., "equal to 100 *chŏn*"). It was proposed on December 6, 1866, by Kim Pyŏng-hak, then the left councillor of state.[39] On December 12, after extensive deliberation by the ranking members of the government, the minting of the new coin was begun at the Kŭmwi regiment under the direction of the Department of Revenue. The minting seems to have lasted until June 15, 1867.[40] The new coin was formally put into circulation on January 15, 1867. To ensure its uniform circulation, new and old coins were to be used in the ratio of two to one.[41]

Two problems soon arose: counterfeiters immediately went to work and the people, particularly the peasants, refused to accept the new coin. The government punished the counterfeiters harshly; following the traditional policy, they were unceremoniously put to death as soon as they were apprehended.[42] To break resistance to the new coin the government sent the large sum of 1,420,000 *yang* in new coins to Kyŏngsang, Chŏlla, Ch'ungch'ŏng, and Hwanghae on July 4, 1867, to pay for the rice which served as capital for the restored grain-loan system.[43] On March 23, 1868, all merchants and shopkeepers in Seoul were summoned before the Taewŏn'gun and ordered to receive the new coin. Furthermore, detailed instructions were put up to guide the people in its use.[44]

By the end of 1868 the new coin had found its way into daily transactions, but it gave rise to widespread inflation, which was accelerated by continued counterfeiting and the importation of Chinese coins worth three to four million *yang* or more.[45] Rigid price control measures affecting all commodities were imposed in an attempt to stem the inflationary tide, but they had limited success.

The Taewŏn'gun also attempted to curb some of the extravagances of the yangban that affected the economy adversely. Their large overcoats and ceremonial gowns with immense sleeves, the two or three foot long pipes, hats the size of parasols tied under the chin with two-foot long hat strings, immense sheets of letter paper, and large quantities of silver utensils were conspicuous signs of the luxurious life of Korea's upper class. Few criticisms had been directed against these extravagances until the Taewŏn'gun launched his vigorous drive against waste and extravagance. He ordered the length and width of their coats and gowns and the size of the hats to be drastically reduced, and yangban who ignored his order were indiscriminately fined. The length of pipes and hat strings was radically shortened, and the costly white leather or silk shoes were replaced by more durable black leather ones. The use of fancy silver utensils such as wine cups, spoons, plates, and chopsticks was reserved for the royal family. Elaborate regulations even limited the use of silk for clothing.[46]

It is difficult to say exactly how successful the Taewŏn'gun's economy program was, and almost impossible to determine with any accuracy the extent to which the program was put into operation. Documents do show that corruption in local governments was checked to a large degree. The government even began to accumulate some surplus funds in its treasury. For example, Minister of War Min Ch'i-sang noted on April 1, 1873, that his department had enjoyed a great increase in revenue during the past few years; he ascribed this to the Taewŏn'gun's wise financial policy.[47]

The Taewŏn'gun appeared to have resolved two of Korea's historical problems with lasting effect. The establishment of the *hop'o* was revolutionary since it equalized the military obligations among the social classes. Ŏm Se-yŏng, who was sent as secret inspector to Chŏlla in 1875, testified that after the introduction of the *hop'o*, extortion ceased.[48] Furthermore, the *hop'o* laid the foundation for the future *hose* (household tax). The *sach'ang* system is rightly regarded as the forerunner of the rural bank, *kŭmyung chohap,* which was introduced during the Japanese colonial period.[49]

Thus, during the Taewŏn'gun's regime the government recovered from its economic decline and regained some of its financial vitality despite unprecedented spending on military and public works. Yet the Taewŏn'gun did not significantly abandon the traditional economic policies and institutions. The economy remained basically agrarian with no steps taken toward commercialization or industrialization.

Chapter V

THE REORGANIZATION OF THE GOVERNMENT

The social and economic ills of Yi Korea had flourished mainly because the central government was unable to control the local governments. In theory, all Yi kings were autocrats; they were the source of all power, civil and military, and they had final authority over all executive, legislative, and judicial matters. In practice, however, their power and authority was limited by the actual governmental machinery, by their consorts, their in-laws, and by an inadequate system of communication with various parts of the country. Of these limitations, the governmental system played the most important role in limiting and checking their power and authority.

In the early years of the Yi dynasty civil and military power were clearly divided. The supreme executive power over civil affairs was delegated to the Council of State (Ŭijŏngbu) to which were subordinated the six administrative departments of appointment, revenue, rites, war, punishment, and works. All military affairs, except for personnel matters, were placed under the jurisdiction of the Military Council (Samgunbu). In the course of time, however, this arrangement underwent many changes until an office called the Board of Defense, or Pibyŏnsa, emerged, eventually absorbing both civil and military power. These changes were bitterly criticized by many who thought the original arrangement ideal. Following is a history of the origins and the development of the three councils.

The Origin and Development of the Council of State

The Council of State had its origins in the Supreme Council (Top'yŏng ŭisasa), which, together with the Board of Civil Affairs (Munhabu), had been the highest organ of the Koryŏ government, and which at the beginning of the Yi dynasty consisted of the highest officials of the Board of Civil Affairs, the Board of Economic Affairs (Samsa), and the Board of Military Command (Chungch'uwŏn).[1] Three councillors (chief, left, and right), two vice-councillors (left and right), and two assistant councillors (left and right) formed the ruling element of the Council of State. In theory the three councillors were equal in rank and power, although the chief councillor acted as the head of the council. In the absence of the councillors, the vice-councillors presided. The assistant councillors aided the senior members. The secretarial work of the council was performed by two secretaries *(sain)*, one auditor *(kŏmsang)*, one recorder *(sarok)*, and a number of clerks.[2]

The official duties of the council were vaguely defined in the *Kyŏngguk taejŏn* (Great code of administration) of 1471, according to which the council was empowered to "oversee all officials of the government, manage all affairs of the state, regulate the forces of yin and yang, and govern the nation."[3] However, both this general definition of the council's role and its specific powers, referred to in the same code,[4] merely reflect the council's nature during the formative years of the dynasty.[5]

Prior to 1864 there were three periods during which the council functioned with full power. In the first period (1392-1413) the council had complete control over the six administrative departments, which did not have direct access to the throne, and directed the transaction of all official business. On May 5, 1414,[6] King T'aejong (r. 1400-1418), apparently alarmed at the growing power of the council, deprived it of its "supervisory power" *(sŏsa* power) and reduced it to a kind of advisory board to the king, leaving it, however, with the right to handle diplomatic correspondence with the Ming court and to review important criminal cases. This action gave the king absolute power, and transformed the six departments into his private administrative chambers.[7]

The second period began on April 28, 1436, when King Sejong restored *sŏsa* power to the council. Sejong upheld that power as the "fundamental law" *(sŏnghŏn)* of King T'aejo. For the first time since the council was established the relationships between the king, the council, and the six departments were clearly defined. In fact, at this time the council's power was increased considerably.[8] However, the "fundamental law" of T'aejo was abolished when another strong king, Sejo, usurped the throne from his nephew, Tanjong, in 1455.[9]

The last time the power of the council was restored was on June 30, 1516, under King Chungjong.[10] The council, however, was soon obscured by a new office, the Board of Defense.

The Military Council and the Problems of Military Command

The predominant feature of the Yi military system in the early years of the dynasty was the clearly defined autonomy of military authority—more precisely, the power of military command—from the civil branches of the government. According to the royal decree defining the governmental organization, which was issued on August 16, 1392, military affairs were put under the jurisdiction of the Department of War and the Board of Military Command (Chungch'uwŏn).[11] The latter agency, however, was soon assimiliated by the Ŭihŭng samgunbu (lit., "Headquarters of the Righteously Rising Three Armies"), or, in short, the Samgunbu (lit., "Three Armies Headquarters"), which I shall call the Military Council. The council had originally been created to command a new royal army consisting of three large corps: the central, left, and right corps.[12] The merger was formally enacted in 1400, and the council was delegated supreme military command. The significant feature of the new military council was that all its members, most of whom were military personnel, were barred from holding concurrent posts in other government departments, notably in the Ŭijŏngbu.[13] Thus, no encroachment of military authority on civil offices was allowed, and military command was completely independent of the civil authority of the government.

The history of the Samgunbu, though brief, paralleled for the greater part the history of the Ŭijŏngbu. The Samgunbu's main problem was its lack of real power. Its independent status and power were gradually attenuated, and its name was frequently changed, until it was buried in oblivion. King T'aejong was the first to attempt to control the power of the council. He tried to subordinate the Samgunbu to other branches of the government, namely, to the Department of War and the Ŭijŏngbu, but later brought it under his personal control.[14] After his death in 1422 the Samgunbu's power was restored. Ten years later, however, the council was permanently dissolved and the long defunct Chungch'uwŏn was recreated to take its place.[15] In 1451 the Three Armies system was dissolved and a new military system was introduced;[16] the army was divided into five regiments *(owi)* and was apparently under the control of the Chungch'uwŏn until 1466, when a new Military Command Office of Five Regiments (Owi toch'ongbu) was established.[17] Largely due to this reorganization, the Chungch'uwŏn was transformed into an office of an entirely different nature, having no connection

with military matters,[18] and was renamed the Chungch'ubu. The authority
of the new military command office was soon absorbed first into the Department of War and then into the Pibyŏnsa. It remained intact, however, almost
until the end of the dynasty, playing a role similar to that of the
Chungch'ubu.[19] At the same time the newly reorganized central army disintegrated, owing to the heavy cost of maintaining such a standing army. More
emphasis was placed on local garrisons, which were made up of farmer-
soldiers, for defence purposes.

The Role of the Pibyŏnsa

The eventful rise and growth of the Pibyŏnsa was primarily related to
Korea's troubles with the Manchu tribes on her northern frontier and with
Japanese pirates along the coast. Since frontier defense was too important to
leave in the hands of provincial authorities, the government created a special
office on May 16, 1517, to handle frontier problems.[20] First named the
Ch'uksŏngsa (Bureau of Wall Construction), it was reorganized under the
name Pibyŏnsa on June 24, 1517. From the start, although it had no permanent status as yet in the government, the Pibyŏnsa was completely independent of either the Ŭijŏngbu or the Department of War. The personnel
consisted of two commissioners *(tojejo),* who were also state councillors, two deputy commissioners *(chejo),* chosen from among frontier
experts, a few administrative secretaries *(nanggwan),* and probably clerks.[21]

The Pibyŏnsa was not made a full-fledged administrative or executive
body of the government until 1572. Its primary function did not extend
beyond recommending policies with regard to the pacification of the fast-
growing Manchu tribes and the Japanese pirates, and to related problems.
Such recommendations, which according to their nature were carried out by
either the Department of War or the Department of Rites, were with few
exceptions put into effect.[22] Between 1517 and 1572 the Pibyŏnsa cooper-
ated closely with the Ŭijŏngbu, the Department of War, and the president of
the Chungch'ubu in joint conferences, usually held before the throne. The
Pibyŏnsa thus did not as yet have unchallenged authority in matters of
national defense.[23]

After 1573 the power of the Pibyŏnsa grew rapidly, particularly in the
realm of personnel matters, as a result of increasing threats from the Manchus

and the Japanese pirates. The Pibyŏnsa was almost solely responsible for the recruitment of new talent and the appointment, removal, and impeachment of provincial governors, naval and military commanders, and magistrates of strategically situated districts.[24] By 1592 the structure of the Pibyŏnsa had undergone many changes.[25] There were further changes between 1592 and 1793.[26] During those years the Pibyŏnsa gradually became the supreme policy-making and executive body of the government, holding the combined power and performing the functions of both the Ŭijŏngbu and the Samgunbu of the early days of the dynasty. It was also empowered to discharge a number of other duties previously not vested in either of the councils.[27] After 1713 four (later eight) of its members were charged with supervising the administration of the eight provinces. The right to recommend candidates for certain strategic posts was statutorily reserved for its governing members.[28]

Naturally the concentration of power in the Pibyŏnsa had a lasting impact on the entire Yi government machinery. For example, the Ŭijŏngbu virtually lost its political significance. To be sure, its senior councillors (and frequently one or two junior councillors) could attend the meetings of the Pibyŏnsa as ex officio commissioners, but other members of the council were left without any duties. The six administrative departments were also stripped of many of their functions.

In the last phase of the Pibyŏnsa's development, between 1800 and 1863, the number of its ruling members increased from some twenty in 1800 to approximately fifty in 1863. At the same time, the relatives of the queens gradually dominated the Pibyŏnsa. The Kim family of Andong, for instance, had fifteen men in the council during the latter years of Ch'ŏlchong's reign. The official record of the Pibyŏnsa covering this period shows that most of the strategic posts were actually rotated among the in-laws and their relatives.[29]

The Reorganization of the Council of State

The Taewŏn'gun's concern with the Ŭijŏngbu was first stated by Dowager Regent Cho on February 20, 1864, at a meeting with ranking officials. She pointed out the irregularity with which government affairs had been managed by the Pibyŏnsa, and instructed the Ŭijŏngbu to share in their management. Chief Councillor Kim Chwa-gŭn and Left Councillor Cho

Tu-sun commented on the fact that the Ŭijŏngbu had been an "office with no duties" since the Pibyŏnsa was established, and proposed to study the reorganization of the council and to present a special report.[30]

Presented on March 18, their reorganization plan called for the division of the administration of various government affairs between the two bodies. The Ŭijŏngbu was given back supervisory power over some forty-three government activities, mostly in the areas of ceremonies, education, personnel, the economy, punishment, and examinations.[31] The Pibyŏnsa was allowed to retain under its jurisdiction only those matters primarily of military significance such as beacon fires, courier service, fortifications, suppression of rebellions, ships, forests, defense of frontier and strategic passes, and transmission of diplomatic papers to China and Japan. Moreover, it was authorized to keep the power of recommending candidates for the posts of naval commander-in-chief (t'ongjesa) of the southern provinces, military commander of P'yŏngan and the northern section of Hamgyŏng, magistrate in Hoeryŏng, Ŭiju, Tongnae, Kanggye, and Cheju, commander of the five regiments, commander of the Sunmuyŏng (a special military command which was established temporarily in time of war), and border inspector (sunbyŏnsa).

The Ŭijŏngbu was granted the power to recommend candidates for the office of magistrate in Kaesŏng, Suwŏn, Kanghwa, and Kwangju, and for the office of governor in P'yŏngan and Hamgyŏng; it was given the right to select various ad hoc officials such as "pacificators" (sŏnmusa) in time of war and rebellion, special investigators (anhaeksa) for specific local problems, military inspectors (ch'allisa), "consolers" (wiyusa), who were sent to disaster areas, and secret inspectors (amhaeng ŏsa). In addition, the reorganization plan specifically permitted many of the senior members (tangsang)[32] of the Pibyŏnsa and its secretarial staff to hold concurrent appointments in corresponding positions in the council.

This arrangement, however, did not last long. On April 23, 1865,[33] a special edict ordered the Pibyŏnsa to integrate completely with the Ŭijŏngbu, which resumed its ancient status as the supreme administrative organ of the state. The internal organization of the new council of state was basically a replica of that of the Pibyŏnsa. The Pibyŏnsa's deputy commissioners and assistant commissioners (tangsang) and the twelve-man secretariat were

48

transferred in a body to the new council. They assumed the new titles *chŏngbu tangsang* (standing members of the deliberating and administrative committee of the council) and *kongsagwan*[34] (lit., "public affairs officials") respectively. All four junior councillors were included in this administrative committee, which was directly controlled by the three state councillors.[35] The minister of works, the commanders of the two metropolitan police head-quarters (Chwap'ochŏng and Up'och'ŏng), and the magistrate of Hansŏng (Seoul) also received statutory appointments to this body gradually.[36] The council's secretariat (Chŏngbu nangch'ŏng) consisted of *kongsagwan* and the regular roster of *sain, kŏmsang,* and *sarok.*[37] All functions of the Pibyŏnsa were taken over by the new council. Strictly speaking, except for the resto-ration of power to the grand councillors, all the reorganization amounted to was a mere change of names.

The Restoration of the Samgunbu and the Reconstruction of the Defense System

The restoration of the Samgunbu was to a large extent an inevitable result of the abolition of the Pibyŏnsa, which left to the new council of state both civil and military power. The deposition of these two powers in the council was undoubtedly unprecedented in Yi history. It repudiated what Kim Pyŏng-hak called the "far-sightedly conceived model of the dynastic forefathers," the separation of the two powers.[38]

The formal proposal for the restoration of the Samgunbu was put forward on June 19, 1865, by Chief Councillor Cho Tu-sun.[39] Although his proposal was approved by the court on the same day, the Samgunbu did not begin to function until April 15, 1868, when the composition of the person-nel was first announced.[40] The new body was empowered to deal with defense and overall military planning. In this it resembled greatly the original Samgunbu. Specifically, the new council was entitled to recommend candi-dates for a number of military commander and magistrate posts in strategic locations.[41]

The ruling element of the Samgunbu, which ranked equal to the Ŭijŏngbu in the hierarchy of government offices,[42] consisted of a president *(yŏngsa),* three vice-presidents *(p'ansa),* three first assistant presidents *(haeng chisa),* and five second assistant presidents *(chisa).* Most of these posts were concurrent appointments. Officials of the first three groups were drawn primarily from those who had served previously as regimental commanders. The *chisa* were generally selected from among the commanders of the five regiments. The routine work of the Samgunbu was handled by the *chisa* (except for the commander of the Suǒ regiment) who held the appointment of senior executive officers *(yusa tangsang).* [43]

The reconstruction of the defense system carried out by the Taewǒn'gun was probably the first major attempt at rearming Korea since the war with Japan in the sixteenth century. The impetus was provided by the French and American invasions. Korean military conditions on the eve of the French invasion in 1866 were deplorable. The military establishments were reduced to five regiments, all located in the capital region, and even these were keeping up a façade with a handful of soldiers. To be sure, there were naval and army bases throughout the country, but these too maintained no troops. This state of affairs explains the government's total reliance on volunteers and tiger-hunters during the French invasion.

The picture changed drastically, however, after this first encounter with the West. Between 1866 and 1873 Korea turned into something of an armed camp. The emphasis was primarily on the construction of fortresses and garrisons, the regrouping of military zones, the establishment of rifle units, the manufacture of war materials, and the reform of existing regiments. Fortresses and garrisons were built throughout the country, particularly along the coast, on strategic islands, and along the northern frontier. The regrouping of military zones was designed to channel military commands more effectively. For example, the Chinmu regiment on the island of Kanghwa was reorganized in December 1866 and given sole command of the general defense of Kanghwa as well as the entire coast of Kyǒnggi, Hwanghae, and part of Ch'ungch'ǒng.[44] Similarly, the defense of the southwestern coastal region of Chǒlla was placed under the command of a new military base established on the island of Chin in January 1867.[45]

The creation of rifle units was largely to the credit of General Sin Kwan-ho, one of the most colorful military figures of that time. The French invasion had convinced him of the superiority of Western firearms, and owing to his efforts and those of the Samgunbu, rifle units were introduced into

50

some 270 districts, mainly between 1871 and 1873.[46] Sin also recognized
the outstanding performance of the tiger-hunters from the north. He first
urged the integration of hunters into the organization of general defense in
a special memorial in March 1867.[47]

As for the manufacture of war materials, the Taewŏn'gun and his generals seemed to have put priority on improving the quality and on introducing
new weapons, for existing Korean arms were quite outdated.[48] Gunpowder
was ordered to be manufactured only during the dry seasons so as to increase
its effectiveness. In June 1867 ten new ships, including four "battleships"
(chŏnsŏn) especially equipped for fast maneuvers, were launched at a shipyard in Ch'ungch'ŏng.[49] In October of 1867 the government announced that
it had succeeded in manufacturing and testing an "underwater rocket"
(suroep'o) built after the model given in Wei Yüan's *Hai-kuo t'u-chih.*[50] This
project was probably undertaken by Kang Yun under the general supervision
of Sin Kwan-ho. Kang later became a military genius in the popular imagina-
tion, and is credited with the invention of a number of new weapons and the
construction of a steamship using charcoal for fuel, on the model of the
General Sherman.[51] Early in 1873 the government also reported that it had
cast a big cannon at the Hullyŏn regiment.[52]

The reform of the regiments was aimed at turning each contingent into
a pure combat unit. Traditionally Korean military units were organized more
for ceremonial purposes than for fighting. Nearly one fourth of the members
of a unit were noncombat personnel—clerks, servants, messengers, honor
guards, and color-bearers. The gist of the reform, which was credited to
General Sin and first introduced into the Hullyŏn regiment in 1867, was to
withdraw all noncombat personnel from the main body of the unit and
reorganize them into a separate auxiliary unit. The regular combat troops,
called *chŏngbyŏng,* were to be subjected to rigorous training and constant
examination so that weak members would be eliminated.[53]

The abolition of the Pibyŏnsa, the reorganization of the Ŭijŏngbu, and
the revival of the Samgunbu were all carried out in a general spirit of revital-
ization, a spirit which found repeated expression in edicts and memorials
with words such as *yusin.* The emphasis on military matters, which had been
discriminated against for centuries, restored to the military class the honor

and dignity that it had enjoyed during the early years of the dynasty. Official documents and private accounts of this period show that the two councils were instrumental in restoring order in the government and that they initiated and realized the manifold reforms that characterize the spirited decade of the Taewŏn'gun.

Chapter VI

THE TAEWŎN'GUN AND THE OFFICIALDOM

Ideally, the system which brought men into government service was to recruit men of talent, virtue, and excellent character. These qualities were believed to be acquired through the study of the Confucian classics, particularly the Neo-Confucianist teachings, and literature. Men who were accomplished in these fields were selected mainly by means of examinations and recommendations. However, there were few Yi institutions that suffered more from a conflict between the ideal and the reality. The recruiting system was in fact impaired by discrimination against classes other than the yangban, against illegitimate sons, men from the northern provinces of Hamgyŏng and P'yŏngan, and descendants of the former royal house of Koryŏ. Between 1800 and 1863, when the government was virtually controlled by the in-laws of the royal house, who were adherents of either the Noron or the Soron, nepotism not only influenced the appointment of officials, but also accelerated the disintegration of the recruiting system.[1]

With the emergence of the Taewŏn'gun many policies were radically changed. The power of the Noron and Soron, especially of the in-law groups, was curtailed, and discrimination was discontinued. Talented clerks, illegitimate sons, and slaves were given official status. These changes were conspicuous evidence of the Taewŏn'gun's determination to reconstruct and revitalize Korean officialdom and bring a certain degree of equality to the social classes.

The majority of the officials in office during the early days of the Taewŏn'gun's regime were carried over from the previous reign. Many were soon replaced by fresh, hitherto unknown men who were either closely associated with the Taewŏn'gun or had gained his confidence with their ability in office. Some were adherents of the Namin and Pugin factions, which had previously been out of power,[2] and others were members of the royal clan.

Following are some rough figures on the composition of the ruling elements of the Pibyŏnsa and the Ŭijŏngbu which succeeded it in 1865. Both bodies included all former and present councillors of state as well as many other ranking officials. It is safe to say that the pattern of composition found in these bodies would be valid for other government agencies during the period as well.

In May 1847 the ruling body of the Pibyŏnsa consisted of thirty-three members. There was definitely one Pugin and twenty-one Noron and Soron, thirteen of whom were in-laws.[3] In April 1857 thirty-two out of forty-nine members of the ruling body of the Pibyŏnsa were adherents of the Soron or Noron; among them were twenty-two in-laws, and only one was a Pugin.[4] In February 1866 the ruling body of the Ŭijŏngbu consisted of sixty-eight members; twenty-five of them were Noron or Soron, of whom at least nineteen were in-laws. The number of Namin or Pugin had risen to ten, and the royal family had four representatives.[5] In February 1873 there were sixty-four ruling members of the Ŭijŏngbu; there were still twenty-one Noron and Soron, of whom fifteen were in-laws. The large number of in-laws reflects the beginning of the influx of the Min family, who were soon successful in forcing the Taewŏn'gun out of power. There were no less than ten Pugin or Namin.[6]

These figures show a continuous decrease in the number of in-laws and Noron and Soron and an increase in the number of Namin and Pugin and members of the royal clan. However, the number of Pugin and Namin in the higher echelons of government never equaled that of the other factions. There is reason to believe that by the time the Taewŏn'gun came to power the lines of many of the early Namin and Pugin had fallen into oblivion. This is also evident from the fact that their representatives in the government during the Taewŏn'gun's reign came from only a few clans. Unfortunately, the backgrounds and ties of the other members of the ruling body are not readily accessible.

Brief biographical sketches of all the councillors of state who served under the Taewŏn'gun further illustrate the tendency to mobility within the officialdom. Between 1864 and 1873 eleven men held senior posts in the Ŭijŏngbu. Kim Chwa-gŭn, Cho Tu-sun, Yi Kyŏng-jae, Im Paek-kyŏng, and Yi Yu-wŏn received their appointments in the early days of the Taewŏn'gun's regime.

Kim Chwa-gŭn (1797-1869), an in-law of the royal house, had served as right councillor once and as chief councillor twice during the reign of King

Ch'ŏlchong. He was again appointed chief councillor on January 16, 1864, but resigned on May 23. Cho Tu-sun (1796-1870), who had served as right councillor and left councillor at least four times prior to the Taewŏn'gun's reign, was appointed left councillor on January 16, 1864, and promoted to chief councillor in April 1865. He stayed in that office, except for a brief interval, until May 26, 1866. Both Kim and Cho were Noron.[7]

Yi Kyŏng-jae (1800-1873), a Soron, had passed the higher civil service examination in 1822 without a spectacular record. Little is known about his early career. In 1845 he became a senior member of the Pibyŏnsa and two years later minister of works. In 1849 he was appointed minister of punishment, and in 1851, magistrate of Seoul. After 1851 he served in several important posts, including that of governor of P'yŏngan (1853), minister of war (1856), assistant left councillor of state (1858), and minister of revenue (1859). It came as no surprise, therefore, when he was appointed right councillor of state on February 9, 1864. He served in this capacity only until July. Then on May 26, 1866, he was called upon to become chief councillor, a position which he presumably retained during the subsequent years.[8]

Im Paek-kyŏng (1800-1865) was born into a Pugin family in 1800 and received the *munkwa* in 1827. His slow advancement may have been due to his factional background. His first major appointment, in 1848, was that of royal secretary *(sŭngji)*. In 1854 he was recommended for the post of magistrate of Kyesŏng, but his candidacy was unsuccessful. In 1858, however, he was appointed minister of punishment, and in 1859 magistrate of Sŭwon. His appointment as right councillor of state on July 18, 1864, must have been a deliberate move on the part of the Taewŏn'gun to bring into the Ŭijŏngbu a man who belonged neither to the Soron nor the Noron. Im served as right councillor until his death in March 1865.[9]

Yi Yu-wŏn (1814-1888) came from a Soron family. He passed the *munkwa* examination in 1841 and climbed the official ladder with unusual rapidity, probably aided by his connection with the in-law families. In 1846 he was appointed secret inspector; in 1850, at the age of thirty-six, he became magistrate of Ŭiju, a post which carried the rank of junior second grade. By 1864 he had held the offices of governor of Chŏlla (1851), vice-minister of appointment (1858), inspector-general (1859), minister of punishment (1860), minister of rites (1861), governor of Hwanghae (1862), and governor of Hamgyŏng (1863). From Hamgyŏng he was called to Seoul to serve as left councillor of state on July 18, 1864. His association with the Taewŏn'gun was short-lived, however; on March 22, 1865, he resigned, and although he served briefly again in the same capacity in June 1868, he gradually drifted to the side of the Min family.[10]

Kim Pyŏng-hak, Chŏng Wŏn-yong, Yu Hu-jo, Hong Sun-mok, Han Kye-wŏn, and Kang No served in the Ŭijŏngbu during the latter years of the Taewŏn'gun's reign. Except for Kim and Chŏng, none of them had been well known before the Taewŏn'gun noticed them. Chŏng Wŏn-yong (1783-1873) was a Soron and had served as chief councillor more than five times prior to 1864. Under the Taewŏn'gun he was chief councillor for only ten days in June 1868.[11]

Kim Pyŏng-hak (1821-1879) occupies a unique place in the history of Yi officialdom and deserves special attention. He was a nephew of Kim Mun-gŭn, King Ch'ŏlchong's father-in-law, and he masterminded a significant part of the Taewŏn'gun's reform program. The fact that he enjoyed the Taewŏn'gun's favor, in spite of the latter's policy of curbing the power of the Kim family, is difficult to explain. He may have earned this favor through his own abilities, but it seems clear that his extraordinarily rapid rise through the official hierarchy was largely owing to his family background.

He received the *chinsa* in 1849 at the age of twenty-eight, but he did not receive his *munkwa* until 1853. His performance in the final examination was not outstanding. Between 1849 and 1853 he seems to have occupied minor government posts. In 1853 he was appointed magistrate of Ŭiju (junior second grade), but was reassigned secretary of the Royal Secretariat. He was one of few men to hold a post of junior second grade at the age of thirty-two. Four years later he advanced to the post of senior member of the Pibyŏnsa. In that same year he moved rapidly from assignment to assignment: from vice-minister of works to vice-minister of appointment, to royal secretary, and finally to vice-minister of revenue. In 1859, after having administered the departments of war, punishment, and works, he held the key posts of magistrate of Suwŏn, chief academician *(tae chehak),* and minister of appointment. All of these posts were of the rank of senior second grade.

From 1860 to 1863, except for a short period as minister of works in 1862, Kim was out of office. The reason is unknown. With the emergence of

the Taewŏn'gun, however, appointment followed appointment. He became
minister of rites on March 3, 1864, minister of appointment on March 12,
and minister of rites on September 29. On February 25, 1865, he was
elevated to the Ŭijŏngbu as assistant left councillor, and on March 29, at the
age of forty-five, he was promoted to become left councillor of state. He
retained this position, with only a brief leave between April 18 and June 5,
1867, until June 19, 1867, when he was appointed chief councillor of state.
His was a rare case in Yi history; he became chief councillor at the age of
forty-six, and served in that capacity for seven years and six months.[12] His
long years of service in the Ŭijŏngbu covered the most crucial period of the
Taewŏn'gun's reign. The various official records show that he initiated many
of the Taewŏn'gun's foreign and domestic policies.

In contrast to Kim Pyŏng-hak, Yu Hu-jo (1798-1876) did not reach the
apex of his political career until the latter part of his life. A Namin, he was
the son of Yu Sim-ch'un, who had served in the Office of Protection of the
Heir to the Throne (Seja igwisa) during the reigns of Chŏngjo, Sunjo, and
Hŏnjong. Yu could trace his ancestry directly to Yu Sŏng-nyong, the chief
councillor during the Hideyoshi invasion. Utilizing the influence of his ancestry, he entered government service, rising to the rank of junior third grade by
1858. He did not receive his *munkwa* until he was sixty. Although most of
his political life after 1858 is not known, it is known that he was recommended for promotion, and that in 1860 he was a candidate for the post of
magistrate of Cheju. In each case he was unsuccessful. Kim Chwa-gŭn, Chŏng
Wŏn-yong, and Yi Yu-wŏn—the men who had recommended him—belonged
to the Noron and Soron, which suggests that factional lines were not as rigid
as they were often thought to be.

In 1865, after long years of inactivity, Yu unexpectedly rose to prominence. On January 1, 1865, he was appointed vice-minister of appointment,
and on December 2, minister of works. On February 18, 1866, at the age of
sixty-eight, he was promoted to right councillor of state, and then on June 19,
1867, he was made left councillor of state. There is no extant record of
Yu's activities as councillor. He resigned sometime in May 1868, apparently
without having drafted any major proposals.[13] One might conclude that his
appointment to the Ŭijŏngbu was merely a favor granted by the Taewŏn'gun
for political reasons.

Hong Sun-mok (1816-1884), a Noron, received the *munkwa* degree with a fair record in 1844. His career was obscure until he was appointed governor of Hwanghae on February 24, 1864. He proved himself an able administrator, and presumably on the strength of his record there, he was called to Seoul on June 6, 1866, to head the department of appointment. By 1868 he had held three other key posts: magistrate of Seoul, a second time as minister of appointment, and minister of rites. Finally, on March 4, 1868, on the basis of his "literary ability, wise counsel, and good reputation," he was nominated for the post of right councillor of state. On November 24, 1872, he succeeded Kim Pyŏng-hak as chief councillor of state, serving in that capacity until the end of the Taewŏn'gun's reign. It is difficult to assess Hong's role in the Ŭijŏngbu, since he was to some degree overshadowed by the powerful figure of Kim Pyŏng-hak. However, there is reason to believe that he was a sound judge of national affairs and conceived some constructive proposals to improve the economy.[14]

Han Kye-wŏn (1814-1882) was born into a Namin family. He received his *munkwa* with a brilliant record in 1835, and was apparently a man of great integrity. Despite his obvious qualifications, however, Han held only minor positions until 1864. In 1862 he was appointed magistrate of Ŭiju, but he was soon relieved. His political fortunes turned decisively on April 4, 1864, when he was summoned to fill the post of inspector-general. On August 19, 1865, he became minister of works; between 1866 and May 14, 1869, when he went to P'yŏngan as governor, he passed through seven key posts: magistrate of Seoul, a second time as inspector-general (1866), minister of rites and chief of the special tribunal (1867), minister of appointment and a second time as minister of works (1868), and left assistant councillor of state (1869).

His administration in P'yŏngan was very successful; he was considered a man with zeal and outstanding ability, and credited with the introduction of wise reforms. As a result, he was asked to serve as governor for one year beyond the normal tenure, which he did. His accomplishments in P'yŏngan won him the position of right councillor of state on November 24, 1872, when he was fifty-eight.[15]

Kang No (1809-1887), a Pugin, was the son of a magistrate of a small district. He received the *chinsa* degree in 1837 and passed the higher civil service examination in 1848. Despite his marked literary talent and his expertise in economic problems, he had a most uneventful career prior to his appointment as magistrate of Tongnae on April 12, 1863. In Tongnae he gained a reputation for unusual skill in administration, and was "discovered" by the Taewŏn'gun. On July 3, 1865, he was promoted to assistant minister of appointment, but was allowed to keep his Tongnae post. At the end of his tenure, on January 10, 1867, he moved to Seoul to become rector of the Sŏnggyun'gwan on the strength of his literary ability. On May 15, 1867, he was made vice-minister of appointment. Late in 1867 he went to Peking as the vice-envoy of the Winter Solstice Mission. On February 2, 1870, he was promoted to the rank of senior second grade, and in August of that year he headed the Winter Solstice Mission to Peking as the chief envoy. Finally, on November 12, 1872, at the age of sixty-three, he was appointed left councillor of state. This was indeed an extraordinary appointment for, without regard for his age or length of service in the government, it had been less than six years since he was promoted to the rank of junior second grade.[16]

Factional background was no doubt a weighty factor in the appointments of all these men. Yet, in most cases, ability too was considered. Only one of the eleven, Yu Hu-jo, was not judged on ability. The officials were judged by recommendations and evaluations of their performance in office. In the past both these methods had been obscured by nepotism, but they were again emphasized by the Taewŏn'gun.[17]

Regardless of his faction or ability, a candidate for the higher offices still had to climb the conventional ladder of advancement;[18] the major difference was the speed with which this was done. Statistics on the eight chief councillors under the Taewŏn'gun, excluding those who had served as councillors in previous reigns, indicate that the average age on attaining a first appointment to the Ŭijŏngbu was fifty-eight, the range being from forty-four to sixty-eight. The average age at which they first reached the junior second grade, a stepping stone to the higher echelons of the officialdom, was forty-nine, the range being from thirty-two to sixty-seven. From the time they passed the civil service examination until they were promoted to the junior second grade it took an average of sixteen years; the range was from one to twenty-nine years. It is probable that in the past the adherents of the Soron and Noron factions reached the junior second grade faster, their factional background working to their advantage.

Historians have contended that there were few Namin and Pugin in the government prior to 1864. This, however, is not entirely correct. The research I have conducted on the years after 1800 reveals that the number of Pugin and Namin in the government was not negligible. A few even held high positions,[19] although none of them were councillors of state. In comparison with the Soron and Noron, however, their promotion was slow, evidence that their factional ties did work to their disadvantage. Most of the Namin and Pugin served in military appointments, which traditionally carried less prestige than the civil posts. Again, the records do not support the belief of some historians that the in-laws were almost wiped out during the Taewŏn'gun's reign.

The Taewŏn'gun and Discrimination

The historical reasons for the Yi dynasty's tenacious discrimination against natives of P'yŏngan and Hamgyŏng, an area commonly known as sŏbuk, or the northwest, are difficult to explain. Some claim that discrimination originated with King T'aejo, who feared the militant and rebellious character of the people from the northwest and therefore wanted to keep them out of important government positions.[20] Others believe that the policy of discrimination began only after the Yi Si-ae rebellion in 1468, which, though local in character, was directed against the government's new policy of appointing officials of southern origin to administrative posts in Hamgyŏng and of restricting the free movement of the populace. After the rebellion the people of the northwest were said to have been forbidden to take the civil service examinations for a period of a hundred years,[21] although on paper official examination quotas were established for each province.[22]

Whatever the reasons, one factor cannot be dismissed: the unique social background of the northwest. In contrast to the south, no rigid class system existed in the north. Many inhabitants were migrants from the south or naturalized Manchu tribesmen, and intermarriage between the two was not uncommon.[23] Confucian education, particularly in Hamgyŏng, was not widespread.[24] For these reasons, the southerners traditionally regarded the people of the northwest as half-civilized barbarians.[25] Edicts and memorials often

referred to them as *wŏnin,* or the "people from the far land." If the government gave rank or position to one of them, the act was considered very
special, one "to soothe the people from the far land."[26]

The Yi government was apparently not insensitive to the unhappy
situation. After the reign of King Injo (r. 1623-1649) there were persistent
efforts to give the people from the northwest more of a chance to hold government positions.[27] However, even when appointed by special order of the
king, they were unable to stay long in office because of constant friction with
their southern colleagues. A good illustration is found in Nam Ku-man's
memorial of June 13, 1686: "I have memorialized many times with regard to
the use of the people from the north . . . No sooner are they appointed . . .
than they are dismissed. Hong U-sŏk was unusually bright and intelligent. He
was appointed second secretary of war when I was the minister. However,
the atmosphere did not permit any northerner to hold such a position. He
was treated as though he were a degraded slave."[28]

The resentment over discrimination finally erupted in violence in
January 1812 with the famous Hong Kyŏng-nae uprising in P'yŏngan. It was
not suppressed until May of that year.[29] Hong Kyŏng-nae charged that the
court had cast aside his province like "filthy earth," and that even the slaves
of the southern yangban referred to the men of the north as *p'yŏnghan*
(lit., "plain men").[30]

The uprising drew due attention to the problem, but did not bring about
any significant change in policy. Nor was there much progress during the
reigns of Hŏnjong and Ch'ŏlchong.[31] As late as 1864 two incidents of discrimination were reported. In May 1864 Yi Chik-hyŏn, the magistrate of
Chaeryŏng in P'yŏngan, apparently insulted the natives by saying, "How can
there be titled men and yangban in the province of P'yŏngan?"[32] In September of the same year Kim Ch'ang-yun, returning home with a newly won
munkwa degree, was attacked by Yi Min-jŏng, the magistrate of Tŏgwŏn in
Hamgyŏng, and Yi's brother.[33]

The Yi government also traditionally discriminated against the descendants of the royal house of the Koryŏ dynasty, the Wang; this was based on
dynastic considerations. When the house of Wang lost its mandate to Yi
Sŏng-gye, many of its members were put to death. A few took refuge in the
countryside or in the mountains and lived under different names. After the
extermination policy was lifted, probably during the reign of Sejong, many

of the Wang returned to Songdo (Kaesǒng), the old capital, where for almost five hundred years their descendants engaged in trade, usually using their original surname again.[34]

In an edict on November 8, 1866, the Taewǒn'gun declared that regional discrimination in the use of men from the northwest in government service had not been a traditional policy of the reigning kings, but had resulted from negligence on the part of officials in carrying out royal instructions. He pledged to undertake a wide search for talented men in the northwest and in Songdo, and instructed the governors of the two northern provinces and the magistrates of Kaesǒng to recommend qualified men, and to refrain from partiality in their choice.[35]

After this edict, a number of specific measures were introduced to recruit men from these regions into the government. In 1869 Kim Pyǒng-hak and the Samgunbu proposed that the number of candidates for the post of liaison officer *(sǒnjǒn'gwan)* recommended from the northern provinces and Songdo be increased; hitherto each province had been allowed to select only one candidate.[36] The post was considered a stepping stone to a military career. In 1870 regulations which permitted soldiers from only a few districts of P'yǒngan to take the provincial military examinations were discarded, and all qualified soldiers were admitted to the examinations.[37] In 1872 it was further specified that all who passed the provincial military examinations in P'yǒngan were free to proceed to Seoul to take the final military examinations.[38] Hamgyǒng was favored by a simialr policy.

In that year there was a renewed effort to bring members of the Wang family and other qualified men from Songdo into the government. On April 12, on the occasion of the king's visit to the tomb of the founder of the Koryǒ dynasty, a special examination was given for the benefit of the Wang and the inhabitants of the ancient capital. Five candidates, among them Wang Sǒng-hyǒp, received the *munkwa* degree, and twenty-five received the military degree.[39] At the same time an edict ruled that members of the Koryǒ royal house who had gained the *munkwa* degree should not be prevented from accepting appointments to the Sǔngmunwǒn (Bureau of Diplomatic Correspondence). Similarly, those who held posts under the favoritism system were not to be barred from becoming commissioners of the royal temples, the Temple of Earth and Grain, various royal tombs, the Kyŏngmo temple, and the Yŏnghŭi temple. Those who held military degrees in the house of Wang should be freely recommended for posts as liaison officers.[40] All of these appointments were considered important steps toward further advancement. On April 13, 1872, the post of tomb commissioner of the Hyŏllŭng, the tomb of the founder of the Koryŏ, was reserved by edict for a qualified member of the Wang family.[41]

The source material at hand is too scanty to allow a full assessment of the Taewŏn'gun's effort to bring more men from the northwestern region and from Songdo into the government. The available evidence, however, gives the impression that his endeavor was more than nominal. During his reign fourteen men from the northwest and from Songdo, most notably Cho Kwang-sun, Ma Haeng-il, Wang Chŏng-yang, and Wang Sŏng-hyŏp, were appointed to posts of considerable importance; all of the appointments were made by special decree.

Cho Kwang-sun (1821-?), a native of Chŏngju, P'yŏngan, passed the higher civil service examination in 1852 and was appointed assistant minister of works by special decree on December 25, 1867. Later he served as royal secretary and censor-general.[42] Ma Haeng-il, the son of a clerk in Kyŏngsŏng, Hamgyŏng, is said to have been a kind of personal representative of the Taewŏn'gun in that province. He served as magistrate in various districts and proved himself an able administrator.[43] Wang Chŏng-yang (1823-?), a native of Kyesŏng, passed the higher civil service examination in 1866 and was appointed assistant minister of war by special decree on February 18, 1867. In 1872 he was promoted to royal secretary (tong pusŭngji), and subsequently rose to be vice-minister of works.[44] Wang Sŏng-hyŏp (1850-?) was Wang Chŏng-yang's son; he passed the civil service examinations brilliantly in 1872 and soon received the highly coveted appointment of first reader (kyori) to the Academy of Literature (Hongmun'gwan).[45]

The available source materials do not present a complete picture of the Taewŏn'gun's policy toward the employment of clerks, slaves, and illegitimate sons. However, clerks with exceptional talents seem to have been encouraged to take the government service examinations[46] and were even selected for official posts without their having to go through the conventional procedures.[47] Many able clerks were apparently recruited into the Taewŏn'gun's working staff and were assigned various important duties.[48]

Slaves were also allowed to take the military examinations. According to a memorial by the Ŭijŏngbu dated December 17, 1866, a certain Han, a public slave serving in a Chŏnju rifle unit, passed the provincial military examination with an excellent record. Since it was unprecedented to give a degree to a slave, the council proposed that the examination be given again, probably in the hope of excluding Han. The court, however, rejected this proposal and ruled that Han should be freed from his slave status and granted the degree.[49]

In the early years of the dynasty illegitimate sons were confined to lowly posts and barred from the formal official class. In later years this rule was eased, although not significantly changed. In his edict of February 25, 1864,[50] the Taewŏn'gun charged that the practice of excluding illegitimate sons from serving in the government without their even being given a chance to display their talents was unnatural. His edict instructed the Department of Appointment and the Department of War to employ such men according to their abilities.

The Taewŏn'gun's policy of giving equal opportunity to men of all social classes was indeed momentous in Yi history. This policy had repercussions long after his reign, for many of Korea's leaders in later years were products of his search for talent who had gained their political training under his rule: for example, Kim Ok-kyun and Hong Yŏng-sik, leaders of the abortive *coup d'état* of 1884; Kim Hong-jip, the chief of the "reform" government of 1894; Ŏ Yun-jung, a brilliant military leader who played a crucial role in the first stage of the Tonghak rebellion in 1893 and served as minister of revenue under Kim Hong-jip.[51]

Chapter VII

THE CONSOLIDATION OF THE ROYAL HOUSE

The Taewŏn'gun's tradition-oriented approach to reform is perhaps most clearly manifested in his attempt to consolidate the royal house and to reconstruct the Kyŏngbok palace. Kojong's succession opened a new era in the long somber history of the royal clan. The Taewŏn'gun introduced a series of systematic measures to restore the royal family's original dignity and position and to build a new foundation for the Yi clan.

In principle members of the royal family[1] were entitled to a number of extraordinary privileges and were appointed to one of the three councils of nobility: the Council of the Royal House (Chongch'inbu), the Council of the Royal Kinsmen (Tollyŏngbu), and the Council of the Royal Sons-in-law (Ŭibinbu).

The Chongch'inbu, established during the reign of T'aejo (r. 1392-1398), was composed primarily of the male descendants of the king down to the fifth generation. Except for the king's sons, all of the members held, in addition to their titles, ranks in the system in which officials of the civil and military classes were graded. Their initial ranks (the lowest being senior sixth grade) and titles varied according to how closely they were related by blood to the reigning king, but theoretically they could all rise to the highest rank, that of senior first grade and receive the title of *kun* (prince). The king's sons were not given a rank for they were above such decoration; they were ennobled as *kun* if they were illegitimate sons, and as *taegun* (grand prince) if they were legitimate.[2]

The Tollyŏngbu was originally founded in 1414 for untitled members of the Yi clan who did not descend directly from T'aejo: the males in the families of the king's mother or the king's wife, husbands of the queen's sisters, and sons of the king's daughters. The number of members was limited, and they were generally not ennobled.[3]

The Ŭibinbu was composed of the king's sons-in-law *(puma),*[4] who were given the titles of *wi, puwi,* or *ch'ŏmwi* according to their rank. The lowest starting rank, the junior third grade, was awarded to the consort of a king's illegitimate daughter.[5]

These nonpolitical groups were equal in rank to the Ŭijŏngbu in the hierarchy of the government. Like the government officials, their members were granted land and other favors in accordance with their rank. Although the three councils were completely independent of the administrative offices of the government, their members were not originally barred from holding regular posts in the government. If a member were to take on a government post, he was generally relieved of his council position.

There were two other institutions for the members of the royal family. One was the Office of the Clan Register (Chongbusi),[6] which was established in 1392 principally to keep and publish the register of the royal clan and to supervise the conduct of royal clansmen. It was also empowered to deal with general criminal cases involving royal clansmen. The second, the Royal School (Chonghak), was established in 1450 (perhaps in 1427),[7] primarily for the education of the children of royal clansmen.

Undoubtedly, these institutions were supposed to promote and protect the interests of the royal family. However, members of the royal family, particularly those belonging to the Chongch'inbu, never fully enjoyed their special rights and privileges, essentially because of the struggle among the princes for the throne during the early days of the dynasty, the inevitable involvement of princes in factional struggles, the growing power of the yangban class, and the rise of queens' forces, that is, the forces of the royal in-laws. To keep princes out of politics and the government, members of the royal house were forbidden to take the civil and military government service examinations after 1471.[8] During the long period of factional strife they were not uncommonly involved in one party or another; between 1495 and 1863 at least sixteen sons and grandsons of kings were condemned to death for high treason—in most cases innocently.[9] By the end of Ch'ŏlchong's reign the Yi house was on the verge of collapse. The sick and feeble king was merely the political instrument of the in-law groups, especially the Kim family of Andong. Even his few remote surviving kinsmen were in exile. It was this precarious and enervated dynastic line that Kojong was called upon to succeed.

The Taewŏn'gun attempted to revitalize the royal clan by introducing a sweeping reorganization of the Chongch'inbu, enabling its ranking members

to participate in the administration of national affairs. He relaxed the regulations on appointments to the council, which now incorporated the
Chongbusi, so that distant members of the Yi clan could be brought in.[10]
This reform of the Chongch'inbu was paralleled in 1869 by the lifting of the
century-old ban on direct descendants of the king—except sons and grandsons
—taking the civil and military service examinations. At the same time,
consorts of the king's daughters and granddaughters were allowed to enter
government service if they showed ability.[11]

Another important measure taken by the Taewŏn'gun was the rehabilitation of disgraced clansmen, both living and deceased. He believed that this
act of "grace" would bring longevity to the king and fortune and harmony
to the dynasty. Yi Se-bo and Lady Sŏ[12] were released from banishment, and
some eighteen princes who had been unjustly condemned for treason and
were put to death were posthumously restored to their former ranks and
titles in 1864.[13] This was followed by the restoration of many long-extinct
important branches of the Yi clan. The missing generations of each house
were usually filled by "adopting" dead men of different generations from
other branch houses.[14] This desperate attempt to augment the strength of
the clan went against orthodox Confucian principles, and was destined to
become a bitter political issue.

These acts of rehabilitation and reestablishment were usually carried
out along with the bestowal of posthumous honors on deceased members of
the royal family and of special privileges on living clansmen. The most
common of such honors was the upgrading of the dead man's titles and
ranks,[15] which had great bearing on the social standing of his descendants.
Numerous living clansmen were honored by being brought into government
service through special examinations or appointments.[16] Except in the early
years of the dynasty, there were probably few periods when so many
members of the Yi clan entered government service.

Along with the members of the Yi clan, descendants of those who had
rendered outstanding service to the Yi dynasty were also given special honors
and privileges. Among the many recipients of such rewards were the direct
descendants of "merit-subjects of the dynastic founder" (kaeguk kongsin)
and of Song Si-yŏl, a founder of the Noron faction and one of the dynasty's

greatest Confucian scholar-statesmen. All of them were awarded the *saengwŏn* and *chinsa* degrees. In 1865 Chŏng To-jŏn, the long-disgraced but once-honored supporter of T'aejo, was rehabilitated. The post of tomb commissioner *(ch'ambong)* of the Kŏnwŏllŭng (the tomb of T'aejo) was to be reserved for his descendants.[17]

In addition, many new laws and regulations designed to raise the traditional status of certain members of the royal family, both living and dead, were introduced. For instance, the consorts of the king's daughters were to be given the rank of senior first grade upon their marriage; they had traditionally been awarded either junior first grade or senior second grade according to their legitimacy. The king's granddaughters would also be appointed to senior first grade when they were formally ennobled.[18] The tomb title of the king's sons or grandsons, who had been designated crown princes but had never ascended the throne, would be raised to *wŏn,* and the title of the tomb commissioner would be changed from *suwigwan* to a more dignified one, *subonggwan.* The tombs of the king's concubines having the rank of *pin* (lady of the first class) would also be called *wŏn.*[19]

Apart from these institutional changes, the Taewŏn'gun also took steps to promote solidarity and fraternity among royal clansmen. He called a grand meeting of the clansmen known as the Chongch'inhoe at the palace on May 9, 1871. Delegates from various branch houses of the Yi clan came to the gathering, which lasted for several days. They attended a royal banquet given in their honor, and the conferment of titles on worthy clansmen; they visited royal tombs and took special examinations. Thereafter the Chongch'inhoe was to be held regularly once every three years. In addition, the Taewŏn'gun requested titled and educated clan members to participate in the royal sacrificial ceremonies that were performed at the beginning of each new year before the Ancestral Shrine of the Royal Clan (Chongmyo). He also brought younger clan members into the palace on occasion to attend the young king.[20]

The reconstruction of the Kyŏngbok palace was the final symbol of the Taewŏn'gun's determination to restore and enhance the failing authority and prestige of the Yi dynasty. The palace[21] was first built during T'aejo's reign. Subsequently, new buildings were added through Sŏngjong's reign

(1469-1494). Palaces of the early Korean kings were traditionally erected on hills, but the Kyŏngbok palace was built in a valley under the general supervision of Sim Tŏk-pu. The name kyŏng pok (ch'ing-fu, or blessing and prosperity) was taken from the Book of Odes by Chŏng To-jŏn. The palace was 10,878 ch'ŏk (one ch'ŏk is a little over thirty centimeters) in circumference, had four main gates and some fifty separate groups of buildings comprising important government offices, temples, and pavilions. The greater part of the palace was destroyed by fire in 1533 and the rest was lost during the Japanese invasion of 1592.[22]

The reconstruction of the palace was first proposed by the regent dowager on April 26, 1865. The following day the proposal was formally adopted at a special meeting of high officials in the face of opposition from Kim Chwa-gŭn, president of the Tollyŏngbu, and Yi Kyŏng-jae, vice-president of the same council, both of whom were apprehensive about the cost. At the same time, the Taewŏn'gun was officially given the power to supervise and plan the reconstruction. A special construction bureau known as the Yŏnggŏn dogam was set up and a large number of leading officials were appointed to it to direct the project. It was originally planned that the construction would be mainly financed by wŏnnapchŏn (voluntarily contributed money), but the government was soon obliged to turn to forced labor.[23]

Actual ground work began on May 14, 1865. To speed up the construction teams of singers and dancers were sent to the site to cheer the workmen. Donors of large sums were usually rewarded with appointments to government posts, promotion to higher positions, or titles and ranks. The Chongch'inbu was constantly urged to conduct its own drive for donations among clansmen. Buddhist-monk carpenters were called up to the capital from many parts of the country.[24]

The rebuilding of the palace took seven years and five months,[25] and cost nearly eight million yang, most of which was "donated" by the public.[26] This was, perhaps, the most ambitious and most costly project undertaken in the history of the Yi dynasty. Although we do not know the total number of men put to work on the construction, one record shows that over 35,000 men were employed at one time during the early stages.[27] Nearly 450 high-ranking officials served at various times in the construction bureau before its abolition in 1872.[28]

The reconstruction of the palace and other government buildings was an attempt on the part of the Taewŏn'gun to inject new life into the failing royal clan, but his efforts were later harshly attacked by his political opponents.

Chapter VIII

THE TAEWŎN'GUN'S CULTURAL POLICIES

The Taewŏn'gun's revival of the Sŏnggyun'gwan in Seoul was his greatest contribution to the field of Confucian education. His reform of the sŏwŏn made a tremendous impact on education as well as on politics and the economy. It is a landmark in the long history of the Yi dynasty.

The History of the Sŏwŏn

The sŏwŏn were private autonomous institutions of higher learning[1] where a limited number of carefully selected yangban students, most of them holders of the *chinsa* degree, prepared primarily for the higher civil service examination.[2] As a rule, each sŏwŏn was dedicated to at least one patron-hero or scholar to whom biannual (spring and autumn) sacrifices were offered.[3] These ceremonies were performed by elders of the Confucian society *(yurim).*

The academies, which were administered by elected officials,[4] were divided into two categories: in the first were a small number of academies that had received their names from the king. For this reason, they were called the *saaek* (lit., "name-grant") academies. They were endowed with three *kyŏl* of land, slaves, and books. Those in the second category were maintained by private donations in the form of land, slaves, grain, and money. Both types of sŏwŏn were free from any obligations to the state.

Besides the sŏwŏn there were many shrines known under various names such as *sa, sau,* or *hyangsa.* They were dedicated to heroes or scholars born in a particular locality.

For nearly a hundred years after the first academy was founded by Chu Se-bung in 1543, the sŏwŏn system played an illustrious role in the propagation of Neo-Confucianism and in reshaping and advancing the education of the yangban. From the early seventeenth century on, however, the system became a growing national problem. The initial function as promoter of education was lost, and every sŏwŏn became a "state within a state." The deterioration of the system was closely connected with the rise and development of factional strife. By 1649, there were 190 *sŏwŏn*[5] in the country; many of them had been dedicated to martyred faction leaders, and they began to be transformed into home bases for the contending factions. Students neglected their studies to compose memorials in defense of the causes of their respective leaders.

As early as 1644, Im Tam, the governor of Kyŏngsang, stated in a memorial: "The students are no longer interested in learning, and those enshrined in the academies are not worthy of such an honor."[6] He then proposed that the government strictly control the establishment of *sŏwŏn*. Despite this warning and many others that followed, 414 additional *sŏwŏn* were founded in the seventy years between 1650 and 1720. This period of mass construction closely corresponds to the years of intensified factional strife (1674-1724), and the destruction and reconstruction of the *sŏwŏn* often paralleled the fall and resurgence of factions. This phenomenon can best be understood with reference to the case of Chŏng Kae-ch'ŏng (1528-1590).

Chŏng, a Pugin "whose learning was pure and superb and deeply respected in scholarly circles,"[7] was at one time charged with treason for having associated with Chŏng Yŏ-rip, who led an uprising in 1589, and died in exile. He was posthumously rehabilitated when his faction returned to power; an academy was built to honor his memory. In 1657 this academy was destroyed at the request of Song Chun-gil, a prominent leader of the Sŏin who were then in power.[8] In 1677, when the Namin, an off-shoot of the Pugin, ruled, Hŏ Mok (a Namin) memorialized King Sukchong, asking that the academy be rebuilt.[9] As a result of Hŏ's memorial, Chŏng's followers were permitted to rebuild the academy. In 1678 it was honored with the award of a name. Then two years later, in 1680, when the Namin were ousted from the government, Chŏng's academy was again torn down. In 1689, when the Namin returned to power, the academy reappeared. Finally, in 1702, almost six years after the Namin lost their last battle against the Noron and Soron, the academy honoring Chŏng was again demolished, never to reappear.[10]

The decay of the *sŏwŏn* was closely allied with the traditional social structure and the rapidly degenerating economic condition of the country. Their position as privileged institutions in the society bore heavily on their fate. In principle, under the traditional social system, the yangban and the lowborn were not subject to the military tax and the *corvée;* the peasant class alone carried these burdens. This pressure on the peasantry steadily increased during the late sixteenth century, when the disintegration of the economic system set in. Unable to bear their increasing hardships, many peasants voluntarily entered the service of yangban households as slaves.

Since *sŏwŏn* land was exempt from tax and those attached to the *sŏwŏn* as guards and servants were traditionally free from the military tax and *corvée,* many hard-pressed peasants entered the service of the *sŏwŏn* for protection. These peasants usually lived in so-called *pokchuch'on* (lit., "happy drink villages") attached to the academies, and maintained a kind of extraterritorial status. In addition, many powerful yangban put their land under the protection of the academies. All these factors made the *sŏwŏn* more like havens for tax dodgers than citadels of learning. To make matters worse, the academies frequently sent out private agents, usually tax escapees under their protection, to extort money and grain from the people. These agents were apparently armed with special warrants, one of the most powerful being the *hŭkp'ae* (warrant stamped with black ink), issued by the Hwayang Academy in Ch'ungch'ŏng; it carried more authority than a government decree.[11] The following quotation, from a memorial presented to King Yŏngjo in 1738 by Pak Mun-su (1691-1756), best describes the conditions of the *sŏwŏn* in the eighteenth century—conditions that remained more or less unchanged until the 1860s:

> If a man becomes councillor or minister, makes his name, and leaves a couple of sons, the rich and those who want to escape military service start to build a shrine for him. Moreover, his sons build a majestic *sŏwŏn* for him, using their influence to obtain permission from the governor and magistrate. Treacherous creatures entering the *sŏwŏn*, afraid of military service, number a few hundred to each *sŏwŏn*. They extort money from the people as though they were officials . . . And they make the *sŏwŏn* a place to steam chickens, slaughter dogs, eat, and become intoxicated. Even the magistrates are afraid of them and refrain from intervening in their affairs. The evil custom of extorting the taxes of dead men and escapees from their kinsmen and neighbors began with the *sŏwŏn*.[12]

The Reform of the Sŏwŏn System

The Taewŏn'gun's reform of the *sŏwŏn* system began in 1864 and was successfully completed in 1871. The fact that this reform was spread out over such a long period, a phenomenon unknown in his other reforms, partly testifies to the difficulties he encountered. An examination of the many edicts issued during this period indicates that the greatest obstacle was the indifference of the officials, particularly the provincial governors and district magistrates. This apathy was actually silent opposition to the reform, since an intricate relationship existed between the *sŏwŏn* and the majority of officials. Their mutual interests had proved a formidable stumbling block to any reform of the system in the past.[13]

The formal introduction of the reform was preceded by the edict of May 27, 1864, issued through the dowager regent, in which the Taewŏn'gun instructed the provincial and the four special district governments to submit special reports on *sŏwŏn* conditions, including information about their land-holdings and "attached persons."[14] The local authorities, however, did not readily respond to this sudden order. The government had only received replies from Kanghwa, Suwŏn, and Kwangju by July 10, when the Taewŏn'gun issued another edict threatening the provincial governments with heavy punishment.[15]

This warning did bring some definite results, but the reports were so poorly prepared that they provided no intelligible guide for immediate action. Nevertheless, on August 28, 1864, the Taewŏn'gun made public his reform plan for the *sŏwŏn* system. In the edict of the dowager regent he stated that those *sŏwŏn* that were dedicated to the same patron and those that were built by families and clans were to be screened. The Ŭijŏngbu was entrusted with the task of investigating the *sŏwŏn* records in the Department of Rites and to make further inquiries through the provincial authorities.[16] This edict was shortly followed by a more significant one, issued on September 17, 1864, in which the Taewŏn'gun announced a more concrete reform plan. He categorically attacked the evil practices of the *sŏwŏn:* the sheltering of military escapees, exploitation and illegal arrest of the "little people," profiteering, and shameful quarreling over food and drink. He said that if the former worthies knew of these evils, they would never find comfort in sacrificial offerings. A "great reform" had to be brought into such age-old and deep-rooted customs "to apologize to the spirits of the former *kunja (chün-tzu)* and worthies." Seven corrective measures were expounded:[17] (1) arrest all those who were suppressing the "little people" under the protection of the *sŏwŏn* and shrines and expel them from the society of the yangban *(saryu);* (2) confiscate all the landholdings of the *sŏwŏn* except those of the name-grant *sŏwŏn* which were to be allowed to keep their three *kyŏl* of tax-free land; (3) enroll in the military register all students and "attached persons" of the *sŏwŏn* above a number to be fixed by the Ŭijŏngbu; (4) enroll all "attached persons" of the miscellaneous local shrines; (5) ban sacrificial offerings at the local shrines; (6) abolish the *pokchuch'on;* and (7) suppress the *sŏwŏn* and shrines dedicated to the same man or built by families and clans.

While these provisions were being carried out, the Confucian society was dealt another blow. The Taewŏn'gun issued another edict on April 24, 1865, ordering the abolition of the famed shrine of the Noron and pro-Ming literati, the Mandongmyo. The shrine had been built at the turn of the eighteenth century in memory of two Ming emperors, Shen-tsung (1573-1620) and Hsi-tsung (1621-1628), for their aid to Korea during the dark days of the Hideyoshi invasion. The edict was informally promulgated, perhaps in anticipation of the bitter reaction it would arouse among the adherents of the Mandongmyo; it was not published in the official gazette *(chobo).*[18]

In protest, Im Hŏn-hoe, one of the "Confucian worthies" *(yuhyŏn)* of the nineteenth century, memorialized for the immediate restoration of the Mandongmyo. This memorial found an echo in all of the southern provinces, the heart of Confucian learning in Korea. On September 15, 1865, a joint memorial by Confucian students from Ch'ungch'ŏng pressed a similar demand. On January 12, 1866, 1,468 students from Kyŏngsang also urged the government to rescind the order. Further protest was expressed by a sit-down strike of memorialists from Chŏlla and the presentation of a memorial on November 13, 1866, by another Confucian worthy, Yi Hang-no, who depicted Korea's spiritual attachment to the Ming.[19] None of these measures, however, were strong enough to alter the decision of the Taewŏn'gun. He argued that privately offered sacrifices to the Ming emperors at the Mandongmyo violated the proper rites.

The Taewŏn'gun did not hesitate to step up his reform program and to see it to completion. This decision apparently grew out of the fact that his orders had not been carried out punctually, and the *sŏwŏn* continued to oppress the peasantry. The edict, issued on October 18, 1868, restated the earlier order that all *sŏwŏn* students beyond a fixed number were to be entered in the military register. This time the Department of War was entrusted with the task of enforcing the order. The Taewŏn'gun also stripped the name-grant *sŏwŏn* of their tax-exemption privilege. To insure the prompt and effective execution of these orders, he placed the management of all *sŏwŏn* affairs directly in the hands of district magistrates where the *sŏwŏn* were located.[20]

The transfer of *sŏwŏn* management, however, was never carried out. Instead, the "direct descendants" *(ponson)* of the enshrined persons took over the administration of *sŏwŏn* affairs, much to the displeasure of the Taewŏn'gun. In the edict of October 4, 1870, he charged the *ponson* with harassing the "little people" with their own factional quarrels, not only loosening national polity, but also endangering the peace and harmony of the nation. He threatened to have those *sŏwŏn* closed and their tablets buried.[21] Within half a year of this warning the Taewŏn'gun moved to screen the name-grant *sŏwŏn* that had apparently not been affected thus far. On April 28, 1871, he pointed out that one man was often enshrined at more than four or five *sŏwŏn,* bringing the total number of name-grant *sŏwŏn* to some 270. He announced that he would order the destruction of all but one *sŏwŏn* for each man who was exceptionally renowned in the field of Neo-Confucianism or outstanding in his loyalty to the dynasty. The execution of this order was entrusted to the Department of Rites and was personally supervised by the Taewŏn'gun.[22]

Presumably to quell any opposition, the Taewŏn'gun had the king explain the significance of this order on May 1, 1871, to the students of the Sŏnggyun'gwan who had participated in a ceremonial visit to the State Confucian Shrine. The students were particularly reminded that the *sŏwŏn* were monuments only to men of exceptional loyalty and to the great masters of Neo-Confucianism.[23] Similarly, on May 5, at a meeting with high officials, the Taewŏn'gun expounded the original aim of the *sŏwŏn* system and its later aberrations. In defense of his latest policy, he cited the cases of Kim Cho-sun and Grand Prince Inp'yŏng. Kim was the founder of the Kim clan, whose members had virtually monopolized government positions for many years. In the Taewŏn'gun's opinion this man deserved a *sŏwŏn*, for he had served the dynasty well. But in the eyes of many Confucian scholars, Kim was an avaricious and corrupt man, and they did not approve the plans. However, when the literati wanted to build a *sŏwŏn* for Grand Prince Inp'yŏng, a direct ancestor of the Taewŏn'gun, the Taewŏn'gun forbade it. No doubt he intended to exhibit the impartiality with which he proposed to effect the screening of the *sŏwŏn*. [24]

The screening of the name-grant *sŏwŏn* was actually done by the Taewŏn'gun himself, and his verdict was officially announced by Cho Pyŏng-ch'ang, minister of rites, on May 9, 1871. Forty-seven *sŏwŏn* were selected; the rest were to be destroyed. [25] It seems, however, that the actual execution of this order was not completed until the latter part of the year, apparently owing to sabotage by local authorities. [26]

The reform of the *sŏwŏn* system was certainly one of the more momentous and historic events in the long history of Yi Korea. A rough estimate shows that between 1864 and 1871 some 3,000 *sŏwŏn*[27] and miscellaneous shrines were destroyed as a result of the reform. By this act almost 100,000 men were added to the military register, and thousands of *kyŏl* of land[28] were recovered for taxation. The radical increase in the number of adults of military age no doubt lessened the demand on the peasantry, although the real extent of the relief brought about by the abolition of the *sŏwŏn* abuses can only be guessed at. Inevitably, the abolition of the *sŏwŏn* became instrumental in the gradual revival of the local Confucian shrines (*hyanggyo*) as educational centers. [29] These shrines, found in almost every district, had played a vital role in the promotion of Confucian education during the early days of the Yi dynasty, but had gradually been overshadowed by the *sŏwŏn*.

The Reform of the Sŏnggyun'gwan

The mass destruction of the *sŏwŏn* induced the critics of the Taewŏn'gun to allude to him as the "Ch'in Shih-huang-ti of Korea," a title which is certainly not justified in the light of the Taewŏn'gun's efforts to reshape and promote "right learning" *(chŏnghak)*. His major accomplishment in the field of Confucian education was the reform of the Sŏnggyun'gwan, which had existed from the beginning of the dynasty, but later had fallen into decline.

Concern about the dilapidated state of the Sŏnggyun'gwan was first voiced by Left Councillor Kim Pyŏng-hak on September 8, 1866, in connection with the Catholic persecution. Kim believed that Confucianism was the fundamental energy *(wŏn'gi)* of the nation, and that as long as that energy was strong and viable no evil influences would be able to penetrate the country. The rise of heretical teaching was an outcome of the decline of that energy. As a means for the promotion of the "right learning," Kim proposed the strengthening of the Sŏnggyun'gwan by restoring the monthly examinations. This suggestion, which found quick approval, included the provision that the accumulated examination scores be published at the end of each year, and that students be rewarded or punished according to their merits.[30]

After this initial measure, on October 17, 1869, the Taewŏn'gun instructed the Ŭijŏngbu, then headed by Kim Pyŏng-hak, to submit a special reform plan for the Sŏnggyun'gwan. He shared with Kim the belief that the national energy could only be strengthened by promoting the "right learning." This edict was accompanied by two others: one concerned the expansion of the Sŏnggyun'gwan dormitories from two houses (the East and West houses) to four (the addition of a South house and a North house); this step would be jointly carried out by the rector of the Sŏnggyun'gwan and the Ŭijŏngbu. The other projected the expansion of the Sŏnggyun'gwan library by the addition of the collection of the Royal Library *(Kyujanggak)*.[31]

The Ŭijŏngbu formally presented the reform plan to the court on October 31, 1869. The first three of the ten provisions dealt primarily with general academic discipline, referring to the regulations of the White Deer Academy (Pai-lu-tung shu-yüan). The other more important provisions described the daily examination *(ilgang)*, the *sunkwa* (lit., "test given every tenth day") system, the rule of attendance, the recommendations of local students, the introduction of special examinations, and the tenure of the officials of the Sŏnggyun'gwan.[32]

The daily examinations, practiced to some degree in the past, would be given in rotation (probably to one or two students each day) to the students

at the Sŏnggyun'gwan and to outsiders on a voluntary basis. The test would
be confined to memorizing two selected Confucian classics, with special
emphasis on understanding the text and on punctuation. The results would
be reported to the throne at the end of each year. The *sunkwa* was used to
examine students and selected outsiders on a more advanced level. It would
focus on two topics at a time, such as essays, poetry, and commentary on the
classics, in order to test their intellectual originality and creativity. The rector
of the Sŏnggyun'gwan would administer the *sunkwa* and the throne would
reward the students at the end of each year.

   The new rule of attendance was designed largely to screen the students.
All students who failed in the required examinations would have to report to
either the Department of Rites or the Sŏnggyun'gwan authorities. Except for
those who went home because of illness or to attend memorial services for
their immediate relatives, students who absented themselves from the
required examinations, or those who were not well "accustomed to reciting"
the Confucian texts or were not "fond of literary composition," would be
suspended from the Sŏnggyun'gwan for a period of one month.

   The recommendation of local students was utilized by the Taewŏn'gun
in his search for "hidden" young talent. Every village was to recommend its
best students to the local magistrate, who, after giving them a stiff screening,
would send one or two to be tested by the provincial government on a
number of specific subjects. Their examination papers would be judged
jointly by the Ŭijŏngbu and ranking government officials, who would then
choose a limited number from among the candidates and send them up to
the capital for the final (probably oral) examination. The students with the
most brilliant records would be presented to the throne, most likely for
admittance to the Sŏnggyun'gwan. The names of the others would be kept
by the Department of Appointment for later employment.

   The introduction of additional special examinations was designed
specifically to provide Sŏnggyun'gwan students with increased opportunity
to take the higher civil service examination, the *munkwa*. Traditionally,
before taking the second test *(poksi)* of the civil service examination the
students had to pass either the academy examination *(kwansi)* or the
chŏrilche, which were usually given four times a year.[33] But to qualify for

even these preliminary examinations, the candidates had to fulfill certain residence requirements: 300 days for the *kwansi* and 50 days for the *chŏrilche*. The new system stipulated a number of special residence requirements, presumably with shorter periods.

The tenure of the Sŏnggyun'gwan officials would be extended under the new regulation. Traditionally, the entire staff from the rector down to the lowest official was subject to constant shifts. Furthermore, concurrent appointments had made it difficult for the officials to devote themselves fully to their work in the Sŏnggyun'gwan.

The Compilation of Legal and Ritual Works

The Taewŏn'gun's final cultural achievement was his compilation of legal and ritual works. Since 1471 the Yi dynasty had used the *Kyŏngguk taejŏn* as its basic legal guide to administration. The code was divided into six sections in accordance with the departmental divisions of the government: appointment *(i)*, revenue *(ho)*, rites *(ye)*, war *(pyŏng)*, punishment *(hyŏng)*, and works *(kong)*. The section on appointment dealt with titles and ranks, the general structure of the government, and the selection and appointment of officials; the section on revenue treated such matters as the census, the land, salaries of officials, housing, government finances, taxation, and money; the section on rites dealt with the government service examinations, the attire of officials, schools, sacrifices, ceremonies, official seals, and foreign relations; the section on war covered the military system, courier service, military examinations, protection of palaces, and arms; the section on punishment[34] was largely concerned with trials of criminals, inspection of prisons, robbery, slave ownership and status, redress of grievances, and private disputes; and the section on works dealt with such matters as bridges, roads, the inspection and repair of public buildings, weights, scales, public inns, and ships.

The code had been supplemented by three major compilations: the *Taejŏn songnok* (Early supplement to the great code)[35] in 1492, the *Taejŏn husongnok* (Late supplement to the great code) in 1543, and the *Sok taejŏn* (Supplementary great code) in 1744. These codes included both new and revised laws which were enacted after the codification of the *Kyŏngguk taejŏn*. In 1785 another code called *Taejŏn t'ongp'yŏn* (Comprehensive code of administration) was enacted. It contained all new laws promulgated after the completion of the *Sok taejŏn* as well as those that had appeared in the four earlier codes. After 1785, however, no major codification[36] of laws was undertaken despite the fact that many new laws were enacted and many of the old laws became obsolete. For this very reason, the Taewŏn'gun personally directed the compilation of a series of important codes. The first of such legal works was the *Taejŏn hoet'ong,* which may be called the New Comprehensive Code of Administration. Completed in 1866, this compilation was an ambitious attempt to incorporate into a single work all new laws issued after 1744 and all previously enacted laws.[37] Other compilations were the *Yangjŏn p'yŏn'go* (Manual for the departments of appointment and war) in 1866, the *Yukchŏn chorye* (Regulations of the six departments) in 1867, the *Samban yesik* (Rules of etiquette for the three classes)[38] in 1866, and the *Orye p'yŏn'go* (Manual on the five rites) in 1868(?).

In great contrast with the sections on appointment and war in the earlier codes, the *Yangjŏn p'yŏn'go,* which was published in two *kwŏn,* dealt in minute detail with matters such as titles and ranks of the civil and military classes, and procedures relating to appointment, tenure, dismissal, and leave. Many of these provisions had been enacted under the Taewŏn'gun. This manual was specifically designed to aid officials of the two departments in their management of personnel affairs. It is one of the most valuable sources for the study of the political structure of the late Yi dynasty.[39]

The *Yukchŏn chorye,* published in six *kwŏn,* was intended to supplement the *Taejŏn hoet'ong,* and dealt extensively with the internal structure and functions of the six departments.[40] The *Samban yesik,* in two *kwŏn,* was one of the most significant works to appear during the Yi dynasty. Compiled by the Taewŏn'gun himself, it discussed, as the name indicates, the etiquette expected of the officials. For instance, the code prescribed how an official of an inferior rank should greet his superior when the latter visited the former. It dictated the proper form of address to be used when officials of different ranks meet on the street and how a high official should dismount from his horse and greet a blood prince when he sees the latter on the road.[41] The *Orye p'yŏn'go,* which was based on the old *Ch'un'gwan t'onggo* (Comprehensive manual for the department of rites)[42] of 1788, consisted of thirty *kwŏn.* It expounded more elaborately on the entries in the section on ritual in the *Taejŏn hoet'ong.*[43]

The Taewŏn'gun's main cultural achievements were his reform of the *sŏwŏn,* the revival of the Sŏnggyun'gwan, and the compilation of legal and cultural works. Certainly these were important reforms, as were the restoration of the original council of state and the elimination of the Pibyŏnsa. The drive against discrimination, the abolition of the military tax and the grain-loan system, and the vigorous campaign against corruption were all courageous measures. However, his efforts lacked persistence and depth and failed to arrest the degeneration of Yi society. Here we find a basic difference between the Taewŏn'gun's approach to Korea's problems and that of some of Korea's early progressive thinkers who urged the development of industry and foreign trade and demanded the abolition of the unequal class system. In the years 1864 to 1873, when Korea's neighbors were entering a new era in history, Korea remained in her ancient hermitage.

Chapter IX

THE NORTHERN FRONTIER AND EMIGRATION

As the traditional orientation of many of his reforms might have led one to expect, the Taewŏn'gun held firmly to the policy of isolation which had characterized Korean foreign relations throughout most of the Yi dynasty. The "opening" of Korea would have been a precondition for all fundamental reform in the country; at the same time, a greater disposition to more basic domestic changes would have provided the incentive to seek contact with the outside world. Between 1787 and 1860 visits by European ships to the Korean coast were rare. One may conjecture that more visits from foreign ships and repeated insistence on treaties and trade would gradually have forced Korea's ruling classes to realize that the world around Korea was changing. However, given the early history of Korea's foreign relations, it is not difficult to understand how by the time of the Taewŏn'gun the seclusion policy had become part of the national philosophy, character, and life.

In the early years of the Yi dynasty Korea considered herself the center of a little universe of Confucian civilization and wealth. This little universe, as opposed to the greater universe with Ming China at its center, comprised many lands and peoples. Korea welcomed tribute-bearing envoys from sundry lords of Muromachi Japan, from chieftains of Jurchen tribes, from kings of the Ryūkyū Islands, Siam, Luzon, and even the far land of Palembang in Sumatra. Many of these envoys and their suites received Korean titles and ranks. This intensive exchange led to foreign settlements on Korean soil, notably Japanese and Jurchen. On the other hand, the activities of Koreans overseas and beyond the Yalu were less significant, although Korean trading ships sailed far on the South China Sea, and one Korean colony was reported to have been founded in the Ryūkyūs.

This lively chapter in Yi history did not last long; Korea's contact with lands in the southeast gradually came to a stop, perhaps by the middle of the fifteenth century, or a little later. At that time even her relations with her immediate neighbors grew stormy, and she gradually retreated into seclusion.

Many factors contributed to making Korea a "hermit nation." From the beginning of the fifteenth century a series of conflicts occurred between

Japanese settlers and Koreans, stirring up the mutual hatred and distrust that were rooted in time immemorial. Then, from the beginning of the sixteenth century, Korea slowly began to restrict both the movement and the trade of the Japanese, ostensibly for security reasons. This policy was pushed to its extreme after the Hideyoshi invasions of the 1590s. The only contact between the two countries was a trickle of trade conducted by Tsushima at Pusan and the periodic exchange of embassies. Such contact was regulated under provisions of the Treaty of 1612 and later supplementary clauses. Changes in this treaty and later agreements were possible only by mutual consent.

Korea's relations with China, particularly with the Ch'ing court, bore equally on her seclusion. After two devastating invasions, in 1627 and 1637, Korea was forced into allegiance to the Manchus. The Treaty of Samjŏndo in 1637 formally established a suzerain-vassal relationship between the Manchu emperor and the Korean king. The founder of the Yi dynasty had voluntarily submitted to the Ming court, but from 1637 to almost the end of Kyŏngjong's reign (1721-1724), Korea was treated no better than a conquered colony. The Ch'ing government intervened high-handedly in Korea's internal affairs, burdened her with heavy tribute demands, and devised means to confine the Koreans within their narrow borders. Those who had earned their livelihood by gathering ginseng and cutting wood in Manchuria were driven out. From the beginning of the eighteenth century Korea was made responsible for warding off pirates. Later, Korean fishing boats were restricted to coastal waters. The Korean government was even held responsible for private disputes between the Chinese and the Korean merchants who were permitted to accompany the tribute missions to Peking. Such was the state of affairs that forced the Korean government to further restrict the movement of people and ships to forestall any provocative incidents that could create difficulties with China. These steps were rationalized as being in the best interests of Korea's safety.

During the Taewŏn'gun's regime Korea's isolation was challenged not only from the sea, but also from the north. The northeastern frontier separating Hamgyŏng from Russia posed a special problem. The geographical setting, the decayed defense system, and great economic difficulties had encouraged Koreans to emigrate to the sparsely populated Russian territory. The emigration was nothing new, but it became a more urgent problem in the Taewŏn'gun's time, when Korea was beginning to feel the pressures of a changing Far-Eastern world.

According to official Russian records,[1] Korean villages such as Yančix, Sidim, Adim, and Krabb were founded in the region of Posjet, not far from the Korean border on the Tumen River, as early as 1864. The same sources also state that Korean immigration into Russia began between 1858 and 1860. However, there are no Korean records of any such emigration prior to 1866. A dispatch from the governor of Hamgyŏng, Yi Yu-wŏn, to the government in Seoul on April 4, 1864,[2] mentions, however, the appearance of Russians on Korean soil. According to this report, on March 20, three Russians and two Chinese crossed the frozen Tumen River, entered Kyŏnghŭng, presented a note to the local magistrate requesting trade relations, and demanded a reply. When they were told that no local official was authorized to reply to such a note, the Russians reluctantly recrossed the river. The magistrate reported the incident to the governor, who concluded that some Koreans at the border must have collaborated with the Russians. Acting on this assumption, the governor ordered Yi Nam-sik, the military commander of the northern section of Hamgyŏng, to track down possible Korean suspects. Yi was also instructed to keep a strict watch on the river and the seacoast. The governor and the magistrate of Kyŏnghŭng did all they could in the circumstances, nevertheless, the court reduced the salary of the governor and the magistrate as well as that of the commander on grounds of negligence. At the same time the governor was ordered to take proper action against any suspect or collaborator who might be apprehended. Several suspects, including a Kyŏnghŭng clerk, were subsequently arrested. In June the clerk and another man who had been charged with crossing the border were beheaded on the bank of the Tumen as a warning against similar transgressions.[3]

This was the first of many such incidents. For instance, in the fall of 1865 a few dozen Russians accompanied by a Chinese interpreter came to the shore of the Tumen to deliver another note to the authorities in Kyŏnghŭng; again their overtures were rejected. On December 19 three

Russians again attempted in vain to approach Kyǒnghǔng. Several days after that seven Russians finally succeeded in making their way to the district headquarters. They asked Magistrate Yun Hyǒp for a permit to proceed to the provincial headquarters at Hamhǔng so that they could present their note directly to the governor, but this request was also refused.[4]

Although the sudden appearance of Russians with requests to trade seems to have had some connection with the Korean emigration into Russian territory, the Korean government did not take note of this movement until late in 1866. On December 1, 1866, seven inhabitants of Paegan, a border village in Kyǒngwǒn district, crossed the Tumen into Russian territory. The next day two more left the village. Four days later, on December 6, several hundred armed men, who were reported to be Chinese but who were presumably Koreans who had emigrated earlier, crossed the Tumen to Paegan and carried away the women and children and family possessions such as cattle and horses. Six more families left the village at this time, bringing the number of emigrants from Paegan to fifteen households totaling seventy-five people by the end of that day. During the incident three natives who attempted to prevent the emigration were wounded by the armed men, and the guard posts on the riverbank were burned down.[5]

Soon after the Paegan incident the Russians constructed huts on the border, presumably to house Korean immigrants. This news reached Seoul on January 18, 1867,[6] and greatly disturbed the Korean government, which seems to have been poorly informed about the new Sino-Russian territorial agreement. In 1715 the Koreans and the Chinese had agreed to enforce the rule forbidding the erection of houses or the tilling of land along the Yalu and the Tumen. This measure was designed to forestall any conflict between the peoples of the two countries. However, the Treaty of Peking (November 14, 1860) delineated a new Russo-Chinese frontier and recognized Russian sovereignty not only over the territories ceded by the Treaty of Aigun (May 1858) but also the vast region east of the Amur, Ussuri, and Tumen rivers. This territorial change did away with the "forbidden land" east of the Tumen.

On January 23, 1867, a small number of Korean guards clashed with a few hundred bandits at the border village of Samdongsa in Kyǒnghǔng. Many of the bandits fled across the Tumen, leaving behind sixty horses and cows, thirty cooking stoves, twenty carts, and a considerable amount of grain.[7] Although the nationality of the bandits was never ascertained, they were no doubt Koreans attempting to emigrate to the Russian zone.

This early Korean emigration into Russia was prompted primarily by the barrenness of the land along the Tumen. The cold climate, little rain, and early frosts all prevented productive farming. Moreover, the area of the old "Six Garrisons" (Yukchin) which comprised most of the northern half of present day Hamgyŏng was more affected than any other part of the country by the military tax, the *corvée* levies, the grain system, and the chronic abuses of the local governments. Large-scale graft, even on the part of the governors and military commanders, was frequently uncovered.[8] The traditional trade between the Koreans and the Chinese at a few border towns contributed further to the economic burdens of the local populace by imposing upon it the cost of maintaining the Chinese officials.[9] And to make things worse, the people in the north had, on the whole, suffered heavier land taxes than other Koreans as a result of faulty and incomplete land surveys.[10]

In those conditions there were two principal ways by which border people might ease their economic burdens. One was to become part-time petty traders, the other was to gather wild ginseng in the neighboring Manchurian hills. The first possibility, however, was practically eliminated by the traditional government policy which restricted free trade and proscribed the use of money in that region.[11] The second was outlawed by both the Korean and Chinese governments.[12]

As a result of these natural and economic hardships, the people constantly moved from place to place, either as beggars or in search of new sources of livelihood, leaving many towns and garrison districts deserted. In 1759 it was reported that the population of Kyŏngwŏn, which several years before had been about 4,000 households, was reduced to half this number. In 1848 Changjin in Hamgyŏng was demoted from the status of district to that of garrison district because of heavy depopulation. Such population changes were also noted in the southern part of the province. For instance, in 1853 it was reported that the population of the eleven old garrison districts under the jurisdiction of Kapsan and Samsu districts had practically vanished.[13]

The illegal movement of Koreans beyond the border had been constantly guarded against by both the Korean and Chinese authorities. As long as this joint cooperation continued there was no opportunity for Koreans to move across the Yalu and the Tumen. But the establishment of the new boundary between Russia and Korea and Russia's protective policy toward Korean immigrants gave the northerners a chance.

The Taewŏn'gun tried to stop this mass migration by attempting to have the houses constructed by Russians removed and the migrants repatriated through the aid of the Chinese government.[14] In the light of past experience this approach seemed proper; houses erected by the Chinese near the Korean border had always been removed at the request of the Korean government.[15] This time, however, the Taewŏn'gun's efforts were useless. One exception was the repatriation of some 450 men who had been wandering in the Hunchun area, the Manchurian region between the Tumen and the Russian border.[16]

The Taewŏn'gun also responded to the emigration by examining basic conditions in the northern region. This led him to introduce a series of military and economic reforms. As previously noted, the primary cause of the migration of Koreans into Russia was economic. It should be added, however, that an important secondary cause was the lack of an adequate border defense system. Although the subject of defense of the northern frontier had received the close attention of the Yi government since its inception, the long period of peace that followed the rise of the Ch'ing dynasty had made defense preparations in the north almost meaningless. As a result, the original military establishments on the northern border had been gradually abandoned, leaving only a few garrison posts. And indeed, the soldiers stationed in these posts were not even permitted to carry guns. Moreover, weak as the garrisons were, they were constantly attacked for constituting a burden on the populace. Even after the first appearance of the Russians at Kyŏnghŭng, no one in the government was seriously concerned over the question of border defense. It was some five months later before the Taewŏn'gun began to take a few half-hearted steps to prepare against further intrusions by the Russians. For instance, on August 23, 1864, the

military commander of northern Hamgyŏng, Yi Nam-sik, was ordered to stay
on duty beyond his normal tenure and the magistrate of Kyŏnghŭng, Yun
Hyŏp, was concurrently appointed commander of frontier defense *(pangŏsa).*[17]

The Paegan and Samdongsa incidents finally brought about radical
changes in the government's policy toward northern defense. On February 24,
1867, shortly after the mass desertion from Paegan village was reported, the
government ordered the first shipment of weapons and ammunition to the
Tumen region. At the same time the military commander of the northern
section of Hamgyŏng was instructed to remain at his temporary headquarters
on the border (at Hoeryŏng?) until July in order that he might supervise the
defenses more closely.[18] These initial measures were soon followed by the
introduction of more systematic defense plans such as the establishment of
rifle units and the reorganization of districts.

The rifle units, the first of which was set up at Kyŏnghŭng in 1867,
were introduced into almost every district of both P'yŏngan and Hamgyŏng.
There were over fifty of them, and each one contained from twenty to three
hundred men. In addition, numerous small guard posts and barriers were
built along the border between the garrison of Hunsul (opposite Chinese
Hunchun) and the littoral of the Tumen.[19] A local gazetteer of Hamgyŏng
gives a graphic description of the physical features of the new defense
system set up along the Tumen:

> In the spring of 1869 . . . thirty guard posts and a wooden barrier
> were erected along the bank of the Tumen for a distance of 150 *i.*
> [Alarm] bells were hung on the entire fence. Still fearing that this
> was not enough, thirty more such posts were added in the autumn
> of 1871 . . . Three to five soldiers were assigned to each post. The
> old and new posts were so closely placed together . . . that even
> little creatures like flying birds and leaping rabbits could not avoid
> them.[20]

The most important areas affected by the reorganization were
Kyŏnghŭng, several garrison districts, and the fertile region of the ancient
"Four Districts" (Sagun),[21] situated between Manp'ojin and old Huju along
the Yalu. The Sagun region, which had become a haven for outlaws for the
past few decades, was reorganized in 1869 into two administrative districts,
Chasŏng and Huch'ang, and opened for colonization to the roving border
people. At the same time, four garrisons (Oetkoe, Chongp'o, Mamahae, and

Ch'up'a) located around this region were abolished, and others in more strategic locations were strengthened. In 1871 the seat of the government of Kyŏnghŭng district was moved to a more safely situated place, the Fort of Mui, several miles north of the original town of Kyŏnghŭng. The latter was then transformed into a fortified garrison. In 1872 two fortresses in Kyŏngsŏng district, Pohwa and Samsamp'a, which seemed worthless from a military point of view, were abolished. In their place a new fortified garrison was established at Tokkumujin near the town of Kyŏngsŏng on the east coast.[22]

In connection with these defense measures, the "Five Household" system, in effect elsewhere in the country, was reintroduced, and the old "roll-call" system *(kwan [jin] mun chungjŏm)* was more strictly enforced. Both, of course, were designed to keep a closer watch over the population.[23]

In the economic sphere, the Taewŏn'gun's main effort was directed toward lightening the burdens of the populace in the north. A special proclamation was issued in the name of the king on December 25, 1869. A vernacular version of this document was to be posted in the villages, particularly in those of the Yukchin region, so that the inhabitants might know that their welfare was cause for royal concern:

> As for grief about the plight of North Hamgyŏng, it has not yet been made known to me where the officials' care and compassion lie. The news of the recent desertion of the people [in the north] is indeed alarming . . . [They] abandon the home of their fathers and mothers and flee to a land where the customs and language are strange . . . Thus, I can only say that the people [in the north] are unable to secure those things necessary for sustaining their lives, for the forced labor is too great, and the oppression is too severe . . . I order the Council of State to instruct the governor of Hamgyŏng and the military commander of the northern section of Hamgyŏng to formulate an opinion . . . and to submit a report [about the following matters]: in the frontier region . . . the taxes and tributes which could be reduced and the various defects [of the institutions] which could be reformed; in the other districts and towns . . . the levies which could be eliminated; . . . the origin of various abuses . . . of the trade fairs [of Hoeryŏng and Kyŏngwŏn].[24]

The measures taken to this effect were mainly recommended by Yi Hŭng-min and Kim Su-hyŏn, two former governors of Hamgyŏng, and Chŏng Chu-ŭng, who was sent to the Yalu region as a border inspector *(ch'alpyŏnsa)* in 1869. The reform program consisted principally of: abolition of the tribute of deer antlers and musk, which used to come from the old Huju region (northeastern tip of the Yukchin area); total or partial cancellation of government grain-loans; discontinuation of taxes on fallow land *(chinjŏn)*; temporary abolition of levies on goods shipped into ports, ships, and salt; increase of the price on cattle (thirty *yang* per head) and pigs (eight *yang* per head) which the government purchased from the districts in the Yukchin area to give to the Chinese at Hoeryŏng and Kyŏngwŏn trade fairs; permission to use money for payment of interest on grain-loans to the local governments, instead of polished rice. In addition to these specific measures, most of which were introduced into the Yukchin region (except the first) between 1870 and 1873, the government extended to a number of distressed districts in the north a special grant totaling more than 100,000 *yang* for relief or similar purposes.[25]

Furthermore, the government took special steps to rehabilitate those deserters who either returned voluntarily or were brought back to their native villages. They were provided with the necessary food, clothes, and land; the taxes and personal debts that they had not been able to pay were all remitted; their land and houses which had been taken over by others were given back to them. Each village was strongly urged by the local authorities to render maximum help to those who were returning.[26]

Thus, the problems of the northern frontier could be effectively met by military and economic policies. The real challenge to Korea's isolation did not come from the north but from countries beyond the sea.

Chapter X

THE FRENCH INVASION

An important factor in Korea's isolation, due to her geographical position, was her lack of direct contact with European thought and institutions. To be sure, from the early sixteenth century Korea possessed a rudimentary knowledge of the Western world which it received from China. Initially the West was much admired for its scientific knowledge, but the penetration of Catholicism into Korea radically changed the favorable image of the West and aroused hostility, for one of the early forms of the Western invasion of Korea was religious.

The Early History of Korean Catholicism

One of the most interesting chapters in the history of Catholicism in Korea concerns its origin. Unlike many other lands, where the Christian religion was first brought by foreign missionaries, in Korea it began with a kind of "self-study" of Christian literature by natives.

The earliest introduction of Christian literature into Korea is usually attributed to Hǒ Kyun (1569-1618), Yi Su-gwang (1563-1628), and Crown Prince Sohyǒn (1612-1645). According to the writings of Yu Mong-in (1559-1623), in 1610 Hǒ Kyun brought back to Korea some Christian prayer literature from Peking. In his *Chibong yusǒl* (Collection of miscellaneous essays), which first appeared in 1614, Yi Su-gwang, who had traveled to Peking a number of times, described in some detail certain books on Catholicism such as Matteo Ricci's *T'ien-chu shih-i* (Véritables principes sur Dieu).[1] It is not certain whether he ever took this work back to Korea. However, in 1645 a copy of it together with an image of Jesus and a number of Chinese converts were brought from Peking to Korea by Crown Prince Sohyǒn.[2]

After this introduction, many young men of various social and professional backgrounds poured into Peking out of curiosity, but primarily in search of new knowledge. Many of these carried home the more easily accessible books on the Christian religion in addition to those on their special fields of learning, and they studied the new doctrine with ardor, spreading it among their friends and kinsmen.[3]

The long period of "self-study" finally reached a climax in 1783 with the baptism of Yi Sŭng-hun, who is said to have been dissatisfied with the mere study of the doctrine. In that year Yi accompanied his father, Yi Tong-uk, who was then secretary *(sŏjanggwan)* to the Winter Solstice Embassy headed by Hwang In-jŏm, to Peking. During his brief sojourn there he visited the South Cathedral (Nan-t'ang), where he was baptized by Father de Gramon and given the new name of Pierre.[4]

After Yi's baptism there followed a period of official suppression. Some elements of Christian doctrine fundamentally conflicted with certain basic ethical and ritual principles of Confucianism. The most heretical element of the Christian religion was its abandonment of the established rite of sacrifice to the deceased. Bitter attacks were also directed against preaching about heaven and hell, which was deluding the people, the critics thought. Many Confucians believed that Catholicism did not take cognizance of the king and the parents, but recognized only God.[5]

These early criticisms, however, did not lead the authorities to ban Christianity. The government's action was mainly confined to proscribing the importation of new heretical books (first in 1786 and repeatedly there-after) and to burning the old ones (first in 1788).[6] Another important factor in the initial suppression of Catholicism was the redevelopment of factional strife. From about 1780 the Namin, who had then returned to power under the protection of King Chŏngjo, and the other factions (notably the Noron and the Soron) began to realign themselves into two new factions called the Sip'a and the Pyŏkp'a.[7] The former consisted of those who lamented the tragic fate of Chŏngjo's father, Crown Prince Changhŏn, who was murdered by his own father, King Yŏngjo. The members of the latter faction, however, justified and supported Yŏngjo's action. Now it happened that a few Catholics in the government belonged to the Sip'a of the Namin. Naturally this religious factor was constantly manipulated by the opposition Pyŏkp'a faction for political purposes.

Thus, the so-called Catholic persecution of 1791 was, in fact, not a persecution. It was an extension of the factional strife between the Sip'a and the Pyŏkp'a, centering around Ch'ae Che-gong, then left councillor of state and the leader of the Sip'a of the Namin. One of the most outspoken prosecutors in the 1791 trial of Catholics was Ch'oe Hŏn-jung, a Namin Pyŏkp'a whose grandson, Ch'oe U-hyŏng, was to play the same role during the Taewŏn'gun's 1868 persecution.[8]

The history of Catholicism in Korea entered another stage when foreign missionaries started to come into the country, and a series of large-scale persecutions began. The first of these missionaries to appear in Korea was a Chinese priest named Chou Wen-mo (P. Jacques Tsiou), who smuggled himself into Seoul in the winter of 1794.[9] Largely as a result of Chou's efforts, the number of converts is said to have increased to nearly ten thousand by 1801. In that year the nation witnessed the first major Christian persecution.[10] This persecution was led by Kim Ku-ju, a powerful leader of the Pyŏkp'a faction of the Noron and a brother of the second consort of Yŏngjo. Among the many victims of the persecution were a number of prominent Sip'a figures of the Namin, including Yi Sŭng-hun.[11] As for Chou, he delivered himself to the authorities in April 1801 and was executed on June 1.[12]

In connection with the 1801 persecution, it is important to mention the famous Hwang Sa-yŏng paeksŏ (lit., Hwang Sa-yŏng's "letter on silk"), which was to leave a lasting impression on the minds of the anti-Christians. The letter, dated October 29, 1801, was written over the name of Hwang Sim on white silk and was addressed to Bishop Govéa in Peking. In the letter the author first described vividly the 1801 incident and then made a proposal designed both to rescue the embittered Korean Christians and to ensure the future propagation of Catholicism in Korea. The proposal consisted of these four important points: (1) economic aid from Western countries for both missionary work and for the populace in general; (2) permission from the emperor of China to send European missionaries to Korea; (3) China's annexation of Korea and the appointment of one of the emperor's sons to rule the country; and (4) the dispatch of a few hundred ships and several tens of thousands of European soldiers to protect the peaceful propagation of Catholicism. This letter, however, was never delivered to the bishop, because Hwang Sa-yŏng was captured on November 5 with the letter on his person.[13]

Despite the loss of their leaders and of many fellow believers, the remaining Korean Catholics gradually began to recover from their ordeal and even succeeded in bringing a few foreign missionaries into the country. One of those given most credit for helping missionaries enter Korea was Yu Chin-gil, a senior language officer of the Bureau of Interpreters.[14] As a result of Yu's indefatigable efforts, between January 1836 and December 1837 three French priests—Pierre-Philibert Maubant, Jacques-Honoré Chastan, and Laurent-Marie-Joseph Imbert—were able to cross the border and to enter Seoul safely, disguised in native dress.[15]

Their mission, however, was short-lived. In 1839 a second persecution on a larger scale took place. On August 13 Imbert was arrested in Suwŏn and on September 6 Maubant and Chastan met the same fate in Hongju. On October 21, after a short trial, all three were executed.[16]

Although the events of 1839 at least temporarily arrested the Christian movement in Korea, many who survived the persecution soon began to continue their evangelistic work with even greater vigor and intensity, and, indeed, in far more favorable circumstances. This was partly due to the fact that the overall situation in the Far East was then rapidly changing in favor of missionary work. For instance, in 1842 the Treaty of Nanking was concluded and the city of Shanghai was opened for residence by Europeans. This gave foreign missionaries easier access to both China and Korea. They could avoid the hazardous journey overland and enter Korea by sea aboard Korean junks furnished by native converts. The second factor was the rapidly deteriorating domestic situation in Korea.

After 1839 the most notable man in the history of Catholicism in Korea was Kim Tae-gŏn, known also by the names of André Kim and Kim Hai-kim. In 1836 Kim (1821-1846), whose father was a victim of the 1839 persecution, was sent to Macao by Maubant to study at the Portuguese seminary. He was ordained in 1845 and returned to Korea.[17] On April 30, 1845, shortly after his return, Kim left for Shanghai aboard a Korean ship; he came back on October 12 with two missionaries: Jean Joseph Ferréol, who succeeded Imbert as bishop, and Marie-Antoine-Nicolas Daveluy.[18] Although Kim himself was apprehended on June 5, 1846, and executed on September 15,[19] the evangelic work under the leadership of the two new missionaries and others who came after them prospered greatly. It is said that by the end of Ch'ŏlchong's reign (1863) there were twelve French missionaries and nearly 20,000 converts in the country.[20]

The Catholic Persecution of 1866

The rise of Catholicism began to affect a number of prominent families, including the house of the Taewŏn'gun. According to Mutel, the Taewŏn'gun's wife was said to have inclined to Catholicism for some time, to such an extent that she once asked a French priest, Simon-François Berneux, to pray for her son, the future King Kojong. Her interest in Catholicism was largely due to the presence in the house of a devout convert called Martha Pak, who was young Kojong's wet-nurse.[21] The Taewŏn'gun himself seems to have had wide contact with the Namin, many of whom were hereditary Catholics. Two of his close associates were Catholics: Hong Pong-ju, a Namin and the son of Martha Pak, and Nam Chong-sam, a Pugin and the son of Nam Sang-gyo, under whom the Taewŏn'gun had once studied.[22]

Thus, the Taewŏn'gun must have had some knowledge at least of the association of his wife, Martha Pak, Nam, and Hong with Catholicism, and perhaps he was even aware of the presence of foreign missionaries. This reasoning is confirmed by a rather significant episode which immediately preceded the persecution of 1866.

An examination of a variety of sources indicates that for some time the Taewŏn'gun had been aware of renewed Russian movements along the northeastern border, a trouble spot since the latter part of Ch'ŏlchong's reign.[23] These movements were also known to two Catholic leaders, Nam Chong-sam and Hong Pong-ju, who decided to take advantage of the Russian menace to make the propagation of Catholicism legal, and to further their own political ambitions. They wanted to prevent the southward movement of Russia by concluding a triple alliance between France, England, and Korea. To this end, Nam, who was a royal secretary, and Hong requested Berneux and Daveluy to sound out the French minister in Peking about the possibility of Korea concluding such an alliance. Meantime, they also submitted to the Taewŏn'gun a formal proposal to this effect.

Nothing, however, came of the plan. The two missionaries failed to show any enthusiasm, for they were little inclined to politics. The Taewŏn'gun showed considerable interest in the proposal, at least in the beginning. Later, however, he changed his mind, probably because he was aware that the conclusion of such a treaty might make China suspicious.

The proposed alliance inevitably exposed the presence of foreign missionaries to the government authorities. Soon, increasing pressure was put on the Taewŏn'gun from the anti-Christian elements in the government to sanction the arrest and trial of missionaries and heretics. Thus the Taewŏn'gun suddenly had to take a very strong stand against the religion of his friends and his son's nurse, when until that time he had appeared indifferent.

The persecution of 1866 began with the arrest of Yi Sŏn-i, a house servant of Berneux, in Seoul on February 19. The servant disclosed the hiding places of Berneux and Hong Pong-ju, and they were both arrested on February 23. By March 23 Nam Chong-sam and eight other French missionaries had also been apprehended and executed together with Berneux and Hong.[24] The number of native converts who fell victim to this first wave of persecution, which lasted until the end of March, never exceeded more than thirty to forty, contrary to the much publicized higher figures. To be sure, in the entire period between the two foreign invasions, more Christians than this were in fact arrested and put to death. Many had treacherously attempted to make contact with French and American ships, ostensibly to assist in meting out punitive action against Korea.

The Prelude to the French Invasion of 1866

Three missionaries who were protected by native converts in the south luckily escaped arrest: Felix-Clair Ridel, Stanislas Féron, and Adolphe-Nicolas Calais. The immediate problem facing them was to inform the French authorities in Peking of the deaths of their nine fellow missionaries and to seek protection for themselves. Ridel, a newcomer, was entrusted with this crucial mission. On June 20, 1866, accompanied by several native Catholics, he left Korea for Chefoo aboard a junk procured with the aid of a few well-wishers. On July 6 they arrived safely at their destination.[25]

Ridel left his companions at Chefoo and went on to Tientsin, where he pleaded with Admiral Pierre-Gustave Rose, the commander of the French Asiatic Squadron, to rescue their two compatriots in Korea. Rose promised the priest that he would sail to Korean shores as soon as his squadron returned from Indochina, where it had been dispatched to suppress a native uprising. His mission successfully accomplished, Ridel hurried back to the waiting

Koreans, whom he soon allowed to return to Korea. Ridel himself went to
Shanghai with three Koreans to await further events.[26]

Although Rose decided to launch an expedition against Korea, he
appeared to have worried about the possibility that the two survivors might
be arrested and executed before his arrival in Korea. Therefore, contem-
plating some kind of diplomatic means by which the two men might be
rescued, he first consulted with the French chargé d'affaires, Henri de
Bellonet. As a result, a note was sent on July 13 in the name of Bellonet to
Prince Kung, the head of the Tsungli Yamen. It will be evident from the
excerpt below that the note was in fact more an ultimatum than a plea for
mediation.

> I grieve to bring officially to the attention of Your Imperial High-
> ness a horrible outrage committed in the small kingdom of Corea,
> which formerly assumed the bonds of vassalage to the Chinese
> empire, but [from] which this act of savage barbarity has forever
> separated it . . . The same day on which the King of Corea laid
> his hands upon my unhappy countrymen was the last of his reign;
> he himself proclaimed its end, which I, in my turn, solemnly
> declare today. In a few days our military forces are to march to
> the conquest of Corea, and the Emperor, my august sovereign,
> alone, has the right and the power to dispose, according to his good
> pleasure, of the country and of the vacant throne. The Chinese
> government has declared to me many times that it has no authority
> or power over Corea; and it refused on this pretext to apply the
> Treaties of Tientsin to that country, and give to our missionaries
> the passports which we have asked from it. We have taken note of
> these declarations, and we declare now that we do not recognize
> any authority whatever of the Chinese government over the king-
> dom of Corea.[27]

On July 16, after a consultation with his yamen associates, Prince Kung
sent Bellonet a carefully worded note:

> I may here observe that since Corea is an out-of-the-way
> country, lying in a secluded corner, and, as is well known, has
> always strictly maintained its own regulations, I am quite unaware
> what has led them to put these missionaries and Christians to
> death . . . Seeing, however, that when two countries come to war
> it involves the lives of their people, as it will in this case—and,

therefore, I cannot but endeavor to bring about a solution of the difficulty between them—as the Coreans have killed a number of the missionaries, it seems to me that it would be best to inquire beforehand into the proofs and merits of the affair, and ascertain what were the reasons for this step, so that, if possible, a resort to arms may be avoided. I . . . suggest such a course for your excellency's consideration.[28]

On July 18 the Tsungli Yamen requested the Board of Rites to send a communication to Seoul, enclosing the French note of July 13, so that Korea might be forewarned. The note was received by the Korean government on August 12. In its reply to the Chinese note, prepared on August 17, the Korean government first explained that the "captured aliens," whose nationality was unknown, were found in the company of outlaws who were plotting treason. Then it argued that if its own people illegally infiltrated other lands to deceive the people and harm the country, they too would certainly be exterminated by the authorities of that country. It denied, however, the killing of any Frenchmen, for "Korea and France were situated far from each other without any contact and there had been no old grudge and dislike between the two countries."[29]

On the other hand, the Chinese note had serious consequences for those Christians who had managed to survive the previous persecution. On August 17 the Council of State advised the Taewŏn'gun that the chief reason why the French received the news of the persecution so quickly was probably that there was communication between the French and native heretics. The council then proposed that all treacherous heretics be hunted down and that all coasts be more strictly watched. This proposal, which was immediately adopted, was followed on September 11 by the formal proclamation of a "royal edict of proscription of heresy."[30]

Meanwhile, as the trouble in Indochina had been settled, the French admiral decided to make a preliminary survey of the Korean coast before launching the formal expedition. On September 18 Rose left Chefoo aboard the flagship *Primauguet*, accompanied by two other ships, the *Déroulède* and the *Tardif*. One of the passengers on the *Primauguet* was Ridel, who had volunteered to serve as interpreter. Two days later, on September 20, they arrived off the coast of Pup'yŏng after a brief stopover at a bay called Naep'o

(Sinch'ang district, South Ch'ungch'ŏng) to pick up a Korean pilot, and immediately started the survey of the vicinity.[31]

This survey, which was undertaken mainly by the *Déroulède* and the *Tardif,* continued until the end of the month. It was conducted along Kanghwa Island, the Han River, and the environs of Seoul. At one point, on September 28, the two ships reached a point from where they were able to see the great wall surrounding Pukhan mountain, north of Seoul, and even part of the city itself. This was the first time that a Western ship had caught a glimpse of the heart of the ancient kingdom.[32]

There was not a single attempt on the part of the Korean authorities to take any belligerent action against the French ships. The high officials in Seoul took a "wait-and-see" attitude, and often remarked that the "way of being kind to strangers" had to be observed.[33] All officials of the coastal districts were strictly warned against any provocative acts toward the "little wretches," and were ordered to make every effort to contrive their peaceful departure from Korean waters. On the other hand, indications of the Taewŏn'gun's active concern over unpredictable events are not lacking.

On September 26, when the *Déroulède* and the *Tardif* approached the vicinity of Seoul with thundering noise, darkening the blue autumn sky with columns of black smoke, the unrest among the populace in the capital was evident. Even the court and government were virtually panic-stricken. In this crisis one of the Taewŏn'gun's faithful military aides, Yi Yong-hŭi, was dispatched to the Han River to stand guard against the intruders. For this purpose Yi, who was then deputy commander of the Ŏyŏng regiment, was given command of several hundred mounted and foot soldiers in addition to his own regimental troops. All other military units around the capital were also put on alert. The main palace and its three gates were placed under special guard; the two metropolitan police forces were ordered to take strict precautions against bandits and thieves inside and outside the capital; and a special proclamation was posted on the city gates calling for "patriotic and loyal" men.[34]

From the precipitous nature of these measures, it is quite clear that the Taewŏn'gun had not taken the French warning nor the note from the Board of Rites seriously. Now, however, he fully understood that the French were neither joking nor bluffing. Several days after the departure of the French ships, on October 9, he ordered 30,000 *yang* to be sent from the royal treasury to provincial naval headquarters for the repair of ships. This is the first recorded indication of the Taewŏn'gun's determination to prepare for the imminent return of the French expeditionary force.[35]

On leaving Korean waters on October 1, Admiral Rose and his ships had returned to Chefoo. Rose had learned the sea route leading to the capital, but he had also learned that the Han River was a difficult course for steamship navigation and that there were probably forts along the banks.[36] In view of these factors, he abandoned his plan to approach the capital from the Han, and instead decided to capture Kanghwa, from where he could block the lower course of the Han. This would mean severing the sea route between the capital and the countryside to the south, thus stopping the flow of tribute rice into Seoul. If successful, such a strategy would result in the starvation of the entire populace in the capital. Then, surely, the Korean government would surrender. In order to carry out this plan, however, Rose needed a considerable number of men and ships in addition to actual combat troops.

On October 5, shortly before his departure for the formal Korea expedition, Rose issued two interesting proclamations addressed to the general public. These reflect his confidence in the outcome of the forth-coming campaign. One outlined the aim of the campaign and the other gave notice of the planned blockade of the Han River:

> The undersigned . . . in furtherance of the measures which have
> been deemed necessary in consequence of the murder of many
> French missionaries by the government of Corea, and by virtue of
> the powers belonging to me as commander-in-chief, hereby
> declares, that after the 15th day of this month the River Seoul,
> by all its entrances, will be held in a state of effective blockade by
> the naval forces under my command. All vessels which shall attempt
> to violate this blockade will be treated according to international
> laws and the treaties in force with neutral powers.[37]

The French Invasion and Campaign

On October 11, 1866, the admiral left Chefoo with his Far Eastern fleet of seven ships (the flagship *La Guerrière,* the *Laplace,* the *Primauguet,* the

2. KANGHWA ISLAND

KAPKOTCHIN ●

△ KANGHWA CITY

✳ MT. MUNSU

SALT RIVER

KWANGSŎNG ●

T'ONGJIN ●

SONDOLMOK

TŎKCHIN ●

● TŎKP'O

MT. CHŎNGJOK ✸ CH'AJI ●

HAN RIVER

SEOUL

MULCH'I

YŎNGJONG

O WŎLMI

● CHEMULP'O (INCH'ŎN)

Déroulède, the *Kien-chan,* the *Tardif,* and the *Lebrethon*) and about 600
men, including the marines from the camp at Yokohama. A day later the
fleet was reported to have already appeared off the coast of Kyŏnggi.[38] The
formal campaign, however, did not begin until October 14, when a few
detachments of marines and sailors supported by four ships and a number of
launches successfully landed at Kapkotchin on the eastern coast of Kanghwa
Island and immediately occupied the fortified village of Chemulchin. Two
days later, on October 16, Rose launched a general attack on the city of
Kanghwa with his entire force and captured it with little resistance from the
Koreans. With this ancient city large numbers of weapons, enormous
amounts of grain and silver, as well as large holdings of priceless books and
government papers fell into the hands of the French. These books are
believed to have become the basis for Maurice Courant's celebrated three-
volume work on Korean bibliography, which opened the way to the serious
study of Korea in the West.[39]

During the initial phase of the invasion, the government in Seoul failed
to show any determined line of action, clinging to the policy of "adapting
itself to the circumstances." On the coast there were only a few attempts
made by the local authorities to subject the French ships to inquiry or to
induce them to leave peacefully with offers of provisions. This passive
approach came to an end on October 15, when the government was informed
of the French occupation of Kapkotchin and sensed the imminent danger to
the city of Kanghwa.[40] On that day Yi Kyŏng-ha, Sin Kwan-ho, and Yi
Wŏn-hǔi were ordered to the Han to work out a strategy of defense. These
three generals were then something like the spirit of the Korean army, and
enjoyed the unlimited confidence of the Taewŏn'gun. The same day an
artillery course was hastily introduced as a special unit of the military
examination.[41]

On October 16, when the government received news of the French
reconnaissance of the city of Kanghwa—the traditional haven of kings and
queens in times of foreign invasions and domestic disorder, an emergency
council was held at the palace to discuss national defense. All current and
former councillors, the minister of war, and the commanders of all military
units attended. The result was the creation of a special Defense Command

known as the Kiboyŏnhae sunmuyŏng, largely in accordance with a proposal by Left Councillor Kim Pyŏng-hak. The primary function of this body was the coordination and direction of general defense. Yi Kyŏng-ha and Yi Yong-hŭi were appointed commander-in-chief *(tosunmusa)* and deputy commander *(chunggun)* of the body respectively.

The power delegated to the commander-in-chief was quite extraordinary. After Yi Kyŏng-ha's appointment was announced, Yi was summoned to the palace, where he was issued the marshal's sword, armor, and helmet and given a special rescript empowering him to wield absolute authority, both civil and military, over the entire officialdom of the coastal region (primarily Kyŏnggi). Thus he virtually became the military governor of the region. Meanwhile, a special army corps consisting of nine generals, fifty-two officers, and 2,021 men, including some 150 mounted soldiers, had been formed and put under the Defense Command. Early in the evening a royal secretary was sent to Yi's headquarters to cheer the army corps with dried foodstuffs provided by the Department of Revenue. These troops were about to leave for the front under the direct command of Yi Yong-hŭi.[42]

In addition to the creation of the Defense Command, the emergency council approved the establishment of a special patrol unit consisting of some 400 men under the command of Sin Kwan-ho. This body was to patrol the entire course of the Han River from the capital down to the sea.[43] Moreover, a drive was inaugurated to recruit volunteers and search for new talent. This movement was designed both to increase the number and the quality of fighting men and to unite the people and boost their morale. Old and incompetent officials were dismissed, and new faces found their way into strategic posts in the government. One of those called into the government was the highly reputed Confucian scholar Yi Hang-no.[44] The recruiting of volunteers was carried out in the capital as well as in the provinces. For this purpose, special commissioners called *somosa* were appointed. It appears that the government was particularly interested in recruiting professional "game hunters" *(p'osu)*, especially the fearless tiger-hunters from the northwest.[45]

The government's attention was also directed toward the mobilization of the so-called peddlers *(pobusang)*.[46] These peddlers, whom legend closely associated with the founder of the Yi dynasty and who had been protected by succeeding Yi kings, played a significant role in Yi history. Their tightly knit nation-wide guild had been known for its inner solidarity and unparalleled devotion to the dynasty. In times of foreign invasions and internal uprisings the peddlers were the first to come to the defense of the dynasty. They fought more gallantly than the army regulars.

Between October 17 and October 20 there was no major confrontation between the French and Korean troops at the front. The activities of the French soldiers were mainly limited to reconnoitering and pillaging nearby villages. The fleet was still circling the island of Kanghwa in its effort to blockade the Han. The Koreans, on the other hand, were steadily building up their strength all along the coast. In particular, the garrisons in strategic places such as Haengjuhang and Yesŏkhyŏn were now heavily reinforced by new recruits and troops transferred from other regions. By October 18 the total strength of the Korean troops deployed along the front line probably numbered no less than five thousand.[47]

On October 19 the Koreans finally moved into an offensive position. General Yi Yong-hŭi brought his force of 2,021 men into T'ongjin and soon occupied the entire right bank of the Salt River *(Yŏmha)*, just opposite Kanghwa Island.[48] Apparently General Yi's original plan was to cross the tiny channel to the island and launch a counterattack against the enemy, but he was unable to find enough boats to do this. Nevertheless, he managed to send a note, designed to be a final warning before the Korean attack, to Admiral Rose's headquarters on Kanghwa. This note reflects much of the philosophy behind the Taewŏn'gun's seclusion policy:

> The people who betray the heavenly principle are doomed to perish. Those who violate the laws of the country must be punished . . . From time immemorial, there has been [in all nations] an established custom according to which people from near and far lands have been treated. This is also the case with our country, which has shown much tolerance and kindness to other people. Officials of our country are ordered to receive and inquire after those who happen to drift to our boundaries, and to treat them as if they were old friends, even if we do not know the names of their countries . . . If they are hungry and cold, they are offered food and clothes. If they are sick, they are cared for with medicine. If they want to go home, we send them home, giving them provisions to take with them.

These are the customs which we have honored generation after generation. Even to this moment we practice them. Therefore, there is no country in the whole world which does not call our country the land of civility. If there be those who infiltrate our land . . . wear our clothes, learn our language, deceive our people and country, and corrupt our customs, we . . . have a law for them. Whenever they are found, they are punished severely. This is the great law which is applied by all nations. You are behaving outrageously. Your present invasion of our cities, killing of our people, and plundering have no justification whatsoever. You betrayed heaven and are so against our laws that there is no precedent to compare with. Heaven has already rejected you, and we have reason to punish you. Furthermore, we hear that you have a desire to practice your teaching in our land. If this is true, it can never be permitted. There is no uniformity . . . and each has what each prefers. Therefore, there is no need to talk about how other people base their principles of justice and wrongdoing. We esteem what we have learned, you practice what you have learned. As a principle, each hands down the teachings of his forefathers. How can you tell us to abandon the teachings of our forefathers and accept those of others? . . . Now we can no longer bear your stubbornness, even with our utmost benevolence. Therefore, we are about to cross the sea, commanding a great army of ten million. Since it is necessary to tell you the reason for our coming to subdue you, . . . we propose that we see each other beforehand. Then, . . . we shall decide who will be the victor.[49]

After the city of Kanghwa fell to the French, Admiral Rose had expected that the Korean government would come to terms. No one, however, had appeared since then. Thus, the arrival of the note was a great relief to the admiral. The letter seemed to have been difficult for his interpreter to grasp—it was written in a typically classical style—but Rose immediately sent a reply to General Yi.

Rose justified the military expedition primarily on the grounds that French missionaries had been persecuted by Korean officials. He also called attention to the French invasion of China, which, like Korea, had banned Christianity, and so was subdued. Then he demanded that the officials responsible for the killing of the missionaries be punished, and that a special envoy be immediately appointed and dispatched to his headquarters to conclude a permanent treaty between the two countries. Lastly, he warned the Koreans about the consequences of rejecting his proposal. The French note was soon transmitted to Seoul, where it was simply ignored by the Council of State, which considered it "contemptuous" and "threatening to China."[50]

The Taewŏn'gun noted the growing signs of unrest and fear among the populace in the capital and the officials in the government. He was also much disturbed by the news of General Yi's change of plans and by several other matters such as the lack of action on the part of his other generals and the incessant looting of the French soldiers in the villages. Confronted with these problems, he sent out on October 22 the famous and dramatic circular letter to the government, proclaiming his determination to drive the enemy out of the country. The letter also marks the intensification and aggravation of his seclusion policy.[51]

> Death and destruction are things which no man and no nation can avoid. This is the eternal law of heaven and earth from ancient times. As for the Western barbarians' invasion, all countries have suffered from it from antiquity . . . For the last few hundred years these bandits never succeeded in such an invasion. However, since China allowed them to make peace a few years ago, they have been hopping about more frequently, causing harm everywhere. Therefore, many people are suffering from their poison . . . Our country was the only land which they failed to invade, because the sage Kija residing in heaven protected us. Now they have come even to our land . . . The thing upon which we can rely is the unity of our minds, so that we may produce the strength of walls. If today our people, low and high, have fear and uncertainty in mind, everything will be ruined, and our national cause will be lost. I have four principles to guide our thinking. Remember them, make a blood oath, and follow me.

The Taewŏn'gun then listed these four principles: "The people who want amity [with the enemy], because they are unable to bear hardship, are the ones who sell the country. The people who desire trade [with the enemy], unable to bear suffering, are the ones who destroy the nation. The bandits are now encroaching upon the capital; the people who abandon it

are the ones who endanger our nation. There may be in the country a magic
force which can call upon demons and spirits to expel the bandits, working
a miracle. But this will be in the future more harmful than the evil teaching
[Catholicism]."

On October 23 the Taewŏn'gun issued a similar edict in the name of the
king to the soldiers and to the general public. He ordered the temporary
suspension of further recruitment of soldiers in order to suppress the unrest
and rumors among the populace. As a means of promoting the morale of the
soldiers at the front, officials were sent out to the homes of the soldiers to
console their families. The Department of Revenue was also instructed to
grant daily necessities to such families.[52]

The Triumph of the Taewŏn'gun and the French Retreat

At the front, meanwhile, military activity in both camps had become
more lively. On October 26 heavy fighting took place between a French
detachment of some 120 men and fifty garrisoners of the fortress of Mt.
Munsu, which is situated on the shore opposite Kapkotchin. This was the
first major clash between the invading force and the Korean army since the
former landed at Kapkotchin on October 14. In the battle, which was fought
on the shore, fifty to sixty French soldiers were claimed to have been shot
down. The Korean casualties were placed at four dead, two wounded, and
two missing.[53]

The Battle of Mt. Munsu was soon followed by fresh bombardments of
the coastal area by the French fleet, which brought heavy damage to many
towns and villages. On November 2 even the naval headquarters of Kyŏnggi
were heavily attacked by two French warships, which also destroyed five
Korean war junks.[54] While these devastating raids were continuing, the
Korean government saw an ever-swelling stream of volunteers pouring into
the capital. By November 1 275 hunters had already been assigned to various
points such as T'ongjin and Mt. Munsu. A total of 4,200 civilian volunteers
had been deployed on the front. The movement of the hunters to the front
line continued until November 9; by then their number had reached 1,175.
In addition, on November 8, 110 "frogmen" arrived at the front from the
naval headquarters of Hwanghae and Ch'ungch'ŏng. Thus by November 9

the fighting strength of the Korean army had increased to nearly 10,500 men.[55]

The invasion was practically brought to an end by what was called the Battle of Mt. Chŏngjok. On November 7 General Yi Yong-hŭi received news that a French patrol had entered the deserted fortress of Mt. Chŏngjok, which was located on the southern coast of Kanghwa Island. The general rather belatedly dispatched a company of his own army to the mountain in order to prevent the French occupation of that strategic spot. This force of about 543 men, under the command of Yang Hŏn-su, crossed the Salt River at night and occupied the mountain fortress. This turn of events was soon reported to Rose by a Korean convert. Rose decided to attack the Koreans at once. Early on the morning of November 8 a French force of 160 marines under the command of Captain Olivier left the city of Kanghwa, taking Ridel along as guide. They arrived at the foot of the mountain around noon and started marching toward the walled fortress where Yang and his troops lay in waiting. When the French troops were about to enter the fortress through the east gate, Yang ordered his troops, hidden behind the east and south gates, to open fire. In this surprise attack the French were said to have suffered nearly fifty casualties, while the Koreans had but one man killed and three wounded. Disastrously defeated, the marines hastily retreated as far as Kapkotchin. To the Koreans this was a signal victory, which was officially celebrated the following day. For his brilliant leadership, Yang was appointed Right Deputy Governor of Seoul.[56]

This defeat forced Admiral Rose to reassess the plans for the expedition. He now realized that the blockade of the Han River had little effect, and he could see small hope of entering into negotiations with the Korean government. On the contrary, he felt that in time the growing Korean army would cross the Salt River in a body and launch a general attack against the virtually isolated French troops at Kanghwa. He was probably painfully aware that the tiger-hunters were a far different breed of soldier than the poorly trained men who had guarded the city of Kanghwa. Lastly, he was worried about the possibility of the Han and Salt Rivers freezing, thus making the movement of his troops difficult. These considerations finally forced the admiral to abandon the blockade and to withdraw from the city of Kanghwa and from the Korean coast. Another important factor which may have influenced him to withdraw was the escape of the two French missionaries. This was reported to Ridel by two Korean converts who came to Kapkotchin.[57]

In view of his decision to leave Kanghwa, on November 10 Rose ordered his troops to set fire to all government buildings and to transfer the war booty from the city to the ships. On the following day the four ships raised anchor and left Kapkotchin for Mulch'i Island, off the coast of Inch'ŏn, from where, on November 18, they departed from Korean waters.[58]

With the withdrawal of the French fleet, the Taewŏn'gun's first war with a Western power ended, and his seclusion policy was vindicated. The Taewŏn'gun and his government were now more convinced than ever that the coming of the French was the result of the treacherous work of the Christians. This can be seen in his policy toward the "heretics," which became more oppressive during and after the invasion. In fact, it may be said that his real persecution of Catholics started after the French retreat. On November 21, in accordance with the proposal of the Council of State, he ordered the Department of Punishments, the city of Seoul, the two censoring offices, the two metropolitan police offices, provincial authorities, and all military garrisons to arrest every "heretic" found, and he promised that anyone who succeeded in arresting more than twenty Christians would be advanced to a higher post.

This clash with the French drove the Taewŏn'gun to introduce a more extreme anti-Western policy, which meant not only persecution of Christians and rejection of relations with the outside (including Japan), but also the banning of all Western goods, even those that came indirectly from China and Japan. The invasion also gave rise to a sweeping reconstruction of the defense system. Finally, his victory over the French led the Taewŏn'gun to misjudge the real strength of the Western powers and their true motives in coming to Korean shores.[59] After 1866 he persistently viewed other Western nations as mere reflections of the hated French.

Chapter XI

THE AMERICAN EXPEDITION

In March 1866, soon after the persecutions, a strange ship was blown
onto the coast of Pusan. On inquiry by the language officer of Pusan, Yi
Chu-hyŏn, it was found to be an American trading ship with eight men on
board on its way home from Nagasaki. The name of the ship, which was
loaded with rifles, rice, and sugar, sounded to Yi like "Sabul." When the
captain asked to purchase some food, the Korean official sent fruit, fish, and
chickens to the ship without charge. This was the first historical record of
Korea's contact with any American.[1]

The Case of the "Surprise"

About two months later, on June 24, 1866, another American ship, the
Surprise, was wrecked on the coast of P'yŏngan, while en route to the
Rȳukȳus from Chefoo. At the Council of State's suggestion, Captain McAslin
and his crew of seven men were treated with great care and kindness by the
local officials, particularly in contrast to the treatment they received later
from the Chinese authorities. On July 5 they were escorted, as they had
requested, by a language officer to Ŭiju, where they were turned over to the
Chinese officials.[2] Although this was no more than the customary treatment
given to shipwrecked persons by the Korean government, the American
authorities were much impressed by what the Koreans had done for the crew
of the *Surprise.* S. Wells Williams, the American consul-general in Peking,
wrote to the secretary of state, William H. Seward:

> On the 24th of June the crew left the schooner in a sinking
> condition, and reached an island . . . On the fourth day a third
> officer came from the capital, giving them abundance of good
> food, tobacco, and even medicines for the sick. After remaining
> in the village for 24 days, a special courier arrived from the
> capital to conduct the whole party to the Chinese frontier . . .
> Meanwhile, they were placed in a government building, under a
> guard, and each man was furnished with a suit of clothes.
> Chickens, beef, corn, and rice were served out to them, and on

three occasions they were invited to dine with the authorities of
the town, when each of them received a catty of tea and a fan.
Two days' journey on horseback from this city . . . brought the
party to a wall . . . in which was the gate that divides Corea and
China . . . Their food was insufficient, and of the poorest quality
. . . The officer at Mukten would give them nothing. Next morning they were again brought before the city authorities, who gave
them in charge to four people, one of whom furnished mats for
sleeping, and the others took them to a kind of lock-up, where
several hundred criminals were detained. The filthiness of the
place was unendurable.[3]

Thus it was no wonder that when the American diplomats in China were first
informed of the tragic fate of the *General Sherman* they were much puzzled
by the apparent paradox of Korean conduct and were hesitant to take any
hasty punitive action against Korea.

The "General Sherman" Incident

Sometime during the latter part of July 1866 the owner of the American
schooner *General Sherman,* a merchant named W.B. Preston, arranged with
Meadows & Co., a British firm in Tientsin, to send his schooner to Korea with
a cargo of miscellaneous merchandise. The officers and crew of the ship
comprised men of various nationalities: Captain Page, American; Chief Mate
Wilson and the owner Preston, American; George Hogarth, supercargo,
British; and thirteen Chinese and three Malays. An Anglican missionary,
Robert Thomas, who had learned Korean from some Korean Catholic
converts at Chefoo, accompanied them as interpreter. The ship's cargo
consisted mainly of cotton goods, tin sheets, glass, and other items. The
schooner left Tientsin on July 29 and stopped briefly for water at Chefoo,
from where she set out on August 9 on her ill-starred last voyage.[4]

On August 16 the *General Sherman* reached the mouth of the Taedong
River and slowly steamed up toward the city of P'yŏngyang, where Preston
hoped to exchange his goods for Korean paper, rice, gold, ginseng, and
leopard skins. At a number of places, both the provincial and local authorities attempted in vain to prevent the ship from going further (even to the
extent of offering provisions). There was no trouble, however, until August
27, when the *Sherman* appeared off the bank of P'yŏngyang. That day

witnessed the first sign of the important clash that was not well known outside Korea until almost the end of the Yi dynasty.[5]

Toward the evening of August 27 six of the *Sherman's* crew were observed aboard a small blue boat going up the Taedong, then swollen with rains on its upper course. They were immediately pursued by Yi Hyŏn-ik, the deputy commander of the P'yŏngyang military headquarters, and two other Koreans in a tiny junk. The Korean boat was attacked by the blue boat, and Yi and his companions were captured and taken to the schooner.

The next morning the schooner moved its anchorage a short distance up the river, firing at random with muskets and guns. Soon five sailors came down from the ship, boarded the blue boat, and started to go up the river. Just about this time the populace of P'yŏngyang, excited over the news of Yi's abduction, began to assemble along the bank, demanding his release. The sailors announced through their interpreter that they would settle the matter after they entered the walled city. This statement infuriated the crowd and the soldiers gathered along the bank. The civilian crowd now started to throw stones at the sailors while the soldiers threatened them with bows and arrows and matchlocks. The sailors managed, however, to escape from the hostile mob and return safely to the schooner. Since the situation was becoming serious, the schooner at last decided to leave the river. It was unable to go far, however, for a sudden drop in the water level made the river no longer navigable. It was at this time that the first clash between the sailors and the Koreans took place and Yi's rescue was effected.[6]

On August 29 the sailors again ran wild, in spite of repeated warnings from the Korean authorities. Many native junks around the ship were damaged and some of the crowd were fatally shot. It was reported that by the following day seven natives had been killed and five others wounded by the random firing. Faced with this uncontrollable situation, on August 31, the governor of P'yŏngan, Pak Kyu-su, determined to end the turmoil by destroying both the steamer and her crew.

The chief offensive weapon of the Koreans was the "flaming" or "burning" junk. As for the *Sherman's* crew, they fought gallantly until they were left with almost no gunpowder and cartridges. On September 2 the ship, which by then had run completely aground, found herself surrounded by the flaming junks and was at last burned. At the very moment when she caught fire, the Reverend Thomas and a Chinese named Chao jumped from the prow of the ship and appealed for mercy, waving a piece of white cloth. They were captured and taken ashore, where they were beaten to death by irate soldiers and civilians. The other crew members were either shot or burned to death in the ship. During this incident the Koreans only lost one man.[7]

Thus ended the *General Sherman* incident. But the incident became an important diplomatic issue, and finally, in 1871, the cause of an American expedition. To an extent, the "private expedition" of Ernest Oppert effected the settlement of the *Sherman* case.

The Voyages of Oppert

For some time after the opening of Japan, a Prussian adventurer named Ernest Oppert entertained a burning desire to open Korea, "the last of the forbidden lands in the East." For this purpose, Oppert made two voyages to the west coast of Korea in 1866, one in March and the other in August, but nothing resulted from these missions.[8]

Then in 1868 Oppert organized a small private expedition at the ill-advised urging of Monsignor Stanislas Féron, who had been attached to the Korean mission for more than eleven years. The object of the expedition was to get hold of the Taewŏn'gun's "family relics" in the belief that this would force the Taewŏn'gun to open the country to free trade and the propagation of the Christian religion. The relics were the remains of the Taewŏn'gun's father, Prince Namyŏn.[9]

Preparations for the expedition began early in the spring of 1868. Oppert acquired two steamers, the *China,* with a capacity of several hundred tons, and the *Greta,* a shallow-draft vessel for river navigation. The members of the expedition were of all nationalities: German (Oppert), French (Féron), American (Jenkins), some ten or twelve European sailors, twenty-five Filipinos, about a hundred Chinese sailors, and several Korean converts. The expedition left Shanghai sometime in April, and before proceeding to the Korean coast, stopped at Nagasaki to purchase muskets.[10]

Late on the night of May 10 the expedition finally arrived at an island called Haengdam on the west coast of Ch'ungch'ŏng. The next morning the party transferred to the *Greta* and steamed toward the bay of Kumanp'o, some thirty miles from the island. Shortly before noon the party landed at the bay and marched toward Tŏksan, calling themselves Russian soldiers. First they attacked the county office of Tŏksan, destroying many buildings and capturing weapons; then they marched across the hills and fields, arriving at their destination early on the evening of May 11. The work of exhumation was undertaken by the sailors, but after about five hours they had only removed the upper part of the tomb. When they started to excavate the main part, they came across masonry which supposedly housed the coffin and the bones. According to Oppert's estimation, it would have taken another five or six hours of work to remove the masonry. At this point the party noticed the appearance of the magistrate of Tŏksan with a force of soldiers and civilians. For this reason, the expedition had to abandon its quest and return to the landing place, Kumanp'o. Boarding the *Greta,* the party returned to the *China,* which had been left at the bay of Haengdam.

On May 13 the party moved to the island of Yŏngjong off the coast of Inch'ŏn. There, calling himself "O, the naval commander of Pirimang,"[11] Oppert presented an inquiring official with a letter to be forwarded to the Taewŏn'gun. The letter was both a defense of his tomb-digging adventure and a request for negotiations:

> To speak humbly, digging up a man's tomb is close to impropri-
> ety. It is however, better than using force. I had to do it because
> you are leading the people into the greatest misery. Although I had
> originally planned to bring the coffin out here, I abandoned the
> plan, for it was an extreme thought. Is not this the way of revering
> propriety? Are there no tools in our contingent for breaking the
> lime [sarcophagus]? Do not suspect that we, the people from the
> far lands, do not have the power to do so. The welfare of your
> country depends on your decision, and if you are concerned with
> the good of the country, why do you not send an envoy of high
> rank to confer on a good plan? If you stubbornly refuse to do so
> . . . your country will face a great danger in a few months.[12]

The letter was soon delivered to the Taewŏn'gun. Instead of replying directly, however, the Taewŏn'gun instructed the commander of the fort to send a note in his own name, formally rejecting Oppert's request to transmit the letter to the Taewŏn'gun and protesting Oppert's unconscionable

114

conduct. But on May 17, before this note reached Oppert, the expedition attempted to break through the gate of the walled town of Yŏngjong. In the clash that ensued with the garrison soldiers two Filipinos were killed, and the others, including Oppert, fled aboard the steamers.[13]

The court and the government reacted to the savagery of Oppert's party with execration, indignation, and bitterness. The anti-Western sentiments and the hatred of Catholicism that had subsided somewhat now suddenly revived. These feelings were not only revealed in reports, memorials, and edicts, but also demonstrated in a number of official acts following the reports of the Tŏksan Incident. The heads of the two fallen Filipinos were put on public exhibition in the capital and in the provinces. The persecution of Catholics was resumed, for the government believed that Oppert was instigated and led into the country by native "heretics." The government also resolved to terminate the age-old custom under which all Western ships drifting to the Korean coast had been shown special treatment, *yuwŏn chi'ŭi,* or "goodwill to strangers."[14] It was during this time that American diplomatic overtures to Korea began. Thus, in historical retrospect, it may be said that these advances were doomed to failure even before they had started.

The Coming of the American Expedition

The man credited with first bringing the news of the tragic end of the *General Sherman* to China was the French missionary, Ridel. Ridel had returned to Korea with the first French expedition as interpreter. On September 20, 1866, while he was on board the warship *Primauguet* anchored off the island of Kanghwa, Ridel received a visit from Song Un-o, the owner of the Korean junk on which Ridel had escaped to Chefoo on June 20. Ridel learned from Song that a Western ship had been destroyed at P'yŏngyang. Song, however, was unable to identify the nationality of the vessel, but soon after the return of the first French expeditionary force to Chefoo, it was learned that the vessel in question was the *General Sherman.*[15]

The French soon transmitted the news to the American legation at Peking. The consul-general, S. Wells Williams, however, doubted the validity of the report regarding the death of the entire crew of the vessel. On October 23 he wrote to the Tsungli Yamen: "A report has been received here from

Chifu that an American schooner, the *General Sherman,* was wrecked . . . and burned by the natives; her officers and crew, 24 in all, being captured by them, but it is not certainly known whether they are still alive or not. It is the usage of the Corean government to deliver all such persons at the frontier of China to her officers, to be handed over to their respective consuls at Niuchwang." At the end of his note Williams requested the Chinese Foreign Office to send orders to the authorities at Mukden to deliver the twenty-four men to their respective consuls, if they had already been handed over by the Korean authorities. This request was promptly granted. The Chinese Foreign Office promised Williams that orders would be dispatched the following morning.[16]

In contrast to Williams's cautious and exploratory step, Meadows & Co. reacted to the news positively and vehemently. The company that had sent the schooner to Korea with her cargo of miscellaneous merchandise, formally wrote to Anson Burlingame, the American minister in Peking, requesting his special assistance in "getting redress" for the wrongs that they believed had been done to the *General Sherman.* Simultaneously, the company asked the British admiral's help in the matter.[17] If the British government had chosen the firm and positive policy suggested by Meadows & Co., Korea might have experienced a combined Anglo-American expedition, and the course of her history might have turned out entirely different.

After receiving Williams's note and examining the original Korean letter to the Board of Rites, the Tsungli Yamen rightly judged that Korea might become involved in a new predicament with Great Britain and the United States. Accordingly, on November 4, Prince Kung and his associates memorialized as follows:

> According to a rumor which has reached us, when France decided to use force against Korea, both Great Britain and the United States endeavored to prevent it. Although France did not listen to them, Korea was able to avoid having many enemies at one time . . . From the time of her use of arms against Korea, France's conduct contradicts her original statement [that] her interest is the propagation of religion. As for Great Britain and the United States . . . they also have been implicated in trouble with Korea lately. Their interest is trade. If after any war [with them], Korea has to settle

her dispute, she will certainly face the problem of paying indem- nities to them. The three countries have already been discussing the [formation of] an alliance. In this [discussion] France has been most active . . . If we decide to make them change their intentions completely, they will certainly raise questions as to the propagation of religion, trade, and indemnities. An examination of the Korean note shows that there is no possibility that she will permit trade and the propagation of religion. At any rate, we have to consider her interest too . . . [Therefore] our Yamen is unable to insist upon pressing Korea [to accept their demands].[18]

The last remark in the memorial is significant, for it reflects the basic policy China held toward Korea during this crucial period. In contrast to Li Hung-chang's policy in later years, the Tsungli Yamen refrained from giving China's alleged "vassal" state any concrete advice or suggestions on such vital questions as the opening of the country for trade and the free propagation of religion. China would have had the opportunity to give guidance when Korea insisted that she, as China's vassal, had "no right of diplomacy." However, China herself was under pressure from without and wished to minimize her engagement. Moreover, the Chinese government was caught between Korea's insistence on maintaining her seclusion policy and the demands of the Western countries for her mediating services between them and Korea. In contrast to conditions a decade and more later, the role of the Chinese government in the 1860s was at best that of a middleman, merely transmitting the gist of the Western notes to the Korean government. Time and again it assured the Western nations that the nature of Chinese-Korean relations was purely ceremonial, and that China had no responsibility for Korea's management of foreign relations and trade.

At this particular time, however, the Tsungli Yamen did propose that the Board of Rites be ordered to send a note to the king of Korea suggesting that he make a circumspect plan to settle whatever disputes Korea might have with the three Western countries. This proposal was approved by the throne, and a note to this effect was subsequently dispatched to Seoul.[19]

The note arrived in Seoul early in December. A Korean reply was prepared by the Bureau of Diplomatic Correspondence (Sǔngmunwǒn) on December 11. It was a rather strong reflection of the mood of the govern- ment, which had just successfully concluded the clash with France; it expressed an unjustifiably high degree of confidence in its military strength. The letter first reminded the Board of Rites that it was already in possession of reports on the burning of the "English" vessel as well as the French invasion. Then it pointed out that the alleged report concerning the destruction of an American ship was unfounded; it was probably a rumor derived from the burning of the "English" vessel at P'yŏngyang. The letter also gave the Korean government's reason for not accepting Oppert's proposals for trade: Oppert did not carry an official note from China. The rest of the letter was largely devoted to attacking France for having waged an unprovoked war and demanding indemnities and the right to propagate Catholicism:

> Before nations under heaven start wars against each other, they
> first investigate the causes for such hostilities. The Frenchmen, how-
> ever, having seen our lack of [military] preparations, intruded into
> Kanghwa, burned the whole city, and purloined our property. They
> were, indeed, a gang of plundering and vindictive pirates. Is it true
> that people who do trade behave in such a manner? Is it true that
> those who want to propagate religion act in such a way? . . . We are
> sincerely and truly grateful for the concern shown by your Board
> and the Yamen in the subject of indemnities. However, it was the
> French who took countless treasures and weapons from our country.
> Therefore, it may be conceivable that we demand indemnities from
> France. On what grounds can she possibly make such a demand on
> us? As for matters such as trade and the propagation of religion, . . .
> they shall never be permitted, no matter how many years our little
> country and her people may suffer from the Western barbarians.[20]

Meanwhile, apart from diplomatic measures, Burlingame decided to take independent action to determine the fate of the *Sherman*. He saw no use in seeking China's help in the matter because the Tsungli Yamen disclaimed all responsibility for Korea. The view of the Yamen, in particular that of Prince Kung, was that the traditional tributary relationship between China and Korea was only a "ceremonial" one.[21]

On November 27, 1866 Burlingame suggested to Rear Admiral H.H. Bell, then acting commander of the United States Asiatic Squadron, that he send a warship to Korea to inquire about the lost vessel. Acting on this suggestion, Bell assigned Robert W. Shufeldt, commander of the warship *Wachusett,* to the mission. On January 21, 1867, the *Wachusett* left Chefoo for the Taedong River, but because the river was closed by ice, the warship turned its course southward and came to an island named Wŏllae off the coast of Hwanghae on January 23. There, Commander Shufeldt gave a note to a native to forward to the local authorities. In the note the commander first acknowledged the kind treatment that the Korean government had shown the shipwrecked crew of the *Surprise,* and then requested the return of the survivors of the crew of the *General Sherman,* if indeed they had been detained by the Korean authorities. Since they were unfamiliar with the case, the local officials were not able to answer immediately, but promised a reply by January 27. Meanwhile, Shufeldt learned from the natives that a Western vessel had been set on fire on the Taedong and all her crew killed. Shufeldt took this information as evidence enough of what had befallen the *General Sherman,* and left the island to report to the admiral without waiting for the reply.[22]

Shufeldt also brought back with him more important news, somewhat inconsistent with the report of the natives, which resulted in a second fact-finding mission. While the *Wachusett* was lying off the coast of the island, a Chinese named Yü Wen-t'ai, who was aboard the vessel, was sent on a mission up the Taedong. According to Yü, he saw a foreign vessel lying on the southern bank of the Taedong and he met a Korean named Kim Cha-p'yŏng who said that he had personally seen two Westerners and two Chinese detained at the governor's office in P'yŏngyang, the rest of the crew having been killed.

In view of this rumor, S. Wells Williams again decided to seek help from the Chinese authorities in securing the liberation of the survivors. To this end, on March 3, 1868, Williams wrote to Prince Kung.[23] On March 10 Prince Kung replied equivocally, refusing to take any direct action. He reminded Williams that although Korea was subordinate to China, all matters such as official ordinances to keep order and interdict trade with foreign lands and the propagation of alien religions were actually carried out independently by Korea and on her own responsibility.[24]

In the meantime, Williams decided to send another warship to Korea to investigate further. At Williams's request the commander of the United States Asiatic Squadron, Commodore J.R. Goldsborough, ordered Captain John C.

Febinger, who commanded the U.S. corvette *Shenandoah,* to carry out the mission. The *Shenandoah* left Chefoo sometime early in April 1868 and arrived at the mouth of the Taedong on April 10. This mission failed to obtain any concrete evidence to support the notion that there were survivors of the *Sherman* in Korean hands.[25]

With the return of the *Shenandoah,* which departed from Korean waters on May 17, all hope of recovering the rumored captives vanished. By that time, however, the question of the *General Sherman* had begun to develop into a far more interesting and significant diplomatic issue. Emphasis now lay on the possibility of concluding a formal treaty with Korea, the primary object being to secure guarantees for the protection of shipwrecked American seamen. It is interesting to note that this question too seems to have started with a fascinating rumor. On April 24, 1868, a few weeks before the return of the *Shenandoah* to Chefoo, Consul-General George F. Seward at Shanghai sent this note to Secretary of State William H. Seward, his uncle:

> Mr. Frederick Jenkins, a citizen of the United States, formerly interpreter to this office, gave me the following information: There are now in Shanghai four Coreans and a bishop for Corea, of the Roman Church. These persons have been sent here by the Corean government. The purpose is to make inquiries concerning the state of feeling existing toward Corea in regard to the alleged murder of French priests and of the crew of the American schooner, *General Sherman,* with a view to determine whether it will be wise for the Corean government to send an embassy to America and Europe to explain those occurrences, and to make desired treaties of amity and commerce. Mr. Jenkins expects to sail with these persons for the Corea in a few days, and believes that the result of the report of the commissioners and of his visit will be the sending of an embassy, as proposed. He expects to return to Shanghai in about a month, and that ambassadors, as indicated, will come with him.[26]

Jenkins was also reported to have informed Consul-General Seward of what befell the *General Sherman:* "The vessel had reached a point in the interior on a river . . . Several of the crew went ashore and became embroiled in a row growing out of the wrongful treatment of some women, and were arrested . . . This excited the people, and they attacked the vessel, killing eight persons and capturing the others, who are still held . . . He expects to bring back with him those of the crew of the *General Sherman* who are still living."[27]

Some explanation of the persons mentioned in the note is needed. Jenkins later participated in Oppert's tomb-digging expedition. The bishop in question must have been Féron, who also went to Korea with Oppert. The four Koreans who called themselves commissioners no doubt were Korean converts who fled to China after the persecution of 1866. One of these men, Ch'oe Sŏn-il, went back to Korea with Oppert as a guide.[28]

It is difficult to conjecture what the real motive behind this fabrication was. One is tempted to speculate that the Koreans, Féron, and probably Oppert and Jenkins were trying to bring the United States and Korea into open conflict. The statement that some of "the crew of the *General Sherman* . . . are still living" was calculated to arouse the hostility of the American officials, who might then dispatch a squadron of "black ships" to Korea's shores. Such a show of force, if it did not provoke an armed clash, might at least secure from the Korean government guarantees of freedom of trade and of the propagation of Christianity.

Whatever the case, Consul-General Seward took this information rather seriously. In a second note dispatched to the secretary of state on the same day he even proposed that in case the proposed Korean embassy were not sent, he should be authorized to proceed to Korea "to ask an official explanation of the *Sherman* affair, and to negotiate a treaty of amity and of commerce similar to those now existing with China and Japan, or such other lesser treaty as may be expedient and attainable without the exercise of show of force." He also pointed out that "the Empire" was independent, although it sent complimentary tributes to Peking.[29]

Both letters were received by the State Department on June 24, and the secretary of state wholeheartedly accepted the proposal for negotiations. On June 26 he replied:

> The President [Johnson] would be highly grateful if a Corean
> legation or embassy should arrive here, authorized to give proper
> satisfaction to the United States for the outrage in question and
> to enter into a treaty. But should this not occur, the time is thought
> a propitious one to send a civil agent to Corea for the purpose,
> first, of procuring a release of any surviving seamen of the *General*

Sherman; secondly, an official explanation . . . with reasonable
reparation and indemnity; thirdly, treaty provision for the opening
of the ports of Corea to the United States and other nations and
for the security of life and property of foreigners in that country
. . . You will endeavour to procure a treaty of amity and commerce
as nearly similar in the provisions to those now existing between
the United States and Japan, as may be found practicable and
expedient.[30]

The secretary of state also stressed that no threat or use of force was to
be made, although, if necessary, the Koreans were to be warned that the
United States would not permit the wrong done to remain indefinitely without redress.[31] The consul-general was given full power to negotiate with the
Korean government,[32] and for this purpose was charged to deliver a letter
from President Johnson to the king of Korea. The letter, dated June 27,
1868, read as follows:

Great and good Friend. The bearer of this letter, Mr. George F.
Seward, Consul-General of the U.S.A. at Shanghai, is by my
direction invested with full power to negotiate, with such plenipo-
tentiary or plenipotentiaries as Your Majesty may be pleased to
appoint, a General Convention concerning commerce and for the
settlement of claims. Mr. Seward is instructed in delivering this
letter to Your Majesty to inform you of the good will which the
people of the United States bear toward you and the subjects of
your kingdom and of their desire to promote friendship and
intercourse between the two countries.[33]

The secretary of state also informed the Navy Department of the
proposed mission,[34] and Admiral S.C. Rowan, the commander of the United
States Asiatic Squadron, was instructed to place a ship at the disposal of the
consul-general.[35] The proposed mission, however, was at least temporarily
suspended by the return of the *Shenandoah.* Captain Febinger reported that,
in spite of his contact with a number of Korean officials at different points
along the coast, he had learned nothing to corroborate either the story of the
four survivors or the other rumor that Korea was disposed to send an
embassy. As a result of Febinger's report, George Seward now abandoned
his earlier stand—negotiations "without show of force"—and began to advocate a "gunboat" diplomacy. Thus, on May 25, 1868, he wrote to Secretary
Seward, "No negotiations, not supported by a considerable show of force,

would be likely to be successful."[36] This letter was received by the secretary of state on July 13. Nine days later he ordered his nephew not to act upon his instructions of June 27.[37] After this, George Seward bombarded his uncle with three more letters, but nothing developed.[38]

Meanwhile, a change of administration took place, with General Ulysses S. Grant succeeding Andrew Johnson as President and Hamilton Fish taking the realm of the Department of State. The question of a treaty with Korea was once again brought to the attention of the administration.

Early in 1870 George Seward was recalled to Washington for a personal consultation with the Department of State. On February 28 Seward met with Assistant Secretary of State J.C.B. Davis and Rear Admiral John Rodgers, the new commander of the Asiatic Squadron. At the meeting Seward proposed that the United States take the following steps: secure a shipwreck convention and, if possible, a commercial treaty; seek China's good offices; and delegate to the admiral the authority to negotiate with Korea.[39] The first two proposals were subsequently adopted, but Secretary of State Fish decided to entrust the negotiations to the new American minister at Peking, Frederick F. Low, because "the political relations between China and Corea are such as to make it desirable to first obtain the good will and possibly the good offices of the Chinese government."[40]

Fish formally announced this decision on April 4 to Secretary of the Navy George M. Robeson. At the same time, Fish requested of Robeson that:

> Instructions may be given to Admiral Rodgers to place himself
> in communication with Mr. Low, soon after his arrival in Chinese
> waters, and to agree with him upon a time when he shall transport
> that gentleman to Corea. It is hoped that the expedition will be
> sufficiently formidable to make an impression upon the native
> authorities, and that Admiral Rodgers will accompany it in person.
> Mr. Low will be instructed to counsel and advise with him with
> the utmost frankness and confidence in every stage of the negotia-
> tion. Should, unhappily, any cause for hostilities occur during this
> mission, it is hoped that the Navy Department will instruct Admiral
> Rodgers in such case to advise with Mr. Low, and to leave with this
> Department the responsibility of war or peace.[41]

Robeson's instructions to Admiral Rodgers were sent on April 16,[42] and Fish's own instructions to Low four days later.[43] Low was to secure a treaty for the protection of shipwrecked seamen. However, "should the opportunity seem favorable for obtaining commercial advantages in Corea, the proposed treaty should include provisions to that effect." For reference, copies of the treaties concluded with Japan at Kanagawa in 1854 and at Yedo in 1858 were included in the dispatch. Fish instructed Low to approach the Peking government in advance to win its goodwill and, possibly, its good offices. In carrying out his mission, Low was further advised to seek, if possible, "the presence and cooperation" of George Seward. There was no mention of the *Sherman* in this note.

Meanwhile, Low, who had arrived in Peking in the early part of May, occupied himself with gathering information about Korea. He had little success. Nevertheless, he was able to draw a fairly accurate picture of the relationship between China and Korea. In his dispatch of July 16, acknowledging the receipt of Fish's instructions and enclosure, Low wrote: "Corea is substantially an independent nation. To be sure, it sends tributes to China annually, but from the best information I am able to obtain, the tribute is sent rather as a *quid pro quo* for the privilege of trading with the Chinese than as a governmental tribute . . . Beyond these arrangements . . . there seems to be no connection between China and Corea. China claims or exercises no control in any way over Corea."[44]

The expedition was tentatively scheduled to depart from Shanghai or Chefoo—the latter, if possible—between the first and the fifteenth of May 1871. This was communicated to Secretary of State Fish by Low in a note dated November 22, 1870. In the same letter he requested full power to negotiate, in order that: "The Coreans may not have any grounds on which to base technical objections, I have, most respectfully, to request that a commission may be sent, by the steamer leaving San Francisco not later than the 1st of March, authorizing me to negotiate and sign on behalf of the United States such a treaty or treaties with the Government of Corea as may be deemed advisable."[45]

It now remained for Low to inform the Korean government of the coming of the American mission. For this, the cooperation of the Chinese government was indispensable. On February 11, 1871, Low visited the Tsungli Yamen and announced that the United States was soon sending a

124

naval expedition to Korea to open diplomatic negotiations. Low's request for the good offices of the Yamen in conveying this message to the Korean government, however, was rejected. The reason given was that China's dealings with "subject-states" *(wai-fan)* were managed by the Board of Rites and the Yamen had no means of direct communication with Korea.[46]

On February 15 Low made a second request, and was rejected again. Finally, on March 7 Low informed the Yamen that he had been appointed envoy to Korea and was going there on board a warship to carry out his mission. He hoped that the Yamen would forward his letter to the king of Korea. This time the Yamen reluctantly acceded to Low's request, explaining this change of attitude in a memorial on March 12: "We have done our best to prevent America's plan to send warships to Korea. Now, in view of her firm determination, the question does not depend on whether or not we forward this letter. If we do not, we are afraid that Korea may not know the reason for their coming, and consequently, may be unable to meet the situation. This is not the way to treat a subject-state."[47]

On March 28 the Tsungli Yamen wrote Low that the Board of Rites had been authorized to send its own note to accompany his letter to the king of Korea. It added that both the letter and covering note had already been transmitted on March 22 to the Board of War for dispatch by its courier to Korea. On this occasion the Yamen again took pains to point out that although Korea was regarded as a subordinate to China, she was nevertheless wholly independent in everything that was related to her government, her religion, and her laws. Therefore, China had hitherto not interfered in any of these matters.[48]

Low's letter to the king of Korea dealt primarily with the protection of shipwrecked persons. Low explained that he was being specially sent to Korea, on temporary duty from his post at Peking, to negotiate matters relating to the protection of American seamen and merchants who might unhappily encounter distress on Korean shores. He expressed the desire to ascertain the reason why the crew of one ship (the *Surprise*) had been rescued, whereas that of another (the *General Sherman*) had been killed. He did not want Korea to be alarmed by the arrival of warships, because they were coming with peaceful intentions. Finally, he expressed the hope that the king would commission a special envoy to negotiate with him upon his arrival three months hence. There was no remark about trade or a commercial treaty in this note.[49]

The letter, accompanied by extracts of earlier memorials by the Board of Rites and the Yamen on the matter in question, was received on April 10, 1871, by the Council of State. In accordance with the council's proposal, it was decided that Low's letter should not be answered, for such a reply would mean "intercourse" *(wangbok)*.[50] The Korean government, however, acknowledged its receipt and expressed its determination to reject the mission in a note to the Board of Rites. The note, which was prepared by the Bureau of Diplomatic Correspondence, embodied the basic tenets of Korea's seclusion policy. It dealt primarily with three points: the *General Sherman* incident, Low's proposal to negotiate for the protection of shipwrecked persons, and trade.[51]

The note began with an account of Korea's historical treatment of distressed foreigners, then described previous cases in which shipwrecked American seamen had been rescued, and recalled details of the *Sherman* affair as already reported to the Board of Rites and explanations that local authorities had given to Shufeldt and Febinger. The note went on to justify the destruction of the *Sherman:*

> Since the people of that country [America] know fully the occasion for the said *[Sherman]* affair and understand the right and wrong of it, there will be no further reason for coming with doubts and suspicion to make inquiry. Why now does the American minister, in his letter, again express ignorance about the rescue of one of the crews and the destruction of the other? He says that the government of the United States has great regard for its merchants and sailors, and therefore will not tolerate other countries to insult and abuse them, as they please. This is indeed a point in which all nations are alike . . . If the American vessel had not abused our people, why would the Korean officials and people have wished to abuse them first?

As for negotiations on the protection of shipwrecked persons, the note rejected this on the grounds that "no subject [*sin,* i.e., Korea as a vassal state] could have diplomatic relations" with foreign countries. Moreover, the note pointed out that there was no need to make special arrangements for such a purpose because, in addition to Korea's own established law for protecting the crews of foreign ships in distress, "she recalls the profound benevolence the Imperial dynasty [Ch'ing] traditionally shows to such distressed people."

However, should anyone not "cherish goodwill and come to commit wanton violence," he would be rebuffed or exterminated. Thus, the vassal state could also "discharge her natural duty of shielding the Imperial dynasty."

On the subject of trade, a subject which was not directly raised in Low's letter, the note declared:

> Heretofore, foreign countries that have been ignorant of the character and products of Korea, have repeatedly pestered us with applications for commercial intercourse. But this is entirely out of the question with our country. That merchants will also find it unprofitable was set forth in a communication to your Board in 1866: "It is universally known that our country is a small land in a corner of the seas; that the people are poor and the articles of commerce are scanty; that gold, silver, and precious stones are not found in our country; that grain and cloth fabrics are not abundant; that the production of our country is insufficient even to meet domestic needs, and if permitted to flow abroad, thus impoverishing us at home, this insignificant land will be in extreme danger and difficult to protect from ruin; that the habits of the people are sparing and plain; that workmanship is crude and poor; and that we have not one single article to justify commerce with foreign nations."

Finally, the note requested the Board of Rites to submit all the facts to the throne, so that the emperor might issue a special edict to exhort and instruct the American minister to overcome his doubts and dispel his anxiety. The note, however, did not reach Peking until Low had departed.

In the meantime the preparations for the expedition had been completed. Low had received from Washington the "full power" he requested earlier. In addition, he had collected all the data that could be found about Korea and her inhabitants. Rodgers also had gathered necessary information regarding the coasts, harbors, and rivers of Korea. The date of departure was set for May 8. The force comprised five warships: the flagship *Colorado,* two corvettes (the *Alaska* and the *Benicia*), and two gunboats (the *Palos* and the

Monocacy), carrying eighty-five pieces of artillery and 1,230 marines and sailors.[52]

The Expedition: Diplomatic Failure and Resort to Arms

The squadron left Shanghai as scheduled, made a brief stopover at Nagasaki from May 12 to May 15, and appeared on May 19 off the coast of Ch'ungch'ŏng. On May 21 it was seen in the vicinity of the Bay of Namyang, Kyŏnggi. This news, however, did not reach Seoul until May 24.[53]

Meanwhile, both the Americans and the Koreans began to maneuver. On May 26 the magistrate of Namyang made his first contact with a detachment of the squadron and asked in writing about their nationality and their motive for coming to Korea. The magistrate, however, was unable to communicate with the Americans, for no interpreter was present. On May 27 three American launches went to Namyang and left with the magistrate a letter written in Chinese, a copy of which was soon transmitted to Seoul. The letter, which acknowledged the magistrate's earlier written inquiries, was a formal announcement of the arrival of "an envoy and an admiral from the Great United States of America for negotiations with a Korean envoy of high rank." It added that since such negotiations needed time the ships would remain in Korean waters until the business was completed.[54]

On May 28 the Korean government decided to send a formal party of inquiry to the fleet, which by then had moved its anchorage to an island north of Inch'ŏn. This decision resulted from the proposal of the Council of State, which had not yet received a copy of the American letter. The party consisted of three interpreters and a clerk. The four men arrived at the anchorage on May 31 and were cordially received by Edward B. Drew, Low's secretary and Chinese interpreter, and John P. Cowles, Jr., acting secretary of the American legation in Peking. Low himself refused to see them because of their lowly rank.[55]

In the course of their conversation, Drew conveyed to the Koreans Low's statement of purpose, largely a repetition of the letter of May 27. The statement added, however, that in the meantime the small vessels of the fleet would do some exploring farther up the river in order that the large ships might move near the capital. It assured that the people on the shore need not be afraid of the ships, so long as those on board were treated with propriety. After a lengthy conversation, the party returned to Seoul bearing official gifts from the Americans, which were soon sent to the Taewŏn'gun. Low later reported that the Koreans raised no objections to the proposed explorations. They were said to have stated that the king desired friendly relations with Americans, though he did not wish to enter into formal treaties.[56]

A written report of the meeting was prepared by the interpreters and immediately transmitted to Seoul by the governor of Kyŏnggi. The American proposals, however, were virtually ignored by the government, which now began to strengthen the defense of Kanghwa. On June 1 Ŏ Chae-yŏn was appointed the deputy commander of the Chinmu regiment on Kanghwa. Several hundred soldiers from other regiments were dispatched to Kanghwa as reinforcements. Four thousand *kŭn* (one *kŭn* equaled 1.32 lb.) of gunpowder, 30 crossbows, 900 arrows, 30 pieces of artillery, and 1,000 *sŏk* of rice were also sent to the island. All these actions resulted from the proposal of the Samgunbu.[57]

At about the same time,[58] Admiral Rodgers had begun the exploration of the Kanghwa-Han River region. The exploration force, under the command of Captain Homer C. Blake of the *Alaska,* consisted of the two gunboats and four steam launches. The main objective was to survey the passage between the mainland and the island of Kanghwa, the shortcut to Seoul. Cowles was assigned to the party as interpreter.[59] The last of these explorations was to be carried out on June 1. Prior to his departure, Captain Black was specifically instructed by Low as follows: If a hostile attack were made, either upon his men or vessels, he was to reply with force and destroy, if possible, the places and the people from whom the attack came. Any advantage gained should not be pursued by landing a force, but he should quietly proceed to the northern part of the island of Kanghwa, and, if practicable, a few miles up the Han River, but not attempt to reach the capital.[60]

With these instructions, the party left anchorage at noon on June 1 and steamed slowly toward the mouth of the Salt River without noticing any signs of hostility from the natives. Around two in the afternoon they approached the sharp bend in the river named Sondolmok, where the tides were high and treacherous. Sondolmok was then the main pass to Kanghwa city, and (probably after the French invasion) all vessels, whether private or public, were strictly forbidden to go northward beyond the pass without a special permit from the proper authorities.[61] Furthermore, the entire coast, particularly in the vicinity of Sondolmok, was far better fortified than at the time of the French invasion.

Unaware of these conditions, the American vessels entered the Salt River. The gunboats and steam launches safely passed Sondolmok, but when they neared the fort of Kwangsŏng, they were bombarded by eight pieces of artillery from the fort. This bombardment was instantly followed by others from the batteries in the Tŏkp'o and Tŏkchin forts, situated near Sondolmok and Kwangsŏng. Although the Korean batteries were soon silenced by counterfire from the American warships, Captain Blake was forced to retreat to the anchorage, mainly because of the damage suffered by the *Monocacy*. On the Korean side, one gunner was killed.[62]

News of this clash was greeted by the government with further intensification of the defense of the Kanghwa-Han area. On June 2, at the suggestion of the Military Council, the region received a few hundred additional soldiers, 1,000 *kŭn* of gunpowder, 15,000 rounds of lead bullets, and 300 *sŏk* of rice. The deputy commander of the Chinmu regiment, Ŏ Chae-yŏn, was ordered to move his troops to the fort at Kwangsŏng, the scene of the June 1 incident. The commanders of two other strategic forts on the banks of the Salt River were replaced by high-ranking generals. Military units outside the Seoul area were ordered to mobilize in secret, perhaps in order to prevent further unrest, which was already visible.[63]

In the meantime the Taewŏn'gun decided to bring a formal charge against the American vessels' unwarranted intrusion of the Salt River and to reaffirm the established policy of seclusion. On June 6, in a note to the American envoy written in the name of Chŏng Ki-wŏn, the commander of the Chinmu regiment, the Taewŏn'gun declared:

> The barriers of defense of a country are important places, within which foreign vessels are not allowed to make their way. This is the fixed rule of all nations . . . Yet, when your honorable vessels ignored the fixed regulations of another country, penetrated an important pass, how could the officers appointed to guard [the closed portals of] the frontier, whose duty it is to take measures of defense, calmly

130

let it go by as though of no consequence? . . . The non-intercourse
of this land with foreign countries is a settled principle, maintained
by our forefathers for five centuries.[64]

To show his "understanding of the hardships" of a long voyage, however, the
Taewŏn'gun sent the envoy "some worthless articles" (three bullocks, fifty
chickens, and 1,000 eggs) for his table.[65]

Low thought that the June 1 incident indicated Korea's determination
to reject any negotiations. The main question in his mind was whether or not
the squadron should abandon its mission and retire without redressing the
wrong done by the Koreans. On June 2 Low wrote to Secretary of State Fish
concerning these difficulties:

The events of yesterday convince me that the government of
Corea is determined to resist all innovations and intercourse with
all the power at its command, without regard to nationality, or
nature of demands made . . . The question now is, what is the safe
and prudent course to pursue, in view of this temporary check,
which the Coreans will undoubtedly construe into a defeat of the
"barbarians," but which, according to the recognized rules of
civilized warfare, was a complete victory on the part of the naval
forces. In estimating the effect it may exert upon our power and
prestige, which will affect the interest of our people in the East,
the situation must be viewed from an Oriental stand-point, rather
than the more advanced one of Christian civilization. If the
squadron retires now, the effect upon the minds of the Coreans,
and, I fear, upon the Chinese also, will be injurious, if not disas-
trous, to our future prospects in both countries. Corea will rest
firmly in the belief that she is powerful enough to repel any of
the Western states singly, or even all of them combined; and this
opinion will be likely to react upon China, and strengthen the
influence of those who insist that it is practicable to drive out by
force all the foreign residents. In view of these considerations, I
cannot advise the admiral to abandon the field without further
attempts at redress for the wrongs and insults which our flag has
suffered; at the same time I am fully impressed as to the inade-
quacy of the force at his command to carry on offensive operations to conquer this people and compel the government to enter
into proper treaty engagements.[66]

In this same letter Low reported to Fish that, in view of these considerations, he and Admiral Rodgers had decided to send to the site of the incident a force sufficient to take and effectively destroy the fortifications as far as the northern end of the island of Kanghwa. By so doing, Low thought he might force the Korean government to come to terms.[67]

Before launching the projected attack, however, Low made one more attempt to persuade the Korean government to accept the American proposal for negotiations. On June 9 Low sent a reply in Drew's name to the Taewŏn'gun's note of June 6, saying that he considered the attack upon the American vessels imprudent on the part of the local Korean commanders, and that he hoped the Korean government would send an official of high rank to confer with him. The note went on to warn the Korean government that, if within three or four days such a person did not appear, the American envoy would conclude that the Korean government had no intention of negotiating, whereupon it would be forced to listen to whatever he (Low) might have to dictate.[68]

Without waiting for the time limit given in his note, Low decided to launch the attack on the following day, June 10. The attacking force consisted of two gunboats, the *Palos* and the *Monocacy,* several launches, sailors from the three corvettes, and 450 marines. It was put under the general command of Captain Blake, while Commander L.A. Kimberly was ordered to direct the landing. Again, as Low said to the secretary of state, the object of the expedition was "simply to take and destroy the forts which have fired on our vessels, and to hold them long enough to demonstrate our ability to punish such offences at pleasure." The landing force was to withdraw after a period of twenty-four hours, or, at the latest, at flood-tide of the day following the capture of the forts.[69]

On the morning of June 10 the fleet left its anchorage and arrived at the bay of Ch'oji, situated near the mouth of the Salt River, shortly after noon. The troops immediately started landing under the cover-fire from the two gunboats. The Korean garrison soldiers offered no resistance, but began to retreat, abandoning the fort. Thus, the fort of Ch'oji was easily captured by the landing force and all its batteries and ammunition completely destroyed. Their initial mission fulfilled, the sailors and marines spent the night by the dismantled batteries.[70]

The next morning the American force resumed the attack on the other forts. The fort of Tŏkchin fell in the same way as did the Ch'oji fort, the Koreans offering no resistance, but apparently retreating to the fort of Kwangsŏng in preparation for a final stand. After dismantling the batteries at Tŏkchin, the Americans launched a general attack on the fort of Kwangsŏng, which was mainly garrisoned by Ŏ Chae-yŏn's troops. The attack was supported by bombardments from both land and sea. Here the Koreans showed no signs of retreat. All the classical arts of battle were displayed, ranging from the storming of walls to fierce hand-to-hand fighting.[71] Low wrote to the secretary of state on June 20: "All accounts concur in the statement that the Coreans fought with desperation, rarely equaled and never excelled by any people. Nearly all the soldiers in the main fort were killed at their posts."[72]

The battle finally ended with the retreat of the Koreans, their losses heavy. Fifty-three were killed, twenty-four wounded, and over a dozen captured. Ŏ Chae-yŏn, his brother Ŏ Chae-sun, and the commander of the Kwangsŏng fort also fell in this battle. Three Americans were killed, including a first lieutenant of the navy, and ten were wounded.[73] On June 12, after destroying all fortifications at Kwangsŏng and bombarding Sondolmok, the American force left the bay of Ch'oji, where they had camped overnight and had been attacked by a Korean detachment. They returned safely to the anchorage.[74]

The battle of Kwangsŏng brought the Taewŏn'gun's anti-Westernism and seclusion policy to a climax. On the very day that the American force evacuated the bay of Ch'oji, he made his famous anti-Western declaration: "Western barbarians foully attack! Should we not fight, accord must be made! To urge accord is to betray the country!" He ordered officials throughout the nation to erect stone tablets engraved with this declaration in the towns and cities. Even the young king was obliged to declare: "If anyone dares to mention accord, he shall be treated as a traitor!"[75]

This was not all. In order to instill a fighting spirit, those who were killed or wounded in the fighting were showered with unusual honors and acclaimed as national heroes. Their children and descendants were also promised special consideration. An outstanding example is that of Ŏ Chae-yŏn. He was posthumously appointed minister of war, honored with the equivalent of a state funeral, and awarded the posthumous title of *ch'ungjang* (lit., "loyal and gallant"). His sons were to be given positions in the government after the mourning period.[76] Then, to prepare for further battle, fresh troops and more weapons and ammunition were sent to the Kanghwa region.[77]

Thus, as Low rightly observed, even the loss of three or four strategic forts and many lives failed to change the Taewŏn'gun's "anti-barbarian" outlook and his seclusion policy:

> I have . . . little hope of bringing the King to any proper terms. Everything goes to prove that the Government from the first determined to reject all peaceful overtures for negotiation or even discussion; and that the recent demonstration, which would have produced a profound impression upon any other government, has little or no effect, favorable or otherwise, upon this. The operations of the 10th and 11th were more significant than those of the English and French in 1858, when the capture of the Taku forts at the mouth of the Peiho River caused the government of China to immediately send ministers and conclude treaties at Tientsin, and yet this government shows no sign which leads to the belief that there is any change in its attitude of defiance to all nations.[78]

In view of these developments, on July 3, after several fruitless exchanges of notes between Low, Drew, and the Koreans (notably Yi Ki-jo, magistrate of Pup'yŏng), the American squadron left its anchorage for Chefoo, arriving there two days later.

For Korea, the price of her seclusion policy was indeed costly. Had she agreed to the moderate demands of the United States at this time, while the Taewŏn'gun still held power, she might have avoided the confusion that engulfed her five years later when she belatedly joined the family of nations.

Chapter XII

KOREA AND JAPAN

Korean and Japanese Relations before 1862

Contact between Korea and Japan in the early Yi period was based on a tribute relationship. Those who profited most from this relationship were the Ashikaga shoguns and their vassals, who sometimes sent over thirty tribute missions a year.

There were commercial and cultural reasons for sending tribute (*chinsang,* lit., "presentation of gifts to a superior") to the Yi court. Any Japanese lord who desired a tribute relationship with the Yi court had to obtain a copper seal *(tosŏ)* bearing his name from the Korean government. When his tribute envoy presented documents authenticated by this seal, his mission and tribute articles[1] were officially received by the government. In return, the Korean government gave the Japanese envoys gifts, mostly rice and cloth. In terms of trade, the rate of exchange between tribute goods and gifts was never favorable to Korea.[2]

The Japanese envoys were treated like state guests. An envoy and his suite were accorded a formal reception and lodged in the East House (Tongp'yŏnggwan), the Japanese guest house,[3] and they lived at the expense of the Koreans for the duration of their stay. When they were about to leave for their homeland, they were granted provisions enough to last them for the journey home.

In addition to regular tribute envoys, Japan also sent two kinds of private traders: holders of Korean titles known as *sujigin* and private merchants or speculators *(hŭngni waein).* The speculators settled along the southwestern coasts and traveled freely even in the interior of the country. At least during the initial period, there were no special rules designed to control the activities of either regular envoys or merchant settlers.

From 1407,[4] however, the Korean government began to adopt measures aimed at controlling the activities of Japanese settlers, private trade ships, and tribute envoys. These measures were taken primarily because the number of Japanese in Korea was growing. In 1439 they numbered 1,300.[5]

In 1414 the government introduced a new law, the *waesa yŏllo pŏp,* which markedly lowered the ranks of Korean officials who received the envoys. Envoys from the shogun and those from vassal lords were welcomed and entertained by departmental heads and by senior officials (assistant ministers and vice-ministers) of the Department of Rites, respectively.[6] In the same year another law was made to try Japanese convicts.[7] By 1418 Japanese settlers were confined to only four ports located in Kyŏngsang: Pusanp'o, Naeip'o (Chep'o), Yŏmp'o, and Kabaep'o; the latter was soon eliminated.[8] In 1421 Japanese tribute envoys were allowed only two routes—later three— to reach Seoul.[9] In 1429 the export of gold, silver, and several other items was prohibited.[10] In 1438 a policy was introduced whereby the Tsushima fief eventually rose to the position of the diplomatic medium between Korea and Japan.[11] Under this policy, only the shogun, the commissioner *(tandai)* of Kyūshū, the Ōuchi daimyo, the Kikuchi daimyo, and a few select daimyo were allowed to send tribute missions. The copper seals of other Japanese lords were useless unless their envoys received special certificates known as *munin* from the lord of Tsushima.

These were rather makeshift measures to control Japanese trade activity, but in 1443 the Kyehae Treaty concluded between Korea and Tsushima subjected Korean-Japanese trade to further control. Under the provisions of this treaty, Tsushima was allowed to send fifty trade ships a year, giving Tsushima virtual monopoly of the Korean trade.[12] In addition to the regular trade the lord of Tsushima and his clansmen were granted a considerable amount of rice each year.

In spite of this restrictive treaty, Korean-Japanese trade flourished during the next sixty years. In July of 1488 the Korean government reportedly paid 100,000 *p'il* of cotton cloth alone in exchange for Japanese goods bought during the three previous months.[13] And the number of Japanese settlers at the three ports where trade was allowed almost doubled between 1467 and 1494.[14]

Table 5: NUMBER OF JAPANESE SETTLERS AT THE THREE PORTS

Year	City	Japanese Households	Japanese Persons	Japanese Temples	Japanese Monks
1467	Naeip'o	300	1200	–	–
	Pusanp'o	110	330	–	–
	Yŏmp'o	36	120	–	–
1494	Naeip'o	347	2460	10	40
	Pusanp'o	127	446	4	7
	Yŏmp'o	51	152	–	–

The growing numbers of Japanese in Korea inevitably brought serious problems. One was the constant dispute between the Japanese and the Koreans over the land that the former were allowed to cultivate. Another was the problem of protecting national secrets.[15] Largely because of these problems, and because of Korea's economic decline, the government began to limit the number of Japanese households to the sixty originally authorized to stay, and to refuse tribute missions from those daimyo who did not send them regularly.[16] In this tense atmosphere, early in 1510, a quarrel between Korean officials on the one hand and the Japanese community and seamen on the other started over some trivial incident, and resulted in the death of several people on both sides.[17] Later in the spring the Japanese in Chep'o brought in some 4,000 to 5,000 samurai and killed the magistrate of Chep'o and three other officials. The disturbance soon spread to other Japanese settlements. As a result of these incidents 272 Koreans were killed, 796 Korean houses were destroyed, and the Japanese were expelled from all three ports.[18]

The enmity between the two countries soon subsided with the conclusion of the Treaty of Imsin in 1512. The main features of this treaty, which left Tsushima at a disadvantage, were: the abolition of Japanese settlements, the reduction of the number of trade ships to twenty-five, and the confinement of trade ships to Chep'o.[19] This treaty was voided by the Hideyoshi invasion, and in 1609 a new treaty, the Treaty of Kiyu, was concluded between Korea and Tokugawa Japan (represented by Tsushima). Though still

3. PUSAN AREA

KYŎNGSANG

TONGNAE

NAKTONG
RIVER

PUSANJIN

CH'ŎRYANG

HARBOUR
OF
PUSAN

YŎNGDO

TSUSHIMA

more disadvantageous to Tsushima, this treaty laid the foundation for subsequent diplomatic relations between Korea and Japan. This treaty and the supplementary agreements were what the Taewŏn'gun and his diplomatic representatives at Pusan called the "everlasting and unchangeable treaties" when the Meiji government decided to ignore them.

The main provisions of the treaty,[20] which consisted of eleven articles, were: (1) the number of trade ships which Tsushima could send were reduced to seventeen "regular" ships *(segyŏnsŏn)* and three "special" ships *(t'ŭksongsŏn)*,[21] there being, in fact, only little difference between the two categories; (2) the king of Japan (i.e., the shogun) was entitled to send two ships a year, with the number of crewmembers limited, as before, according to the size of the ships; (3) all ships were to carry permits authenticated by a special seal, and they could call only at the port of Pusan; (4) any ship violating these established regulations was to be returned.

Trade was carried out under highly elaborate procedures. The ships came to Pusanp'o at a specified time. Following certain fixed regulations, the officials of the ship and the Tsushima representatives at Pusan (later Ch'oryang) delivered both tribute articles and goods for public trade to the Korean representatives at the port. Then the Korean officials paid the Japanese in the originally prescribed commodities (rice and cloth) and other specifically requested articles. The officers and crew of the ships were allowed to stay in the Japan House (Waegwan) for a specified period (about eighty-five days) and were provided with all necessities for daily living, again for a fixed period. The officers of the ships were also entitled to be formally received by the Korean government according to set rules.[22]

The role of the Tsushima fief as intermediary between Japan and Korea during the Tokugawa period is important, apart from its purely commercial aspect. The lord of Tsushima was allowed to send two classes of envoys to Korea.[23] Envoys of the first class known as *taech'asa,* or grand envoys, were sent to inform the Korean government of important events such as the death or accession of a shogun.[24] Envoys of the second class known as *soch'asa,* or petty envoys, were sent on such occasions as the death of a Korean king or the return of shipwrecked Korean seamen.[25]

A *taech'asa* and his suite of over twenty men, exclusive of some seventy seamen, were received at the Japan House by Korean protocol officials called *chŏbwigwan* and *ch'abigwan,* who were usually sent down from Seoul. The envoys were accorded five different receptions, remained as official guests for five days, and could stay another fifty-five days. At one of the receptions they normally presented four different letters from the lord of Tsushima, written in a prescribed form and accompanied by token tributes or gifts, to the vice-minister of rites, the assistant minister of rites, the magistrate of Tongnae, and the commander of the Pusan fort. The Korean officials had to present letters and gifts to the lord of Tsushima in return. Although these gifts were generally regarded as a personal exchange between the lord of Tsushima and the prescribed Korean officials, the gifts presented by the protocol officials, known as *chŏbwigwan sayedan* and *ch'abigwan sayedan,* were more important, and were in fact provided by the government.[26] The entertainment of Japanese envoys was thus a great economic burden and became an important factor in the deterioration of Korean-Japanese relations in the nineteenth century. The treatment of petty envoys was not much different from that accorded grand envoys except that there was no exchange of letters or gifts between the lord of Tsushima and the Korean vice-minister of rites, and no protocol officials were sent down to Pusan from the capital.[27]

The Japan House, where Korean protocol officers received Japanese envoys, was a trading and diplomatic agency of Japan. It was located near Pusanjin, but was moved in 1678 to Ch'oryang, a few miles north of Pusan.[28] Its walled compound, encompassing several hundred acres, housed a shipyard, office buildings, warehouses, stores, restaurants, and handicraft shops. The residents included the head of the House (Kor. *kwansa* or Jap. *kanshi),* a number of trade officers (Kor. *tae'gwan* or Jap. *taikan),* interpreters, merchants, and servants. No one was allowed to enter the compound without permission from the Korean authorities. All diplomatic business and trade was transacted at the Japan House between the Japanese officials and the Korean representatives, among whom were one language officer *(hundo),* usually one assistant language officer *([hundo] pyŏlch'a),* and thirty junior interpreters *(sot'ongsa).* The language officers were under the direct jurisdiction of the commander of the Pusan fort and the magistrate of Tongnae, who were in turn supervised by the governor of Kyŏngsang.[29] To a great extent the success of diplomatic negotiations between the two countries depended on the language officers.

Although the primary function of the Japan House was trade and diplomacy, it was also authorized by the Korean government to run a small market[30] where the Japanese could buy their daily necessities from a selected number of Korean merchants six times a month.

Korea sent her own missions *(t'ongsinsa)* to Yedo, customarily within three years after the accession of a new shogun was announced, provided such a mission was invited by the Bakufu through Tsushima. Between 1607 and 1810 Korea sent twelve missions, each consisting of some 400 to 500 men. The first eleven missions were received at Yedo and the last one at Tsushima in 1810, in accordance with the Bakufu's request.[31] The reason for the change in location[32] was largely due to Japan's inability to support the mission's long and expensive procession across Japan. After 1810 Korea mi might have sent three more such missions, but she was no longer in a position to finance them. Thus, each time a mission was invited, she had to postpone it.

Korean-Japanese Relations in the Decade of the Taewŏn'gun

Korea's relations with Japan in the decade of the Taewŏn'gun began with two almost forgotten episodes. One was Japan's proposal to mediate between Korea and her two Western adversaries, France and the United States. The other was Yabe's one-man cry for the conquest of Korea. The first episode marked the end of the relatively peaceful relationship between Korea and Tokugawa Japan; the second led to a diplomatic tragicomedy, and characterized the new relationship between Korea and Meiji Japan.

The proposed mediation between Korea on the one hand and France and the United States on the other is primarily attributed to Shogun Tokugawa Keiki, who did not want to see Korea get involved in an uneven conflict with the Western powers. The shogun's desire to mediate was first disclosed on March 12, 1867, when he met Léon Roches, then French minister to the shogunate, at the Castle of Osaka. Roches raised no objection to Keiki's proposal. Thus encouraged, the shogun sent Rōjū Itakura Katsushige and another of his aides to the French minister on the following day to discuss the matter further. Roches, however, had suddenly changed his mind, and declined to accept the shogun's mediation on the grounds that

140

the Korean question had to be settled by negotiations between the Chinese government and the French minister in Peking.[33]

In spite of Roches's refusal, the shogun decided to proceed with his original plan.[34] On March 15 he appointed the vice-minister of foreign affairs, Hirayama Keichū, to head the projected peace mission to Korea.[35] Shortly after his appointment, Hirayama presented a lengthy letter to Rōjū Itakura, outlining the general course his mission should take in negotiations with Korea.[36] Perhaps recalling Japan's own struggle with the West, and not wishing to see a repetition of that struggle in Korea, so close to home, Hirayama proposed that a warship and two battalions of escort soldiers be brought to display the "military might" of Japan. He also proposed that the Bakufu allocate funds for "bribing" the Korean delegates sent to Japan for final negotiations should his mission be initially successful.[37]

Meanwhile, other members of the peace mission were appointed. They included Metsuke Furuga Chikugo-no-kami and nine specialists in Confucianism and foreign affairs.[38] On May 10, in accordance with customary practice, the Bakufu authorities sent an official note to Tsushima fief to announce its intention of sending Hirayama, now minister of foreign affairs, and Furuga to Korea. They also instructed the lord of Tsushima to inform the Korean government in advance of the dispatch of the mission.[39]

On July 30 the lord of Tsushima, Sō Yoshitatsu, dispatched a messenger to Korea with a note to the Korean Department of Rites. This note was to be formally presented first to the magistrate of Tongnae by a Tsushima official, Nii Magoichirō, in the capacity of a petty envoy. The Taewŏn'gun ordered the magistrate to reject the mission saying that Korea was unable to receive such a mission because of "a bad crop, epidemics, hardships attendant upon the foreign invasions, and the absence of precedence" for receiving an envoy for mediation purposes.[40]

Despite the refusal, the Bakufu did not abandon hope, and it even set a tentative date for the departure of the mission.[41] By the beginning of November, two separate notes, one from Shogun Keiki to the king of Korea and the other from Hirayama and Furuga to the *shissei* (regent [?]; lit., "the one who holds power in the government"), were prepared and approved by the shogun himself.[42] Hirayama and Furuga then received their credentials and prepared to leave,[43] but the occurrence of the Meiji Restoration left the exact date for the departure of the mission unsettled. Yet there was no change in the Bakufu's plan, since the new government had approved it. Moreover, the conduct of foreign affairs was still entrusted to the former shogun.

On December 1 the former shogun was finally able to obtain an imperial edict sanctioning the sending of the mission to Korea. Simultaneously, Hirayama and his suite were ordered to depart. The party left Yedo aboard the warship *Banryū* on December 20 and arrived at Osaka on December 26. On the following day they went to Kyoto for final instructions from the shogun. Their departure, however, was delayed again, this time by the war between the loyalists to the former Bakufu and the Satsuma-Chōshū forces. After this interruption, the ill-fated mission was never given serious consideration again.[44]

Although the Japanese mediation mission failed to materialize, it is nevertheless possible to determine the Taewŏn'gun's attitude toward it. Sometime during October 1867 the Bakufu informed the Tsushima fief of the tentative date for the departure of the mission. Naturally the Tsushima authorities in turn reported this to the Korean government through the Japan House at Ch'oryang. The Taewŏn'gun was puzzled by this report because he thought the subject had been closed after he rejected the Bakufu's proposal in July. Sometime in December 1867 he instructed the magistrate of Tongnae to send a formal note to the lord of Tsushima reaffirming Korea's position. The note read as follows:

> For the past four or five months, we have assumed that your [plan to send] envoys had been abandoned. Now, your note refers to that subject anew . . . Is this because our plea to you was not sufficient, or is it because your handling of the matter is too thoughtless? Of course, we realize that the Bakufu's desire to send such a mission is the manifestation of the sincerity shown to a neighbor . . . Nevertheless, . . . we are obliged to think about various difficulties which may arise from receiving the mission and sending it home. The treaties between our two countries have been passed down from our forefathers and have been honored for the past 300 years . . . They shall also be observed by posterity. There is no clause in our old treaties regarding the Bakufu's mission. Once part

of our agreement is broken, it will be difficult to preserve the rest of it . . . As for the Western ships that have recently appeared here and there, we have each pursued our own policy toward them. [For example,] your country opened Nagasaki to [foreign] trade, and our country drove [the French] away from Kanghwa. Yet each of us informed the other of what had been done. Now, the defenses of our coasts are well prepared, so that there is no need for your country to worry. Why then should your Bakufu trouble itself about unpredictable events and send a mission across the sea? Furthermore, all diplomatic affairs between our two countries have been managed solely by your [Tsushima] fief. This is an old agreement which cannot be changed.[45]

This note emphasized the unalterable nature of treaties, the importance of precedent, and the enduring position of the Tsushima fief as the traditional diplomatic channel between Japan and Korea. Korea's insistence on these points later became the major stumbling block to the preservation of friendly relations between Korea and Japan.

In retrospect, it would seem that the Bakufu's projected mission and Korea's negative reaction to it did not affect greatly the continuation of diplomatic relations between the two nations. The Yabe Incident, on the other hand, as we shall see, apparently did much harm to these relations. It might also be suggested that the Taewŏn'gun's bitter reaction to the proposed mediation mission might be ascribed to this incident.

Sometime early in 1867, close to the time the shogun first disclosed his intent to mediate, a Japanese Confucian scholar named Yabe Junshuku took up temporary residence in Hong Kong and wrote articles on Japan for the local newspapers. One such article, published in *Chung-wai hsin-wen* of January 17, 1867, in Canton, was mainly devoted to the progress being made in the new Japan. At the end of the article the author presented a highly distorted account of the historical relationship between Japan and Korea. Moreover, he stated that Japan was now preparing for the conquest of Korea.[46] Other newspapers seem to have carried more detailed articles on the historical relationship between the two countries. Yabe was reported to have said that the three ancient kingdoms of Korea, known as the *samhan,* had belonged to Japan, and that the king of Korea used to go to Yedo to see the *taikun* once every five years, without fail.[47]

The newspapers which carried Yabe's articles were soon forwarded to the Tsungli Yamen by local authorities.[48] The members of the Yamen, already concerned over events in Korea such as the persecution of missionaries, the French expedition, and the burning of the *General Sherman,* were greatly alarmed by Yabe's articles. Most of all, they worried about the inevitable danger to China that might arise from Japan's occupation of Korea. This is evident from a secret memorial presented by Prince Kung and his associates on March 20:

> For the past several years, Japan has been at war with England, France, and others . . . According to what we have learned recently, Japan has been defeated and has made peace with them. She has subsequently begun to exert herself and to display a militant spirit, to learn to build warships, and to travel to various countries. Her ambition is not small. The newspapers are already reporting on her numerous armaments, her warships, and her plan to quarrel with Korea. We have thought for some time that these reports were true. Although Korea is a little country, she has had quarrels with France and England [America]. Their desire was simply to propagate religion and develop trade [but] because France and England [America] are contending with one another, neither of them will be able to occupy that country. However, there is nothing to restrain Japan. No one will be able to guarantee that she is not avariciously seeking the territory of that country. If Korea falls into her hands, the calamity will indeed be great, because of [Korea's] proximity to China . . . If Korea fights Japan, the calamity she may suffer will be much greater than that caused by French soldiers.[49]

The Tsungli Yamen proposed that the Board of Rites be instructed to dispatch a confidential note to the king of Korea to explore any dissonance between the two countries, as a first step toward preventing possible catastrophe. Accordingly, the Board of Rites entrusted such a note together with copies of the Yabe articles to the returning Winter Solstice Mission for delivery to the Korean king.[50] The Winter Solstice Mission, headed by Yi P'ung-ik, returned to Seoul on April 10, 1867,[51] and presented the Chinese note to the king and his father. Not only the Taewŏn'gun, but apparently almost every one else in the government was alarmed by the Chinese inquiry and enraged at Yabe's statement. The following day the Ŭijŏngbu proposed to the Taewǒn'gun that the government dispatch an immediate answer to the Chinese inquiry to set straight Yabe's distorted account of Korean history. The Taewǒn'gun instructed the Ŭijǒngbu to draft a reply in the name of the king.[52] In its reply, the council pointed out that there was not a single reference in Korean historical records to corroborate Yabe's account of the "subjugation of the three kingdoms to Japan." It was also noted that Yabe's version of the Hideyoshi invasion was totally distorted, and that the insulting assertion concerning the visits of the Korean kings to Japan and the sending of tribute to the *taikun* were entirely without foundation. As for the alleged "discord between the two countries," it was emphasized that Korea had long maintained friendly relations with Japan and that any rupture had always been reported to the Chinese emperor.[53]

At the same time a note was sent to Tsushima to ask the Bakufu for a formal explanation of the Yabe statement. The Korean note[54] was presented to Rōjū Itakura in Yedo by a Tsushima representative on June 16, 1867.

Although the Yabe Incident ended officially with the Bakufu's formal denouncement of Japan's alleged "invasion plan" as unfounded rumor,[55] its impact on the Taewǒn'gun and his associates undoubtedly lasted for a considerable period of time. They feared that another Hideyoshi invasion was imminent and they must have regarded Yabe's claim that Korea sent tribute to Japan and that the king of Korea paid personal homage to the *taikun* as a great insult to Korea.

The Conflict between Tradition and Innovation

Relations between Korea and Meiji Japan in the decade of the Taewǒn'gun's rule were characterized by conflict between tradition and innovation. In the eyes of the leaders of the new Japan the recognition of Tsushima as the diplomatic intermediary between Korea and Japan, a major symbol of the traditional relationship, was incompatible with the rapid political, economic, and social changes at home. Korean leaders, on the other hand, regarded that tradition as eternal and the only legitimate basis upon which relations with Japan could be maintained. Given the two antithetical conceptions and actual circumstances, the relations between the two nations, already greatly strained, inevitably entered into conflict.

In the early period of the Meiji Restoration there was no visible evidence of change in the acceptance of the traditional role of Tsushima as diplomatic intermediary. This was largely due to the new government's preoccupation with other more urgent aspects of national affairs. Thus, on February 8, 1868, when the management of foreign affairs was formally taken over by the new government, Korean affairs were excluded from its jurisdiction— Tsushima's hereditary right to conduct relations with Korea was still recognized.[56] On April 15, 1868, Tsushima's right was reconfirmed formally when the Dajōkan, the newly established Council of State, appointed the lord of Tsushima, Sō Yoshitatsu, assistant minister of foreign affairs so that he might continue in his traditional role as intermediary.[57] On May 14 the Foreign Office ordered Sō to send an embassy to Korea to inform her of the restoration in Japan.[58]

Neither the Dajōkan nor the Foreign Office, however, was familiar with the true nature of Tsushima's traditional role or the elaborate diplomatic formality. Hence, before launching any new policy toward Korea, the Meiji government first had much to learn from Tsushima. Indeed, much of Japan's new forward policy toward Korea was initiated by the lord of Tsushima and his retainers.

Tsushima did not wish to continue to play the role of diplomatic intermediary in the traditional system, for she was made virtually a tributary state of Korea, and was economically dependent on Korean largesse. Sō and his ambitious retainers were determined to change that humiliating system. On May 27 the Tsushima authorities submitted to the government a paper dealing with the origin and development of Tsushima's management of Korean-Japanese relations and describing the established diplomatic procedures and formalities. The paper was accompanied by a memorandum urging reform of the traditional conduct of Korean-Japanese relations.[59] The memorandum warned, however, that Tsushima's economic problems had to be solved before any reform could be introduced. By "reform" (sasshin) the Tsushima authorities no doubt meant elevating Tsushima's status vis-à-vis Korea and improving the performance of its diplomatic functions in the name of the imperial government.[60]

Since the inauguration of a new policy toward Korea involved economic problems, the new government was in no position to offer Tsushima a satisfactory answer to its proposal. The Foreign Office, nevertheless, instructed the Tsushima authorities to discuss the matter with the representatives of the Foreign Office in Osaka, who had jurisdiction over "Korean affairs" (as far as policy matters were concerned) beginning in June (29?) 1868.[61] Accordingly, the lord of Tsushima sent Ōshima Masatomo, Tsushima's leading Korea expert, to Osaka. There Ōshima expounded his views on "relief and reform" before the Foreign Office representatives, insisting that the solution of the economic problem had to precede the reform of diplomatic procedures. The Foreign Office, however, assigned priority to reform, and Ōshima finally yielded to the Foreign Office after three lengthy conferences between July 1 and July 6, 1868.

The attempted reform had four aims: The first was to avoid using, in diplomatic notes, characters that appeared in the names of emperors and kings of the five generations preceding the reigning sovereigns. Prior to this, the Japanese were not allowed to use characters found in the name of any king of the Yi dynasty. The second was that the seals which Tsushima had received from Korea be replaced by a new seal issued by the imperial government, inscribed with "Gaikoku Jimukyoku" (The Foreign Office).[62] The third was the elevation of the title and rank of the lord of Tsushima to raise his diplomatic status vis-à-vis the Korean officials with whom he communicated. The fourth was to use the title *tennō* (emperor) in official letters to the king *(wang)* of Korea, raising the status of the Japanese sovereign above that of the Korean ruler.[63]

Thus committed to a system of "reformed formality," the Tsushima fief now began to perform its new role as diplomatic intermediary between the Meiji government and Korea. Its first mission was to send an embassy to inform the Korean government of the new events in Japan, as ordered on May 14 by the Foreign Office. The official notes which the ambassador was to carry were drafted by the members of the Foreign Office and the Korea experts from Tsushima in accordance with the new procedure.[64] On August 16, in response to Tsushima's request, the title and rank of its lord was raised from "Jū yon'i-ge jijū ken Tsushima-no-kami" (Lord of Tsushima and Chamberlain, junior fourth rank) to "Jū yon'i-jō Sa-Konoe ken - shōjō Tsushima-no-kami" (Lord of Tsushima and Brevet Major General of the

Left Imperial Guards, senior fourth rank). Simultaneously, Higuchi Tetsusaburō, the chief retainer of the lord of Tsushima, and Kawamoto Kuzaemon, a Korean expert, were respectively appointed chief ambassador *(taishū taisashi)* and vice-ambassador *(tosenshu).*[65]

The mission of the new embassy was indeed important, for the establishment of a new relationship between the Meiji government and Korea depended upon its success. The unilateral discarding of the *tosŏ* and the adoption of a Japanese seal was a momentous event in the history of the relations between Tsushima and Korea. It was almost unimaginable that the Korean government, which always looked for ways of refusing irregular envoys, would receive an ambassador with documents stamped by a Japanese seal.

In these circumstances, the Tsushima fief decided to dispatch an advance messenger *(kanji saiban)* or petty envoy to Pusan to obtain Korean recognition of the new seal. The Korean expert, Kawamoto, was relieved of his former appointment and assigned to this mission.[66] On November 13 Kawamoto left Tsushima for Pusan, carrying with him two important notes: one to the Department of Rites, the other to the magistrate of Tongnae and the commander of the Pusan fort. The letter addressed to the Department of Rites ran as follows:

> In our country times have changed completely. Political power has been restored to the imperial house *(kōshitsu)* . . . A special ambassador . . . shall bring you news of that event . . . I was . . . summoned . . . by imperial edict *(choku),* and the court . . . raised my title and rank . . . and appointed me to manage diplomatic affairs with your country . . . and also granted me the official warrant and seal . . . The letter [67] which the ambassador will present to you bears the new seal . . . Although the old seal can not be easily abandoned, it has to be done because of a special order from the court. How could there be a principle by which the public interest may be harmed by the private one?
>
> Taira no Yoshitatsu, Courtier, Lord of Tsushima, and Major General of the Left Imperial Guards of Japan[68]

The man who was directly responsible for nearly all negotiations with the Japanese was An Tong-jun, the language officer of Pusan *(Pusan hundo)*. Although we do not know much about An's early background, we do know that he was a career interpreter of Japanese and a persevering and somewhat rapacious man with ultra-nationalist inclinations. His single-minded devotion to the Taewŏn'gun gained him the regent's lasting trust. He was undisputedly the co-formulator and administrator of the Taewŏn'gun's "Japan policy."

A second man was Chŏng Hyŏn-dŏk, magistrate of Tongnae and An's superior officer. In theory, the Pusan language officer was to act according to the magistrate's instruction. Since Ch'oryang, the site of the Japan House, fell under Chŏng's administrative jurisdiction, he had supervisory power over the activities of the House, such as trade and the opening of markets, and its residents, in addition to his nominal diplomatic function. Although Chŏng seldom participated in direct negotiations, all official reports on diplomatic discussions with the Japanese were transmitted by and through Chŏng to the Department of Rites or the Ŭijŏngbu. Kim Se-ho, the governor of Kyŏngsang, and thus Chŏng's superior, was a Pugin and a close associate of the Taewŏn'gun. His participation in Korea's handling of the Japanese problem was confined to advising the Taewŏn'gun, Chŏng, and An.

When Kawamoto, the petty envoy, arrived at the Japan House, he had a preliminary consultation with Koma Itaru, the head of the House. On January 30, 1869, he had his first interview with An Tong-jun and An's aide *(pyŏlch'a)*, Yi Chu-hyŏn, at the House.[69] Kawamoto showed the two language officers a copy of the advance note *(saiban shokei* or *chaep'an sŏgye)* addressed to the Department of Rites, and explained briefly about the restoration in Japan. An's response to the Japanese plea to have the notes forwarded to the Department of Rites and the magistrate of Tongnae was predictably little short of violent. He considered the use of the term "imperial house" and "imperial edict" perverse and insolent. He also regarded the arbitrary discarding of the *tosŏ* and its replacement by one of Japanese contrivance as a "matter of urgent alarm," and demanded Kawamoto's immediate departure from Korea.

On the day following this tense meeting, the special ambassador, Higuchi, arrived unexpectedly in Pusan. On February 2, 1869, An Tong-jun went to the Japan House to learn from Higuchi more about what Kawamoto had told him, but the ambassador merely reiterated Kawamoto's words and requested in vain that he be accorded the treatment due a formal envoy.[70]

Fruitless negotiations of this kind between the two parties continued until December 11, 1869. There is no need to go into the details of all these discussions, but a few of the more important points should be mentioned.

First, the attempt to have the advance notes accepted by An Tong-jun was formally abandoned by April 29, because the Japanese were not sure how long the negotiations for this preliminary step would last.[71] These advance notes were primarily designed to obtain Korean recognition of the use of the new seal in the ambassador's note (*taisashi shokei* or *taech'asa sŏgye*). The logical procedure, therefore, was to present the advance notes before the ambassador's note. Second, the Japanese negotiators, consisting of Koma, Kawamoto, Urase Saijo (interpreter), and the ambassador, decided to try and persuade An Tong-jun to accept the ambassador's note, for a Tsushima envoy could not be formally received by the Korean government until his credentials were examined and found acceptable. Accordingly, on April 29, the Japanese met with An and told him that they had decided to withdraw the advance notes, in view of An's objections. They then pleaded with him to accept the ambassador's note and present it to his government. They allowed that such a step was extraordinary, but, they argued, that if the Korean government accepted their proposal the lord of Tsushima could save face vis-à-vis the new Japanese government. An Tong-jun, however, pointed out that there was no precedent for accepting an ambassador's note without first accepting the advance notes, but he said that he could not give them a final answer until he had seen the magistrate of Tongnae, his superior.[72]

Upon receiving An's report of the new Japanese proposal, Chŏng dispatched a summary report to the Ŭijŏngbu and asked for instructions. More than six months passed before the requested instructions arrived from Seoul. During this period An and Chŏng presumably sent confidential reports to the Taewŏn'gun and received personal instructions from him. On November 17 An went to the Japan House and reported to the Japanese that the Ŭijŏngbu had sent a reply the previous day and that their attitude toward the Japanese proposal was distinctly negative. Seoul had instructed the magistrate to order the "irregular envoys" to leave the country. Moreover, the Korean government declared that it had not the slightest intention of accepting the ambassador's note, even if the ambassador stayed for ten years.[73]

This view was reasserted on December 11, when An addressed two memoranda to the Japanese ambassador. In one An listed the primary reasons why the government refused to receive the Japanese ambassador. These were: Tsushima's violation of the treaty by sending an irregular envoy and by discarding the *tosŏ,* and Japan's lack of sincerity. In his second memorandum An pointed out a number of characters and terms used in both the advance notes and the ambassador's note which he considered improper. Specifically, he argued that the use of the additional title "Brevet Major General of the Left Imperial Guards" was against precedent; the insertion of the word *ason* between the titles of the lord of Tsushima was extraordinary; the replacement of the honorific *taein* (great man), which was traditionally used by the lord of Tsushima in addressing the vice-minister of rites, with the new term *kong* (gentleman) was also unprecedented; terms such as "imperial house" and "imperial edict" could only be used by the Chinese emperor; the use of *shi* (private) was difficult to understand, since no government could engage in diplomatic relations with a "private person."[74]

It is important to note that evidence exists that the Korean government was willing to consider some of the Japanese demands. On April 14, 1869, the head of the Japan House suggested that he might ask his fief to delete from the note those words which Korea objected to.[75] Although An Tong-jun was not enthusiastic about the suggestion at that time, it would seem that this proposal was later transmitted to the Ŭijŏngbu through Chŏng. According to the *Ilsŏngnok* (Jan. 14, 1870), the council memorialized as follows:

> A report from the magistrate of Tongnae . . . says: "The chieftain of Tsushima calls himself in his note 'Major General of the Left Imperial Guards.' Although there might be a precedent for a case like this, for the two characters *a-son* . . . there is none . . . I ordered the language officers to reprimand him and to make him revise the note and present it [anew]." The change in his title . . . violates the regular rules and forms. How can . . . the 300-year-old treaty allow such a change? We wish to reprove him in a separate letter and have him amend his note.[76]

In this memorial there was no mention of terms such as *kō* or *choku* or even of the seal. The magistrate only wanted to have the characters *a-son* removed, whereas the Ŭijŏngbu wanted to have the new title deleted from the note. Although it is not clear which note was in question, it would seem that if the Japanese had been willing to make minimal revisions, the Korean government might have agreed to accept the notes as amended. On the other hand, the Ŭijŏngbu might also have had in mind to reject Tsushima's arbitrary use of a new seal, for example, in a separate action, should further developments so dictate. At any rate, the Ŭijŏngbu's proposal, which was immediately approved, was not mentioned either by An Tong-jun or by the magistrate, for two possible reasons: First, the Taewŏn'gun might have sent secret instructions to An Tong-jun ordering that all Japanese notes which did not conform strictly to precedent be rejected, even though amended in some respect. This is an unlikely reason, however, for if he had intended to reject even a revised note, he would not have approved the Ŭijŏngbu's proposal. On the other hand An Tong-jun might have disregarded the Council's order, because he had already given his own final and formal answer to the Japanese in the two memoranda cited above. In any case, the question of accepting an amended note soon came before An again.

The An-Urase Compromise Plan

With An's two memoranda, not only was the ambassador from Tsushima rejected, but also the "reform" plan. Those primarily responsible for this unfortunate state of affairs were the lord of Tsushima (by now governor of Iwabara) and Ōshima Masatomo. Ōshima in particular, as the real initiator of the plan, felt personally responsible, and he tried to redeem the situation. Through Kido Kōin, an old friend, he obtained permission from Tokyo to send another Korean expert from Tsushima, Urase Saijo, to Korea to propose a compromise plan. Ōshima's plan was to accept at least temporarily the demands of the Korean government: the elimination of the controversial terms and the withdrawal of the new Japanese seal. The main objective of this plan was to open formal diplomatic relations between Korea and Meiji Japan. The question of the Japanese seal could be settled later by a formal treaty.[77]

Bearing Ōshima's compromise plan, Urase arrived at the Japan House early in June 1870. At the meeting with An Tong-jun on June 11, instead of going directly to the heart of his mission, Urase began by noting the consequences that the diplomatic impasse had created in Japan. Since the ambassador's note had been rejected, the former lord of Tsushima was in an extremely embarrassing position; he would soon be relieved of his post as governor of Iwabara because of his failure in handling Korean affairs; and there were some radicals in the government who were advocating punitive action against Korea. Urase assured An, however, that no such action would be taken, for a few people like Ōshima Masatomo were doing their best to mollify the extremists.

In reply, An assured Urase that he personally was willing to do anything to remove the "bottleneck" and expressed his deep sympathy for the people of Tsushima. Encouraged by An's amiable manner, Urase then turned to the main subject, the compromise plan. After an exchange of views on the plan, An and Urase agreed on the following terms: (1) the ambassador's note would be amended; (2) the term *kō* (imperial) would be changed to *chōtei* ("the court"); (3) the ambassador's note would be stamped with the old Korean seal; (4) the future form of diplomatic notes, the use of the Japanese seal, and other such matters would be settled by formal negotiations between the two countries; and (5) future diplomatic relations between the two countries would be carried on in the names of the two governments on a basis of equality.[78]

In accordance with established routine, the "compromise plan" had first to be submitted to Chŏng Hyŏn-dŏk, who would in turn dispatch his own report on the plan to the government in Seoul. If the Korean government approved the plan, An would formally ask Urase to amend the ambassador's note. In view of the formalities involved, An promised Urase that he could expect a final answer by July 8, 1870.[79] In normal circumstances the government would almost certainly have sanctioned the An-Urase plan, for decisions on Japanese affairs were generally based on An's recommendations. The plan, however, came to naught as a result of a trivial incident, the so-called Max von Brandt Affair.

Late in May 1870 the North German minister to Japan, Max von Brandt, undertook an inspection tour of the coastal regions of Chūgoku, Shikoku, and Kyūshū. At the end of his tour von Brandt suddenly decided to take "a little trip" in the vicinity of Korea. He took with him Nakano Kyotarō, an interpreter provided by the Nagasaki authorities.[80] On the morning of June 1, 1870, the warship *Hertha* carrying von Brandt and his party arrived at the bay of Pusan. She was the first foreign steamship ever to reach that highly secluded seaport and the Japan House.[81] To die-hard traditionalist Korean officials, the appearance of the German "black ship" in the heart of Kyŏngsang and at the "south gate" of the kingdom was most alarming. Upon the news of her arrival, troops and officials rushed to the harbor. They were more alarmed than surprised to find several Japanese on the scene, among whom was Nakano, a former interpreter at the Japan House. Shocked and angry, Chŏng sent An to the head of the Japan House to lodge a formal protest against Nakano's presence aboard the Western ship and to announce that the strange ship would have to depart immediately, leaving behind all Japanese passengers. An also reminded the head of the House that the reason the Korean authorities did not exterminate the "Western demons" was because they feared to burn up indiscriminately both "stones" and "jades."[82]

Although von Brandt and his ship left the following day without resisting the Korean demands, the Korean government interpreted the incident as a hostile act. When the Taewŏn'gun received Chŏng's report on the incident he began to suspect that the Japanese and the Westerners were conspiring against Korea. On June 10 he instructed the Department of Rites to send a strongly worded note of protest to Tsushima: "Even children and women know that Korea is on friendly terms with your country . . . Nakano, however, transgressed the boundary of our land, bringing in the barbarian ship. His move was mysterious and secret; he disappeared suddenly like lightning. We are making a strong inquiry into the reason for this event . . . so that bandits' invasions may be prevented in advance."[83] Simultaneously, the government sent a summary of the Brandt Affair to the Board of Rites in Peking. It pointed out that there was substantial reason for suspecting a Western-Japanese complot against Korea.[84]

While the memory of the Brandt Affair was still fresh the report on the An-Urase compromise plan reached the Taewŏn'gun and his associates. Not surprisingly, the Taewŏn'gun ordered that the proposed amendment of the

154

ambassador's note be rejected.[85] This decision was formally conveyed to the Japan House on July 13. An then told Urase that the government's policy had been completely altered by the "incident of the foreign ship." Although Urase explained that Nakano was aboard the ship strictly in a private capacity, An pointed out that his government could not accept such an explanation.[86]

Thus ended the seventeen-month-old Meiji government's first attempt to open diplomatic relations with Yi Korea through Tsushima. This bitter experience began to raise serious doubts about Tsushima's usefulness as a diplomatic medium. The new regime had completed its initial consolidation of power; the nation itself had undergone vast changes both in political organization of its central and provincial governments and in its physical strength and national goals; many talented men had gradually found themselves in responsible positions in the government, particularly in the Foreign Office. Korea was no longer considered a mere rice bowl upon which the existence of Tsushima depended, but was regarded by many young dreamers in Japan as a stepping stone to the conquest of the continent. The idea of the conquest of Korea spread rapidly among the Japanese leadership.[87] In the face of these changes, the age-old diplomatic role of Tsushima inevitably fell victim to the centralization of the new age. The history of the relations between the two nations during the ensuing years is a record of Korea's response to these developments in Japan.

The Sada Mission

The *hanseki hōkan* or the "return of the land and people to the emperor," which became effective on July 25, 1869, wrought another significant change in Tsushima's role in Korean-Japanese diplomacy. On October 27 the Dajōkan decreed that the management of Korean-Japanese affairs was to be formally transferred from Tsushima to the Foreign Office.[88] However, two further decrees issued on November 17 and 26 allowed Tsushima to resume its original role under the direct supervision of the Foreign Office. The reasons for this change were Tsushima's protest against the decree of October 27 and the Foreign Office's unfamiliarity with Korean affairs.[89] This joint management lasted until September 8, 1871. During this period the primary objectives of the Tokyo government were to prepare itself for the eventual takeover of the handling of Korean affairs and to open a direct line of contact with the Korean government.[90]

While Tsushima endeavored with the sanction of the Foreign Office to re-establish relations with Korea, the Foreign Office took its own first major step in an active Korean policy. In December 1869 it decided to send to Korea three young officials: Sada Hakuchi, Moriyama Shigeru, and Saitō Sakae. All three apparently were followers of Ōshima Masatomo.[91] Their specific assignments were divided into twelve categories that were largely concerned with the study of the traditional Japanese relationship with Korea, and such matters as her armaments, seaports, customs, economic and political conditions, and her relationship with China and Russia.[92]

The three officials left Yokohama on January 18, 1870, pretending to be Tsushima officials. At Nagasaki they picked up a well-known Korea expert, a Kurume physician, Hirotsu Hironobu, and then proceeded to Iwabara, Tsushima, where they landed on February 27. After spending some twenty days studying the origin and development of Tsushima-Korean relations, they left Iwabara on March 10 for Ch'oryang where they arrived on March 23.[93]

Although the time they spent in Korea was brief, their report[94] to the government seems to have attracted great interest among those concerned with the Korean question. The Tokyo government based much of its immediate future policy toward Korea on this report.

After his return to Tokyo, Sada, who left Korea in April, presented his fanatical plan for "the conquest of Korea":

> Korea casts dishonor upon our empire . . . She must be subjected! If she is not, the imperial dignity cannot be established . . . We should immediately dispatch an envoy to Korea . . . and thirty battalions of our troops. If . . . she does not . . . apologize for her crime . . . the imperial envoy should immediately leave the capital and our grand army should march into the capital . . . and within fifty days, the king will be captured . . . Russia also keenly watches Korean affairs, and Mexico [America?], intensely desirous of her gold and rice, also intends to conquer her [Korea]. If our empire loses this golden opportunity and gives Korea to these Western

bandits, it will be the same as losing our lips and teeth. Then, the
mouth will be cold . . . Now the Ministry of Finance spends
200,000 *yen* a year for Ezo, without even knowing when that
region will be opened. Korea is not only rich in gold, but also
abundant in rice and barley. If Korea falls into our hands, her
people, gold, and grain can be used for [the opening of] Ezo . . .
Therefore, the conquest of Korea is vital for . . . *fukoku kyōhei*
[enriching the nation and strengthening the army] . . . Our
problem is that we have too many soldiers; . . . there may be the
danger of civil war. Now, fortunately, we have a Korean enterprise.
If the soldiers are used for this, their repressed spirits will be
relieved.[95]

Although Moriyama and Saitō were not as extreme and fanatic as Sada,
they were, nevertheless, strong advocates of a "forward policy."[96] At the
time Sada's plan was dismissed as an academic argument, but it did have a
few powerful supporters in government circles such as Yanagihara Maemitsu
and Kido Kōin.[97] The *seikanron* of Saigō Takamori and Itagaki Taisuke was
in fact close to the Sada line.

The Yoshioka Mission

In spite of the rising cry for the conquest of Korea, the Tokyo government decided, contrary to its agreement with Tsushima, to attempt direct
negotiations with the Korean government. This decision was made largely as
a result of Urase's report on his negotiations with An Tong-jun. After careful
study of the Urase report, which was received by the Foreign Office on
September 13, 1870,[98] Foreign Minister Sawa Nobuyoshi and Vice-Minister
Terashima Munenori concluded that what the Korean government really
wanted was the opening of direct negotiations between the two governments
under the principle of equality, eliminating Tsushima as an intermediary.[99]
Therefore, on September 20 Sawa and Terashima submitted a joint proposal
to the Dajōkan asking that the Foreign Office be authorized to send its own
mission to Korea, carrying documents with the Foreign Office seal rather
than that of the former lord of Tsushima.[100] This request was soon granted.

On October 12, 1870, Yoshioka Kōki, the second assistant minister of
foreign affairs, was appointed to head the mission, and Moriyama Shigeru
and Hirotsu Hironobu were named to assist him.[101] Their specific assignments

were to persuade the Koreans to recognize the Meiji government and to
arrange for the mutual exchange of formal ambassadors.[102] They carried two
notes, one from the foreign minister to the minister of rites and the other
from the assistant minister of foreign affairs, Murayama Sakura, to the
magistrate of Tongnae and the commander of the Pusan fort. This time all
provocative terms such as "imperial house" and "imperial edict" were carefully avoided.[103]

Late in October, Yoshioka and his party left Tokyo, arriving in
Ch'oryang on December 24, 1870,[104] after spending some sixteen days at
Iwabara. They were accompanied by Urase and another interpreter, Hirose
Naoyuki. The principal figures of the Japan House were then Namba
Azumi,[105] the acting head of the House, and the rejected ambassador,
Higuchi. Upon his arrival at the Japan House, Yoshioka first consulted
Higuchi and Namba on the appropriate course to take in executing his
mission. Then he sent Urase and Hirose to An Tong-jun to arrange a formal
meeting for him with the Japanese delegation.[106] At this time, however, An
rejected the request on the grounds that they were not from Tsushima.[107]

Faced with this hopeless situation, Yoshioka decided to plead with the
former lord of Tsushima to exert his influence to break the impasse. Sō
Shigemasa was then governor of Iwabara, a fact that the Korean government
did not know. Sometime in April 1871, in his new capacity, Sō wrote to the
magistrate of Tongnae and the commander of the Pusan fort:

> Since medieval times the reins of our government have been
> placed in the hands of military men. Consequently, foreign affairs
> have also been under their management. However, now everything
> has changed . . . I have recently learned that you have refused to
> see them [the Yoshioka party] because you have never seen some-
> one from the Foreign Office before . . . Since all diplomatic matters
> are now managed by the Foreign Office, it is a matter of course that
> that office sends its men and letters to your country . . . I wish you
> will receive them and hear what they say, without rejecting them
> under the pretext of precedents.[108]

Although this letter too was at first rejected, it was finally accepted on
September 12.[109]

In the meantime, on May 17, 1871, nearly half a year after the arrival
of Yoshioka's party, An Tong-jun had gone to the Japan House and allowed

himself to meet the "Foreign Office men" on an informal basis. An's sudden
thaw was largely due to Urase's efforts. At the meeting Yoshioka revealed to
An the general content of Sō Shigemasa's letter, adding his own remarks on
the significance of the restoration and the function of the Foreign Office,
Japan's negotiations of a treaty with China, and his wish to meet with the
magistrate of Tongnae and the commander of the Pusan fort to talk about
renewing Japan's old friendship with Korea. An, however, refused to commit
himself to arrange a meeting between the Japanese delegation and his
superiors since such a practice was not permitted under the old treaty. He
defended his position with a rather specious line of reasoning: "Our country
has also undergone many changes in political organization . . . Diplomatic
functions previously performed by the Department of Rites have been
transferred to the Council of State or the Department of War, but diplomatic
communications are still dispatched in the name of the Department of Rites
. . . This is evidence that we should hold fast to the old treaty."

An did promise Yoshioka, however, that a report of their meeting would
be sent promptly to the magistrate and the commander.[110] He also asked that
the Foreign Office, like the shogunate, carry on diplomatic relations with
Korea through the Sō family.

Although the Korean attitude toward the Yoshioka mission was clearly
manifested during the May meeting, the formal statement of rejection did
not come until the latter part of the year. In the ninth month (October 14
to November 12) of 1871 Magistrate Chŏng wrote to the former lord of
Tsushima, marking the end of another episode in diplomatic comedy: "His
Excellency, Lord of Tsushima and Major General of the Left Imperial Guards
of Japan, Taira: Of late I have been informed that many things have changed
in your country, and that a new Foreign Office has been established to
manage diplomatic affairs between our two nations . . . The coming of
members of this office to the Japan House is an event without precedent.
Therefore, no further words shall be said about them."[111]

The Sagara Mission and the Protest Demonstration

Despite the failure of the Yoshioka mission the Tokyo government
decided to send still another mission to Korea. The new mission would inform

the Korean government of the *haihan chiken* (abolition of fiefs and establishment of prefectures) which was proclaimed in August 1871, since this change directly affected the joint control of Korean affairs by Tsushima and the Foreign Office. On September 8 Sō Shigemasa was relieved of his role as intermediary and on the twelfth he was appointed Assistant Minister of Foreign Affairs so that his name could be used in dealing with the Koreans.[112]

The new mission was entrusted to a former chief retainer of the Tsushima fief, Sagara Masaki, who received his Foreign Office appointment on January 16, 1872. To avoid further conflict with the Korean authorities Sagara was especially instructed to act in the capacity of a personal representative of the Sō house.[113] Yoshioka, who still remained at the Japan House in Pusan, was authorized to decide the course of action of all Japanese in Pusan should the Sagara mission be rejected. Moriyama Shigeru and Hirotsu were also appointed to assist the mission.[114]

On February 21, 1872, Sagara left Iwabara on the steamship *Manjumaru,* accompanied by Moriyama, Hirotsu, Urase, and possibly Hirose, and landed in Pusan (Ch'oryang?) on February 22.[115] From the outset the prospects for the success of this mission were dim. The main reason, strange to say, was their arrival on a steamship.

The Korean authorities disliked steamships, which they tended to associate with the West. Fukami Rokurō (Masakage), then head of the Japan House, was aware of this fact and had informed An in advance of the coming of the *Manjumaru.* An, however, firmly refused to allow any steamship into the harbor at Pusan. Only a short while after this warning was delivered the *Manjumaru* suddenly appeared in the harbor. The magistrate indignantly ordered the Korean merchants not to trade with the Japanese and even threatened to halt the supply of necessary provisions to the Japan House until the ship left.[116]

As a result, the *Manjumaru* left Pusan on February 24, taking along Higuchi, but leaving the Sagara mission behind. On February 26 the Korean authorities further demanded of the Japanese that no more steamships be sent to Korea since they might be mistaken for Western ships. At the same time the "Foreign Office people" (Moriyama, Yoshioka, and Hirotsu) were ordered to leave Korea.

The immediate duty of the Sagara mission was to present the two letters from Sō Shigemasa to the vice-minister of rites and to the magistrate of Tongnae and the commander of the Pusan fort. Both letters were chiefly concerned with the deprivation of Tsushima's hereditary right to manage Korean affairs, Sō's appointment to the Foreign Office, and Japan's desire to renew her friendship with Korea.[117]

These letters had no better luck than their predecessors. On April 27, perhaps unable to dismiss the Japanese entreaty outright, Chŏng sent Ko Chae-gŏn, who was then acting language officer *(ka-hundo),* to the Japan House to accept the copies of the original letters. (It should be remembered that until the copies were examined and found acceptable, the originals could not be submitted and accepted, and a mission could not be formally received.) On that occasion Sagara asked Ko if he could arrange a meeting between Chŏng and the Japanese delegation.[118] On May 6 Ko reported to the Japanese that the magistrate was so alarmed by the content of the letters that he was unable to make the decision alone. Chŏng had decided to report to the government through An Tong-jun, who was then in Seoul because his father had died. Sagara was promised that he would be given an answer within thirty days.[119]

The Japanese, however, were greatly concerned at the length of the waiting period. Yoshioka, Moriyama, and Hirotsu in particular felt that it was highly unlikely, in view of past experience, that they would receive the promised answer within the thirty days. They also thought that if Korea could not decide about the letters[120] on her own and had to consult with China, they might have to wait several more months before they could be received. They, therefore, decided to repatriate, at least temporarily, all residents of the House except for a number of officers and a few ships until they obtained a favorable answer from the Korean government. This action was apparently intended as a mild protest. On May 9 they dispatched a note to Tokyo asking for instructions.[121]

While waiting for instructions to arrive, Sagara received some unexpected news from the acting language officer on June 16. Ko told Sagara that the magistrate of Tongnae had received a confidential letter from Seoul, and the main purport of the letter was that the matter of the Japanese letters was so important that An Tong-jun had been ordered to lay aside his mourning and resume his post to deliver the decision orally to the Japanese. An was expected to arrive in Ch'oryang around June 30.[122]

On June 28 An arrived in Tongnae. On June 30 he held his first official meeting with Sagara, Fukami, Urase, and Hirose at the Japan House. The three Foreign Office men were excluded from the meeting since they were still "irregulars." At the conference Sagara first briefed An about the main objectives of his mission and the progress of the negotiations with Ko. Then he asked An about the decision of the government. An replied that the question of accepting such important notes could only be decided by "public opinion," and that it was yet premature to announce when such a decision would be reached. With this bewildering statement, the Sagara mission came to an end.[123]

Before departing for Tsushima and Tokyo, however, Sagara and the other officials decided to launch a protest against Korea's policy. The protest, known as *waegwan nanch'ul* (lit., "breaking out of the enclosed compound of the Japan House"), involved some fifty people. They left the compound without permission at midnight on July 1, 1872, and entered the walled town of Tongnae at sunset on July 6, after a five-day journey which covered only a few miles. The demonstration was ineffective; they never saw the magistrate, and instead were charged with violating the law. Finally they left Tongnae early on the morning of July 11 and returned to Ch'oryang on the same day. On July 20, after leaving behind a lengthy protest note, Sagara, Yoshioka, Urase, and Hirotsu left Ch'oryang.[124]

The Hanabusa Mission

When the management of "Korean affairs" was formally transferred to the Foreign Office on September 13, 1871, the first thing that the Foreign Office had to do was to take the Japan House out of the control of the representatives of Tsushima. The requisition of the House meant replacing the House personnel, terminating the arrival of trade ships, and settling Tsushima's debt to Korea. In particular, the dismissal of the personnel, numbering nearly 200, had become a serious problem by the early part of 1872. By that time the trickle of trade between the Japanese and the Koreans had virtually been suspended, thus depriving the former of their only means of livelihood.

In view of this situation, on September 20, 1872, the Japanese government appointed Assistant Minister of Foreign Affairs Hanabusa Yoshitada to carry out the formal requisition of the Japan House.[125] Hanabusa was especially empowered by imperial edict to repatriate officers and residents whose presence was not vital, to terminate the sending of trade ships, to settle Tsushima's debt to Korea, and to return shipwrecked Koreans.[126] Hanabusa was accompanied by four Foreign Office officials, one navy officer, and three army officers.[127] On September 30 they left Shinagawa aboard the warship *Kasuga,* accompanied by the steamship *Yūkōmaru* carrying two infantry platoons.[128]

On October 16 the party landed at Pusan after an extended stopover at Iwabara, where they inspected the records of Tsushima's Korean trade and took custody of the Korean seal. On October 17 they took over the Japan House. Most of the former officials of the House were ordered to return to Tsushima, but a few, such as Fukami and Hirose, took employment in the Foreign Office and were reassigned to the House.[129]

Next, Hanabusa turned to the settlement of Tsushima's debt, that is, to finish delivering promised goods, and the surrendering of shipwrecked seamen. These duties involved negotiations with the Koreans, and the prospects for such negotiations were dimmer than ever. Since the Sagara mission's protest, Fukami, the head of the House, was boycotted by the Koreans and thus was unable to perform his duties. Moreover, An absented himself from Ch'oryang.

Despite such discouraging circumstances, Hanabusa, in Hirose's name, announced to the new assistant language officer, Hyŏn P'ung-sŏ, the arrival of his party, which included Tsushima interpreters. At the same time he proposed a meeting. As expected, this proposal was flatly rejected on the grounds that the interpreters came on steamships, again bringing the "men of Yedo" (Foreign Office men). The "men of Yedo" were ordered to depart with their ships from Korean waters. Acting on Hyŏn's suggestion, the magistrate of Tongnae also ordered all Korean merchants to boycott the market at the Japan House, cutting off the supply of provisions to the officers of the House.[130]

Meanwhile, the secret dismissal of the two ranking trade officers *(taikan)* was reported to Hyŏn—probably by the repatriated trade officers themselves, disaffected by Hanabusa's action. On October 19 Hyŏn declared in brief but sharp notes to all former trade officers that the return of the ranking officers to Tsushima was tantamount to closing the Trade Office (Taikan-sho). He charged the Japanese with disregarding the interests of another country, for the Trade Office was far behind schedule in delivering merchandise promised by Tsushima. With this note he also sent a long list of undelivered goods with a total value of about 24,182 ryō.[131]

Hirose sent a memorandum in reply saying that the promised merchandise had been brought to Ch'oryang and that he wanted Hyŏn to come to the Trade Office to make a settlement, and that he, Hirose, had been appointed acting chief trade officer. He also requested Hyŏn to accept thirteen shipwrecked Koreans brought from Tsushima. But Hyŏn refused to accept either the men or the merchandise so long as the steamships remained in the port. One reason for Hyŏn's hesitation was that An Tong-jun was then absent in Taegu.[132]

Since Hanabusa's presence with the steamships only delayed the settlement of the debt and the reopening of the market, he and his party left Ch'oryang on October 25 leaving behind eighty-two Japanese, most of whom were merchants.[133] Even his departure, however, did little to relieve the tension. On the contrary, relations between Korean officials and the Japan House daily became worse. Hyŏn and An, who returned from his post in November, persistently refused to receive the merchandise on the grounds that it was sent by the Tokyo government.[134] They persisted in not recognizing Fukami. Finally, two incidents brought matters to a head between the two nations. One was the p'yomin ("shipwrecked men") incident and the other was the infiltration of Tokyo speculators into Pusan.

Early in February 1873 Hirose requested An and Hyŏn to accept some ten shipwrecked men who had been picked up at sea by the Japanese and were detained at the Japan House. The two language officers, however, were ordered by Magistrate Chŏng to ignore the request. On March 11 the shipwrecked men escaped from the detention quarters in the House. Chŏng sent his aides and soldiers to the House and accused the Japanese officials of having released them. The Japanese paid no attention to this protest, aware that the escape had actually been encouraged by Korean authorities.

Although it would appear to have been a trivial incident, the Japanese government felt highly offended.[135]

The second incident was far more serious. On the night of May 17, 1873, three agents of Mitsukoshi, one of the new Tokyo *zaibatsu,* were smuggled into the Japan House with a large amount of merchandise. They were soon detected by Korean authorities and denounced as contrabandists. Guards were stationed around the House and along the waterfront of Pusan.[136] On June 22 Magistrate Chǒng posted a warning to all Korean junior interpreters *(sot'ongsa)* and waterfront guards. This warning was actually intended for the Japanese:

> We want to adhere to the 300-year-old treaty, whereas they want to break it . . . Although they adopt their institutions from other [Western] countries they feel no shame. Because of changes in their appearance and customs, they shall no longer be called Japanese . . . Contraband has been prohibited by both Tsushima and our country. However, seeing what they have been doing of late, it can be rightly said that their country is lawless . . . However, there is still law in our country, and we practice it within our national boundary. If those who are living in the Japan House want to do things according to law, they shall never be troubled. If they do things against the law, they shall be constrained . . . They shall take the consequences for whatever may happen.[137]

This pronouncement is significant in that it helped to kindle the *seikanron* ("argument about the conquest of Korea") of 1873 in Japan. When a copy was forwarded to the Foreign Office, the deputy vice-minister, Ueno Keihan, who was then in charge of the Office, proposed to the Dajōkan that special measures be taken in response to the Korean provocation. The prevailing opinion in the Dajōkan was that Japan should send troops to Korea to protect Japanese citizens and that she should dispatch a special envoy to negotiate directly with the Korean government. The leading figures of the group that advocated this "forward policy" were Saigō Takamori and Itagaki Taisuke. Ordered to work out an appropriate policy, Sanjō Sanetomi, the Dajō Daijin, proposed the so-called *Chōsen shuppei* ("dispatch of troops to Korea") to the Dajōkan. The following remarks, made by Sanjō on that occasion, depict the general feeling of the Japanese leaders toward Korea:

They say that "because of changes in their appearance and customs, they shall no longer be called Japanese . . . " This is indeed preposterous. They already call our country "a lawless land," and say that we shall have to take the consequences for what will happen to us . . . It is difficult to imagine what sort of oppression our people [in the Japan House] may encounter, if some unexpected . . . incident breaks out . . . [The current incident] can no longer be tolerated; it has to be settled by sending troops . . . At this time, we should send a few contingents of the army and several warships to protect our people. If anything untoward occurs, an order should be given to the Kyūshū *chintai* [army base] for reinforcements. In addition an envoy should be sent to negotiate . . . [138]

As the proposal shows, Sanjō planned to send troops and an envoy simultaneously. However, this was opposed by Saigō who wanted to go first as an envoy. He feared that sending troops might make the Koreans suspect that Japan was using the incident as a pretext for swallowing up Korea. His view was shared by other councillors such as Itagaki Taisuke, Ōkuma Shigenobu, Oki Takato, Etō Shimpei, and Gotō Shōjirō.[139] The return of the Iwakura mission in September and the appointment of Iwakura Tomomi as acting head of the Dajōkan, however, changed the balance of political forces in the Japanese government. The belligerent Saigō and his followers were driven out of the government, and the moderates eventually gained the upper hand. Thus, the *seikanron* was dropped as the government's policy toward Korea.

Chapter XIII

THE OPPOSITION MOVEMENT
AND THE FALL OF THE TAEWŎN'GUN

An ineradicable opposition movement to the Taewŏn'gun's regime
began as early as 1866. His "heretical" economic and cultural reforms pro-
voked the conservatives, and the upsurge of Catholicism and the threats of
foreign invasion during his reign created an atmosphere of national crisis.
Ironically, the opposition movement was patterned after the traditional form
of factionalism that the Taewŏn'gun had endeavored to combat. One of the
leading forces of the movement was the king's in-laws, or the "Queen Min
faction,"[1] led and supported by political malcontents.[2] Another was a group
of ultra-conservative Confucian literati, most of whom were only coinciden-
tally faithful followers of the Noron faction. Each of these groups had its
own peculiar reasons for opposing the Taewŏn'gun, and each played a
different role in deposing him. The growing independence of the young king
also played an important part in the Taewŏn'gun's downfall.

The Queen Min faction was primarily interested in seizing power.
Preoccupied with intrigues, it enlisted politically disgruntled individuals[3] and
defended the self-righteous, anti-Taewŏn'gun literati, usually from behind the
scenes. The literati had no political program or even ambitions of their own;
they were dissatisfied with most of the Taewŏn'gun's policies, which they
thought incompatible with Confucian principles and the established laws of
the dynasty. Their chief weapon was the memorial, which they used openly
and fearlessly to attack the Taewŏn'gun's "non-Confucian" policies. More
than anything else, these memorials caused the Taewŏn'gun's regime to
finally crumble. One way to force him to retire was to continually criticize
his policies. This tactic might well be called "moral assassination by
memorials." No ruler of Confucianist virtue would have the courage to
dismiss his father from power; at the same time, no man of virtue would stay
in power in defiance of public criticism. Therefore, it was very much to the
advantage of the Queen Min faction to lend generous support to the literati.

On October 16, 1866, a few days after the French expeditionary forces
landed on Kanghwa Island, the Taewŏn'gun appointed a former inspector

(changnyŏng) named Yi Hang-no (1792-1868) as associate assistant secretary
of the Royal Secretariat.[4] This move was apparently designed to rally the
Confucians to the support of his foreign policy; instead, it marked the
beginning of his downfall.

Yi Hang-no, whose pen-name was Hwasŏ, was born in a small hamlet
named Pyŏkkye in Yanggŭn, Kyŏnggi.[5] One of the Confucian giants of the
late Yi period, he was said to have been gifted with an exceptional aptitude
for learning, reading the *Book of History* at the age of twelve. However, he
never cared to take the Civil service examination and make an official career
his life's ambition. On March 6, 1840, the government in Seoul first learned
of his name: Hwasŏ and nine others were especially recommended as the
outstanding Confucian scholars of the country.[6] By virtue of this recommendation, Hwasŏ was appointed a tomb commissioner, but he never served in
this capacity.[7]

For some time Hwasŏ's fame had been attracting young Confucian
scholars from many parts of the country. Among his disciples, the most
celebrated were Ch'oe Ik-hyŏn (1833-1906), Kim P'yŏng-mok, Hong
Chae-hak (1848-1881), Yu Chung-gyo, and Yu In-sŏk.[8] Hwasŏ and these
followers revived and led what might be called the "Chonhwap'a" (lit.,
"Revere-China school").[9] In the face of foreign invasion and Catholicism
they thought that the most urgent Confucian mission was to promote the true
principle of *chonhwa yangi* ("to revere China and expel the barbarians").[10]
By "revering China" they meant the study and application of the Confucian
classics for the perfection of the "principle of the five cardinal relationships
(osang) and the five virtues *(osŏng)*."[11]

Perhaps Hwasŏ was appointed to his influential post because of his anti-
barbarian sentiments and his influence over Confucian society in Korea. Four
days after his appointment, on October 20, 1866, he submitted a memorial[12]
which was designed primarily to advise the king on how he should rule the
country during the crisis of foreign invasion and suggest measures that should
be taken to combat the barbarians and their heretical religion. But the most
significant points in the memorial were the sharp criticisms leveled at the
Taewŏn'gun's "public works" *(t'omok)*, specifically the construction of the
Kyŏngbok palace, and the financial policy, that is, the introduction of new

168

taxes. This was the first time that a government official had publicly criticized any project or policy of the Taewŏn'gun.

The Taewŏn'gun showed neither bitterness nor resentment at Hwasŏ's memorial. On the surface at least he encouraged criticism of his policies, perhaps as an astute political gesture. On October 21 he promoted Hwasŏ to the post of vice-minister of works. At the same time, however, one of his aides secretly approached Hwasŏ and asked him not to bring up again the subject of "public works" and the "rule of extortion" *(yŏmjŏng)*.[13]

Nevertheless, on October 30 Hwasŏ wrote another memorial in which he quoted a famous saying of Mencius: "Words of benevolence *(jen-yen)* do not affect [the well-being of] men as deeply as a reputation for benevolence *(jen-sheng)*."[14] He declared:

> What does *jen-sheng* mean? It means the abolition of all public works, an end to rule by extortion, great attention to remonstrance, means for using men of virtue, detachment from selfish desire, and the elimination of superficiality and covetousness, so that the entire nation may know the true heart of Your Majesty.[15]

Remarks such as "selfish desire," "superficiality," and "covetousness" were no doubt directed at the construction of the palace and the new taxes. As for "remonstrance," it must be noted that during the entire period of the Taewŏn'gun's rule (except for his last days) only a few such as Hwasŏ dared speak out against his policies. The censoring offices themselves were virtually deprived of much of their traditional function of "remonstrance," largely because inspectors and censors were given such brief tenure that they hardly had time to perform the duties of their offices before they were transferred. Between January 13, 1864, and December 16, 1873, according to the *Ilsŏngnok,* the censor-general was replaced at least 183 times, an average of once every twenty days, while the inspector-general was replaced 193 times.

Even this memorial did not bring disfavor upon Hwasŏ. He resigned from his post soon after the presentation of the memorial, but he was soon assigned to the pre-reform Military Council as a senior officer. He resigned from this post too and determined to retire from his short-lived official career.

On November 14, 1866, when he formally retired, he presented a final memorial, which was almost entirely concerned with the restoration of the

Mandongmyo. In this memorial Hwasŏ pointed out that Ming China and Yi Korea were historically bound by the relationship of sovereign and subject, and that Korea was much indebted to the former in the dark days of the Japanese invasions of 1592-1598. Unfortunately, the Ming had fallen to the barbarian Manchus. The Mandongmyo was not only the symbol of Korea's commemoration of that historical relationship, but also the expression of Korea's everlasting gratitude to the Ming, and the symbol of her determination to fight the barbarians. Therefore, the true way to "revere China and expel the barbarians" was to restore the Mandongmyo and cultivate the principle of the sovereign-subject relationship.[16]

Within two years of his retirement, on April 10, 1868, Hwasŏ died at the age of seventy in his native Pyŏkkye.[17] His views on "barbarians" and the Taewŏn'gun's regime, however, were faithfully disseminated by his disciples, the most prominent of whom was Ch'oe Ik-hyŏn.[18]

In September 1868 Ch'oe, whose pen name was Myŏnam, was recalled to the government after a lengthy retirement[19] and was appointed inspector at the age of thirty-five.[20] The reason for this appointment is not known, but it may have been arranged by the Queen Min faction to capitalize on the anti-Taewŏn'gun stand of the Hwasŏ school. At any rate, following the footsteps of his late master, Myŏnam opened his own anti-Taewŏn'gun campaign on November 23, 1868, by presenting the first of a series of memorials. In it he listed as urgent matters for the king's attention: the abolition of "public works," "the rule of extortion," "the new coins," and "the gate tax."[21]

The memorial apparently upset the Taewŏn'gun. On November 27, 1868, Censor Kwŏn Chong-nok, one of the Taewŏn'gun's faithful followers, was instructed by the Taewŏn'gun to present a counter-memorial denouncing Myŏnam for "disgracing the name of Hwasŏ, using vicious words, and failing to define his duty to the sovereign." The counter-memorial went on to demand Myŏnam's banishment. But the king, now reaching maturity, defended Myŏnam, saying that his memorials should be overlooked because they were written by an "ignorant country man," and therefore, it was unnecessary to punish him so severely. He then dismissed Myŏnam from the Censorate. Four days later, however, Myŏnam was promoted by special decree to the senior third-grade post of *tojŏng* in the Council of the Royal

Kinsmen.[22] The king's action on this occasion clearly showed the veiled
enmity between the Taewŏn'gun and the Min faction which the king tended
to support. The feud became more intensified as the king reached maturity,
the point at which he might rightly expect to assume the reins of government.

In the meantime, perhaps in a move to isolate the king from the Mins,
the Taewŏn'gun assigned two relatives of the queen to provincial posts. On
December 17, 1872, Min Sŭng-ho was appointed magistrate of Suwŏn,[23] and
on May 1, 1873, Min T'ae-ho was sent to Haeju as governor of Hwanghae.[24]
However, on October 30, 1873, perhaps by direct order of the king, Min
Sŭng-ho was recalled to Seoul to head the Department of War. He replaced a
faithful admirer of the Taewŏn'gun, Min Ch'i-sang, who in turn was
appointed to Min Sŭng-ho's Suwŏn post.[25] On November 29 the gate tax
was abolished by royal decree; the same day, Myŏnam, who had been in
retirement since February 6, 1869, was appointed associate assistant secretary
of the Royal Secretariat.[26] There is no doubt that these actions, particularly
Myŏnam's appointment, constituted a challenge by the opposition faction
to the authority of the Taewŏn'gun.

On December 14, 1873, prior to his departure for the capital, Myŏnam
presented a second memorial from P'och'ŏn. The crucial part of the memorial
runs as follows:

> In recent years, the government has changed the old established
> laws . . . and councillors and ministers have neglected their duty of
> presenting their views [on affairs of government] to the throne.
> Censors . . . have also refrained from speaking ill of [the manage-
> ment of] the government. In the government, true doctrines [on
> rites, for example] are no longer heard, whereas the false ones
> have gained great vogue. Adulatory and dissolute individuals have
> achieved their objects, while men of upright conduct have been
> discarded. Living souls have been ceaselessly exploited as though
> they were meat and fish. The principle of human relationships has
> perished and morals no longer exist. Those who serve the public
> regard such things as a perversion; those who serve their private
> interests call them opportunity.[27]

This rather slanderous memorial was undoubtedly meant to be a direct attack
upon the Taewŏn'gun; expressions such as "their private interests" were
unquestionably aimed at him. The consequences of the memorial, therefore,
were quite significant.

Since Myŏnam was not in the capital at the time, the normal procedure was for the memorial to be presented through the governor of Kyŏnggi, Kim Chae-hŏn. The governor, however, showed it first to the Taewŏn'gun, who, upon seeing it, became so incensed that he immediately ordered the governor to return it to Myŏnam. Furthermore, he instructed Yang Hŏn-su, commander of the Kŭmwi regiment and a disciple of Hwasŏ, to warn Myŏnam that his memorial was too improper to be presented, and that Myŏnam should resign on the pretext of illness, either his own or his parents'. Otherwise, the Taewŏn'gun threatened, the government would take stern action against him. However, the king and his in-laws were soon informed of the incident and managed to obtain the original copy of the memorial from its author by dispatching a clerk of the Royal Secretariat to P'och'ŏn. The king praised the memorial as a "manifestation of true loyalty" and promoted Myŏnam to the post of vice-minister of revenue.[28]

Members of the Taewŏn'gun's party reacted strongly to the memorial and the king's action. On December 15, the day after the memorial was made public, Kang No, a Pugin, and Han Kye-wŏn, a Namin, respectively the left and right councillors, submitted their resignations to the throne. The following day Hong Sun-mok, a Noron and the president of the Council of the Royal Kinsmen, and members of the Censorate (the chief, Pak Hong-su), the Inspectorate (the chief, Hong Chong-un), the Academy of Literature, and the Royal Secretariat did the same. All the resignations except those of Kang, Han, and Hong were accepted.[29]

This mass resignation was followed by countercharges against Myŏnam. The first to speak openly against him were An Ki-yŏng, the vice-minister of punishment, and the former assistant censor, Hŏ Wŏn-sik. In their memorials, submitted on December 27, the two men categorically denounced Myŏnam's charges as unfounded, while they eulogized various reforms that were brought about during the ten years of the Taewŏn'gun's regency. An and Hŏ demanded that the throne banish Myŏnam on various counts; instead, they themselves were exiled.[30] Also on December 27, at the Royal Lecture held at Chagyŏng Hall, Lecturer Yi Sŭng-bo and Kwŏn Chŏng-ho, a ranking official in the Academy of Literature, charged that Myŏnam's memorial contained no truths whatsoever, but only hypocritical and wild remarks.

They also denounced the king for praising Myŏnam as an "honest" and "upright" man.[31] Moreover, the entire student body of the Sŏnggyun'gwan, indignant at Myŏnam's remark concerning "the destruction of the principle of human relationships," left their classes in protest. For this, the leaders of the protest movement were banished and many were forbidden to take the civil service examinations, probably for a limited period only.[32]

After the first wave of counterattacks, the anti-Taewŏn'gun party came into the open and launched an all-out offensive. On December 18 the new inspector, Hong Si-hyŏng, addressed a memorial designed to reply to the memorials of An and Ho. It demanded the restoration of the Mandongmyo and the *sŏwŏn;* the abolition of the *hop'o,* the *kyŏlchŏn,* and *wŏnnapchŏn;* a ban on miscellaneous levies; and the invalidation of Chinese coins. Furthermore, it attacked the Taewŏn'gun's appointment of men of lowly birth to government posts. For this memorial, Hong Si-hyŏng was immediately promoted to the coveted post of second compositor of the Academy of Literature. Two of his demands, the abolition of the *kyŏlchŏn* and the *wŏnnapchŏn,* came into effect immediately.[33]

The final blow to the Taewŏn'gun's regime came on December 22, when Myŏnam submitted his third memorial.[34] In it he virtually demanded that the Taewŏn'gun go into retirement. He expounded his demands from a historical as well as a Confucian point of view. He generally agreed with Hwasŏ on the significance of the Mandongmyo as described in the latter's memorial of November 14, 1866, but he raised an interesting argument about the *sŏwŏn:*

> Those who advocated the abolition of the academies alleged that they accomplished no worthy result but only brought about abuses. This argument is not valid. When Tzu-kung [one of Confucius' disciples] wanted to discontinue the sacrifice of live sheep, Confucius said: "Sheep may be dear to you, but to me this *li* [ritual or ceremony] is dear!"[35] This remark implies that as long as the offering of sheep was continued [even without formal ritual], there was hope that the formal ritual might be restored some day. Now, if the abolition of academies continues, learning is in grave danger of perishing forever.

In essence, then, Myŏnam held that even if the academies had many faults, they were still indispensable as a medium for learning.

As for the adoption of deceased clansmen, or what Myŏnam called "dead spirits" *(kwisin),* it was unprecedented. It has been mentioned previously that a number of the important branch houses of the royal clan had ceased to exist. The Taewŏn'gun had transferred living members of other less important houses and their ancestors to the discontinued houses. Myŏnam charged that this act violated the principle of human relationships and the ancient code of rites. He asserted that the innovation was designed by selfish persons who sought profit and privileges through the succession to important lines endowed with large amounts of land.

On the matter of "traitors"[36] Myŏnam took a stand which no doubt reflected his own factional background:

> At the beginning of your reign, the licentious coterie achieved their goals, and heterodox doctrines were in great vogue. Without inquiring into right and wrong, and without distinguishing between loyalty and treason, every one who bore the name of traitor was rehabilitated on the premise that such an action would produce a spirit of harmony. If those who should be pardoned are pardoned, it will bring about harmony. However, if those who should be pardoned are not pardoned, or those who should not be pardoned are pardoned, harmony will certainly be impaired. On the list of the pardoned appear the names of men whose treason should never be condoned . . . [Han] Hyo-sun[37] of the Kwanghae-gun period [r. 1608-1623], and Yi Hyŏn-il and [Mok] Nae-sŏn, who took part in the events of 1689.[38] As a result of this act [the pardon of unforgivable crimes] . . . sovereign-subject and father-son relationships have been destroyed, and the call of the public for heavenly judgment and punishment was neglected . . . This being so, how can harmony persist and fortune come to Your Majesty?

On the use of Manchu coins Myŏnam raised two objections: one objection was according to principle, which demanded the rejection of barbarian things; the other was according to established economic doctrine, which for Myŏnam meant that a surplus of coins would imperil the traditional "equalization" *(sangp'yŏng)* or balance of commodities and money (or other medium of exchange) and cause Korean goods to flow into China.

Lastly, Myŏnam boldly indicated the man responsible for all these wrongs, and proposed measures that had to be taken if the king was to be a

sage-king like Yao and Shun, if he was to secure eternal blessings for the
dynasty, and if he was to bring tranquillity to the nation and the people:

> All these upheavals in our established laws and institutions
> occurred in the days when Your Majesty was still too young to take
> the helm of state affairs. Therefore, they are not faults which are
> ascribable to Your Majesty, but to those officials who were especially
> entrusted with state affairs. They are the ones who obscured Your
> Majesty's sageness, wielded power, and amassed fortunes . . . I pray
> Your Majesty may, from this moment, exert the power of the
> sovereign, . . . strive diligently, be alert to [the dangers of] heretical
> doctrines and to being misled by men of power.

The events following the presentation of this memorial were melodramatic.
No sooner had Myŏnam presented this memorial than he left the capital for
his home in P'och'ŏn, not anticipating the consequences which were to
follow. The Taewŏn'gun's followers demanded that the king punish the
memorialist severely. The king, recognizing the impropriety of the memorial,
was compelled to banish Myŏnam.[39] Hong Sun-mok, Kang No, and Han
Kye-wŏn were not satisfied with such a light sentence; on December 23, in a
joint memorial and a special audience sought during the night, they appealed
to the throne to put Myŏnam on formal trial. On the same day other
members of the government, mostly from the Academy of Literature, the
Censorate, and the Inspectorate, presented joint memorials declaring that
Myŏnam had neglected his duty as a subject and had himself betrayed the
principle of human relationships; they demanded that he be tried. These
petitions, however, were rejected by the young king.[40]

Meanwhile, a rumor spread that the Taewŏn'gun was planning bodily
harm to Myŏnam. On December 24 the king appointed Yang Hŏn-su, a
friend of Myŏnam and a disciple of Hwasŏ, and Paek Nak-chŏng commanders
respectively of the left and right metropolitan police headquarters as a means
to ensure Myŏnam's personal safety.[41] That same day the councillors
renewed their demand for judicial proceedings against Myŏnam and finally
managed to make the king yield.[42] On December 25 Myŏnam was arrested
while en route to his home, by an official of the Special Tribunal at
Nuwŏnjŏm, brought back to Seoul, and imprisoned at the Tribunal.[43] The
trial opened at the Special Tribunal on December 27, but it was a mere

formality, since by royal command no flogging was permitted. On December 28 the trial itself was suspended, probably owing to the influence of the queen and her relatives.[44] The king's final verdict on the trial was that Myŏnam's memorials were the products of an ignoramus from the country-side and entirely incoherent! Despite repeated demands for further trial from State councillors and others including members of the Royal Secretariat, the Academy of Literature, and the two censoring bodies, Myŏnam was banished to Cheju island, where he remained until March 16, 1875.[45]

The king and his in-laws took advantage of the situation and began to take over the government. During the evening Royal Lecture of December 23 the king announced to the councillors the "royal decision to conduct all state affairs."[46] On December 30 Hong Sun-mok, Kang No, and Han Kye-wŏn were relieved of their posts, and on January 1, 1874, Yi Yu-wŏn was appointed chief councillor of state.[47] On January 19 Pak Kyu-su and Min Kyu-ho were appointed respectively right councillor and vice-minister of appointment.[48] Thus, the chief posts in the government were gradually taken over by members of the Min faction and the opportunists associated with them.

While this was going on, the Taewŏn'gun had quietly left the capital to retire to his mountain resort at Samgyedong outside the North Gate of the capital. Many of his faithful followers were now removed from the political scene, either temporarily or permanently. Myŏnam's leading critics such as Cho Wŏn-jo, Hong Man-sŏp, Ki Kwan-hyŏn, Kwŏn Chŏng-ho, and Paek Kyu-sŏp were banished to remote southern islands or to the north. Even Han Kye-wŏn was banished on February 4, 1874.[49] A noteworthy fatality of the political strife was An Tong-jun; he was beheaded on April 9, 1875, allegedly for abusing his office.[50] Anyone who continued to take the side of the Taewŏn'gun was punished with either execution or exile. For instance, on February 4, 1874, Pak U-hyŏn was banished to a southern island for having criticized the king for being unfilial.[51] On December 1, 1874, Yi Hwi-rim was also exiled because he had suggested to the king that the Taewŏn'gun should be asked to return to the capital from his self-imposed exile.[52] On April 10, 1875, four Confucian leaders from Kyŏngsang who had appealed for the return of the Taewŏn'gun were also banished.[53] On July 20, 1875, four other Confucian leaders from various provinces who had made the same appeal were beheaded.[54]

The Taewŏn'gun's political career did not end with his retirement. He continued to play a vital, yet controversial role in Korean politics almost until his death in 1898. During the decade of his regency he had striven to preserve the traditions of Yi society. After his fall from power his career differed greatly in ideals and spirit. It was largely conditioned by various interacting elements: the resurgence of corruption in the government, the intensified activities of the Min faction, Korea's rapid economic deterioration, and the coming of foreign powers and their subsequent meddling in Korea's internal affairs. There was no effective political leadership to cope with this situation.

The Taewŏn'gun gradually relinquished his antiforeignism and to observers on the scene he seemed to be the only political personality able to rally diverse interests. For this reason, the Taewŏn'gun found himself in and out of the political scene.[55] However, the disparity of interests and the difference of objectives between him and his supporters in each case prevented a durable partnership. In the end he was no more than a political instrument of contesting foreign powers. Thus ended the life of a man whose personal fortunes had closely followed the meandering path of Korean history in the second half of the nineteenth century.

EPILOGUE

Hardly any period in Korean history has become more intimately linked to the name of a man than has the brief period, 1864 to 1873, with that of the Taewŏn'gun. Such neat dates and the focus on a single person, however, should not obscure the fact that historical figures are inseparably bound to a historical context. As personally forceful as the Taewŏn'gun may have been, he should be seen as the executor of a historical development that did not start with him. In the face of the most momentous uprisings in the history of the Yi dynasty, reform had been clearly on the upsurge during the reign of King Ch'ŏlchong. This pattern came to an undoubted climax in the early 1860s and reached far into the 1870s, even after power had slipped out of the Taewŏn'gun's hands. In other words, there is much more continuity than the emphasis on the Taewŏn'gun's decade would suggest.

Even prior to 1864 the times had become ripe for reform. True, many of the Taewŏn'gun's reform measures were not received enthusiastically by the officialdom and were challenged outright by an active opposition movement, but this opposition seems to have been directed not so much against reform as such but against some of the Taewŏn'gun's initiatives that were felt to be incompatible with the traditional value system. Many of his measures were undone after his fall, but the reform movement went on. It may therefore be reasonable to suggest that if King Kojong had ascended the throne as an adult, the course of Korean history of that decade would not have been very different. The Taewŏn'gun owed his prominence to timely circumstance, and he rode the tide of reform proudly and vigorously. It is somewhat hazardous, however, to try to determine what exactly the Taewŏn'gun's role in the reform movement was, and from what source he derived his power to steer it along a course very much determined by his will. In earlier times, the mere title of *taewŏn'gun* had carried no power. To be sure, the Taewŏn'gun was never a *de jure* regent, and his person, at least as far as the official records are concerned, was entirely hidden behind Dowager Cho, who was the rightful regent until 1866, and the young King Kojong. The three-way relationship between them is not at all clear. Did the Taewŏn'gun derive his extraordinary powers not only from the fact that he was the father of a child king, but even more from the circumstance that his title granted him an official standing without forcing him into the power structure, thus giving him great liberty to work from behind the scenes almost at will?

The author of this book had perhaps such a hypothesis in mind when he set out to determine the Taewŏn'gun's role in the reform movement. The Taewŏn'gun is certainly pictured as the source from which the impulses for change emerged. But if this was indeed the case, it is nevertheless very difficult to find a common denominator underlying the reform programs. No contemporary terminology other than the word *yusin,* "restoration," which was used occasionally seems to have labeled the reform events of the decade. True, the Taewŏn'gun was a Confucianist who reportedly felt some affinity to the Sirhak school, but on the whole his program seems to have had less of a philosophical base than, for example, the T'ung-chih Restoration in China. The direction of change, therefore, was not consistent, but swung back and forth between, even in Confucian terms, orthodox measures and policies that revealed the individuality of their author. To the latter would belong his "unorthodox" way of choosing the people with whom he surrounded himself. The general aim of his efforts was the restoration of the royal house and government apparatus to the condition of the first decades of the dynasty. In this way he was not an innovator, but a restorer.

It is in this light particularly that the Taewŏn'gun's foreign policy should be seen. However much he was later blamed for his seclusion policy, he was only the guardian of a diplomatic tradition mired in etiquette and ceremony that precluded circumspect adjustments to developments in the outside world. To the Taewŏn'gun, as to the majority of Koreans at that time, the world outside Korea, except China, did not have any relevance to the Korean situation. What was more, relations with it would not only have violated traditional concepts but would have been detrimental to Korean ways. Challenged by enemy ships appearing along the Korean coast in the late 1860s and the early 1870s, the Taewŏn'gun was called upon to verbalize tenets of foreign policy that had been transmitted and gone untested since the time of the Japanese invasions at the end of the sixteenth century.

The Taewŏn'gun's reform movement was most dynamic on the home front. There his adjustments cannot be termed marginal. On the contrary, his

reforms did away with many of the "marginal adjustments"* that had helped
to keep the dynasty in balance for almost five hundred years and aimed at
establishing a new equilibrium of political and economic forces. In the light
of later events much of the Taewŏn'gun's restoration work looks like a futile
exercise in historicism. Coming unwittingly on the eve of Korea's opening to
the outside world, many of his achievements were later swept away, leaving
but little influence on later developments, by a storm which had been gathering while the Taewŏn'gun was at the helm of power. He survived, but many
of his policies were soon rescinded. The reform movement did continue,
albeit at a different pace and in a different spirit, even after he had gone into
retirement.

These might have been some of the conclusions Dr. Choe would have
drawn, had he lived to see the book through to its completion.

Throughout this book he devoted much attention to providing background information on socio-economic history which would enable the
reader to see the Taewŏn'gun's time in historical perspective. Korean
economic history, however, is an especially thorny subject, for the line
between theory and practice is in many respects so fragile that distinguishing
that which has been accomplished from that which was intended is difficult.
From the beginning of the dynasty there had been no clear-cut new basis
upon which the economy could be rebuilt. True, a number of new theories
and rules were conceived to abate and rectify some of the worst economic
evils of the late Koryŏ dynasty, rules that were proclaimed and later even
codified, but the impression remains that too many old customs and
practices were only buried temporarily during the flourishing first century
of the dynasty, to reemerge at a later date. New research conducted by both
Korean and Western scholars—too late for this book to consider—has contributed to a more differentiated picture of the economic scene and shown
that the variables in space and time are so numerous that some of the
presentations in this book may stand on too narrow a basis. Cases in point
would be the complex problems concerning the growth of private ownership
and of inheritance of land. Too, the social status of the cultivator of that
land has been put into new perspective.

*See James B. Palais's paper, "Stability in Yi Dynasty Korea—Equilibrium Systems and Marginal
Adjustments" (prepared for the Conference on Tradition and Change in Korea, Seoul, September 1,
1969).

The unexplored field of Korean history is awaiting more research from which more trustworthy conclusions can be ventured, not only to give us a deepened knowledge of Korean history, but also to help us draw fruitful comparisions with developments in China and Japan. This book is but a small beginning. If it stimulates research, its purpose will have been fulfilled.

Zurich, January 1971   Martina Deuchler

NOTES

Abbreviations Used in the Notes

CS	*Chōsen shi*
FRUS	*Papers Relating to the Foreign Relations of the United States, 1867-1871*
ISN	*Ilsŏngnok*
IWSM	*Ch'ou-pan i-wu shih-mo*
KS	*Kojong sillok*
MHBG	*Chŭngbo munhŏnbigo*
NGB	*Dai Nippon gaikō bunsho*
PBTN	*Pibyŏnsa tŭngnok* ("b" after page nos. refers to lower half of the reproduced page)
SMTN	*Sunmuyong tŭngnok*

Introduction

1. The title "Taewŏn'gun" was given to the father of a king who succeeded to the throne from a branch of the royal house. This title had previously been conferred upon the father of King Sŏnjo, Grand Prince Tŏkhŭng, and the father of King Ch'ŏlchong, Grand Prince Chŏn'gye, but only Yi Ha-ŭng came to be commonly known as the Taewŏn'gun.

I. *Social and Economic Conditions in Yi Korea before 1860*

1. For details of the 1391 reform and related background, see *Koryŏsa* (The history of Koryŏ; Seoul, 1955), 45:14b, 36b; 78:20b-42b; 118:3ff.; 137:29, 39. This study of the historical development of the three basic economic systems of Yi Korea is a preliminary survey of the subject, and therefore open to change as my research progresses. No adequate study of these subjects has yet been undertaken. For the earlier development of the *kwajŏn* system, see Fukaya Toshitetsu, "Sensho no tochi seido ippan: iwayuru kadenhō wo chūshin to shite" (A study of the land system of the early Yi dynasty with special emphasis on the so-called

degree land system), *Shigaku zasshi* (Journal of history), 50.5:47-82 (May 1939);
50.6:32-78 (June 1939); "Kadenhō kara shokudenhō e" (A study of the rank
land system and the service land system), ibid., 51.9:1-42 (September 1940);
51.10:1-29 (October 1940); Sudō Yoshiyuki, "Kōraichō yori Richō shoki ni
itaru densei no kaikaku" (The reform of the land system from the Koryŏ
dynasty to the early Yi dynasty), *Tōa gaku* (Orientalica), 3:115-191 (1940);
"Raimatsu Sensho ni okeru nōsō ni tsuite" (The estates of the late Koryŏ
and early Yi dynasties), *Seikyū gakusō* (Korean studies quarterly), No. 17:1-80
(August 1934); Yi Sang-baek, *Han'guk sa: kŭnse chŏn'gi p'yŏn* (A history of
Korea: Early pre-modern part; Seoul, 1962), pp. 344-410. For a general study of
the Yi land system, see Pak Si-hyŏng, *Chosŏn t'oji chedo sa* (Studies on the
Korean land system; P'yŏngyang, 1961), vol. 2.

2.   The *kongsin* system originated in China and was imported into Korea presumably
     during the Silla period. It was used widely during the Koryŏ and Yi dynasties.
     Those who performed special services for the state or the dynasty—for instance,
     in helping to found the dynasty, to enthrone a king, or to suppress internal
     rebellion—were given the title of *kongsin*. During the Yi period *kongsin* were
     usually divided into three or four classes, each endowed with various privileges.
     For a brief account of the Yi *kongsin*, see *Kuksa taesajŏn* (A dictionary of Korean
     history; Seoul, 1962-1963), I, 137-138.

3.   Under the 1391 reform the small properties of the local yangban apparently were
     not expropriated by the state. See *Koryŏsa, 78:39b.* A discussion of the merit-
     subjects in the fifteenth century can be found in Edward W. Wagner, "The
     Literati Purges," unpublished Ph.D. thesis (Harvard 1959).

4.   See, for instance, *T'aejong sillok* (The annals of King T'aejong), 22:21ff; 24:25b;
     Chŏngjong sillok, 1:4b; *Sejong sillok,* 39:14, 32b.

5.   For calculations of the size of the *tu,* see Pak Si-hyŏng, II, 402-404.

6.   *T'aejong sillok,* 3:7bff.

7.   Another record puts the total *kongsinjŏn* at 21,200 *kyŏl,* ibid., 5:26ff.

8.   This figure is based upon information in ibid., 4:10.

9.   The most regular recipients of special award land were the official members of
     Korean missions to the Ming court. The awards usually ranged from ten to sixty
     kyŏl. See, for example, *Sejo sillok* (The annals of King Sejo), 3:13b.

10. *T'aejong sillok,* 7:14bff.

11. Ibid.

12. It seems that further grants in home provinces were temporarily stopped because some official circles protested. See *T'aejo sillok* (The annals of King T'aejo), 7:7b-8.

13. *T'aejong sillok,* 34:6. See also ibid., 18:5; 28:13b-14, 15b; 31:36, 40b-41; 34: 3ff., 9b, 26b. In 1431 the *kwajŏn, kongsinjŏn,* and *pyŏlsajŏn* were ordered to be retransferred to Kyŏnggi (see *Sejong sillok,* 51:11). It is unlikely, however, that this order was ever implemented.

14. By 1449 (thirty-two years after the transfer of the *kwajŏn*) almost half of the land in the three southern provinces was reportedly taken up by estates of government officials. See ibid., 124:2b. Two *sillok* records dated 1456 and 1457 also show how landholdings of government officials had spread. See *Sejo sillok,* 3:21b-22b; 7:16b-18.

15. Under the *tunjŏn* system each magistracy was given six to ten *kyŏl of* land. See *Sejong sillok,* 26:3b; 32:18; 35:15b. The colonies were usually cultivated by slaves and poor peasants. In theory the income from the colonies was to finance the local governments and postal stations. Beside the local governments, military garrisons and postal stations also had their colonies. Furthermore, there were *tunjŏn* directly run by the state. For further information, see *Kyŏngguk taejŏn* (The great code of administration; Keijo, 1934), 2:8b-9; *MHBG,* 145:2b-20; Pak Si-hyŏng, II, 49-60.

16. *Sejong sillok,* 109:4b.

17. This figure includes gifts to certain palace employees such as eunuchs. See *Tanjong sillok,* 8:17a-b, 21b-22; 9:4b-5b, 9b, 37b-38; *Sejo sillok,* 2:18a-b, 20b-21, 37a-b; 3:13b, 21b-22b; 6:25-26; 43:44b, 61-63b, 64; 44:10a-b, 21a-b, 46b; *Yejong sillok,* 1:43a-b; 2:17b; 5:28b-49; *Sŏngjong sillok,* 9:35b-36; 11:15b-16, 18; and *Chungjong sillok,* 1:11-12, 12b-13, 16, 17b, 18b, 19a-b; 4:4. The 360 new merit subjects included those who were later removed from the *kongsin* list and those who received the *kongsin* title more than once.

18. *MHBG,* 43:15-19b.

19. The maximum was later reduced to 225 *kyŏl.* See *Sejong sillok,* 31:10b; 76:6b; 88:3; 91:4; *Kyŏngguk taejŏn,* 2:9.

20.   In 1458 the amount of *tunjŏn* for magistracies was raised from the previous
      range of six to ten to twelve to twenty *kyŏl*. In 1460 the amount of *tunjŏn* for
      garrisons was standardized, ranging from ten to twenty *kyŏl*. See *Sejo sillok*,
      13:37; 19:12. It seems that by 1466 state colonies were also founded through-
      out the country. See ibid., 23:2; 40:21; Pak Si-hyŏng, II, 58-60.

21.   This figure is based upon *MHBG*, 189:1-11.

22.   *Sejo sillok*, 39:34b.

23.   There is no official record indicating when this system was abolished. It probably
      died out naturally not long after 1512, for prior to this year memorials were
      frequently presented asking that the issue of office land be curtailed. After 1512
      few such memorials appeared. See *Sŏngjong sillok*, 165:5, 10;166:1; 169:3a-b;
      Chungjong sillok, 16:34a-b. The shortage of *chikchŏn* seems to have risen quite
      a bit earlier. According to a memorial by the Department of Revenue in 1477,
      the government was short by 975 *kyŏl* in granting service land to provincial
      governors, provincial military and naval commanders, and other high-ranking
      provincial officials. See *Sŏngjong sillok*, 84:27.

24.   Princely estates were established for both the living and the important deceased
      members of the royal house, such as sons and daughters and mothers of kings.
      If the estates were for deceased members, they financed the maintenance of the
      tombs and memorial services. The landholdings of the members of the royal
      house either belonged to them and were tax-exempt, or were lands on which
      they, not the government, had the sole right to collect taxes. For a more detailed
      study, see *Tochi seido chizei seido chōsa hōkokusho* (Reports on the land and
      tax system; Keijo, 1920), pp. 119-184. Thirty thousand *kyŏl* is a rough estimate
      based upon the Pibyŏnsa record for 1860. See *PBTN*, 247:476-482. The *sillok*
      gives almost unlimited information on the development and dreadful abuses of
      the palace estates. See for example, *Injo sillok*, 1:6, 15; 2:4b; 3:31, 37b-38; 8:3;
      11:42; 12:10b-11; 18:59b; 19:56; 20:1; 36:24b; *Hyojong sillok*, 2:40; *Hyŏnjong
      sillok*, 1:46b; 2:20; 3:1-2, 13, 18, 43b; 4:42b, 46b; 5:24, 26, 31, 34, 37, 42b, 44-
      45, 48-49; 6:1-2, 6b, 9b, 11, 23; 7:23, 25, 34-35, 42-44; 8:21b; 11:18; 15:7b;
      22:2b; 30:34b; *Sukchong sillok*, 12:15, 25, 33; 13a:19b; 14a:36; 19:11b, 40b,
      41, 42; 22:14; 34a:37; 34b:24; 37:7, 9, 14, 16, 32. See also *Man'gi yoram
      chaeyong p'yŏn* (Guide to royal administration: section on finance; Keijo, 1937),
      pp. 243-268; *PBTN*, 247:476-482.

25.   Most of the colonies were owned by various offices of the central government
      and military outfits located in the Seoul area. These colonies were usually
      founded with wasteland and land grants from the state which financed them. But

like the palace estates, they rapidly expanded by encroaching upon other fields. See *MHBG*, 144:2b-20; *Sŏnjo sillok*,55:30b; 57:33; 63:20-21; 72:4b; 120:15; 127:33b-34; *Injo sillok*, 11:3b; 12:11; 27:16b; *Hyŏnjong sillok*, 3:36b-37, 42b; 7:35, 42b; 9:31, 36; 18:31; 20:33b; 21:17b; *Sukchong sillok*, 5:42; 6:10-11, 26-27, 31-33; 7:24, 25; 9:1, 48b-49; 13a:14-15; 14a:5b-6, 36; 14b:27; 15a:49; *Kyŏngjong sillok*, 13:15.

26. *Hyŏnjong sillok*, 6:17b.

27. Most of these palace estates charged double the official rate. See *Sukchong sillok*, 27:25a-b, 47b.

28. Ibid., 47:33b-34; *MHBG*, 144:10b-11, 13; 145:3-15b.

29. See *Man'gi yoram chaeyong p'yŏn*, pp. 202, 239-274.

30. *Koryŏsa*, 80:20-23; *T'aejong sillok*, 2:5b; *MHBG*, 166:1-3; *Richō jidai no zaisei* (A study of Yi finance; Keijo, 1936), p. 323; *Sejong sillok*, 86:29b. For general information on the grain-loan system, see *Shakanmai seido* (Studies on the grain-loan system; Keijo, 1933).

31. In 1458 it was first established in Ch'ungch'ŏng. See *Sejo sillok*, 12:9b-10. See also *MHBG*, 166:3b; *Richō jidai no zaisei*, p. 323.

32. This office was established on an *ad hoc* basis whenever relief was undertaken on a large scale. According to available records, it was established in 1516, 1541, and 1661. See *Chungjong sillok*, 26:36; 67:2b-3, 10b; 95:28, 42, 48, 57; *Hyŏnjong sillok*, 6:10b. See also *MHBG*, 222:1, which treats the later development of this office.

33. In 1807 some 561 such funds were recorded. Nearly ten million *sŏk* of grain was handled. See Pak Si-hyŏng p. 346; *Man'gi yoram chaeyong p'yŏn*, pp. 773-837. For more detailed explanation of each grain-loan fund, see *Shakanmai seido*.

34. For general rules on the actual operation of the grain-loan system, see *Man'gi yoram chaeyong p'yŏn*, pp. 455-459; *Sok taejŏn* (Supplementary great code; Keijo, 1938), *kwŏn* 2: part on finances, section on granaries *(ch'anggo)*.

35. *Richō jidai no zaisei*, pp. 329-366; *MHBG*, 167:1-7b.

36. For further references on these problems, see *Chŏngjo sillok*, 4:58b; 10:56bff.; 25:51; 48:27, 32; 52:25ff; *Sunjo sillok*, 6:46; 13:15b; 14:11b-32; 20:19b; *ISN*, Chŏngjo 10.1.22, 12.5.25, 14.3.10, 18.12.26, 23.5.11; *PBTN*, 199:40b, 133;

205:542, 939bff.; *MHBG*, 167:11-14, 17-22; Chŏng Yag-yong, *Kyŏngse yup'yo, kwŏn 7:* On the land system *(chŏnje);* Chŏng Wŏn-yong, *Kyŏngsan chip* (Collected works; 1895), 9:15b-17, 29-30, 40b-42.

37. In spite of the almost unlimited source material, few satisfactory studies have been made so far on this important system. The present work is merely a brief sketch of some salient features of the development of the system. For additional references, see Tagawa Kōzō, *Richō kōnōsei no kenkyū* (A study on the tribute system of the Ri dynasty; Tokyo, 1964), pp. 637-729; Ch'a Mun-sŏp, "Imnan ihu ŭi yangyŏk kwa kyunyŏkpŏp ŭi sŏngnip" (On the *ryang-yeok* and *gyun-yeok* assize in the late Yi dynasty), *Sahak yŏn'gu* (The study of history), No. 10:115-130 (April 1961), No. 11:83-146 (July 1961); Yi Sang-baek, *Han'guk sa: kŭnse chŏn'gi p'yŏn*, pp. 228-234, 412-424; Yi Sang-baek, *Han'guk sa: Kŭnse hugi p'yŏn* (A history of Korea: Later pre-modern part; Seoul, 1965), pp. 209-240; *Richō jidai no zaisei*, pp. 197-198, 246-270; Pak Si-hyŏng, II, 256-269, 356-366.

38. For the earlier relationship of regulars and reserves, see for instance, *T'aejo sillok*, 11:3; *T'aejong sillok*, 7:21b-22; *Sejong sillok*, 18:19b; *Sejo sillok*, 14:17b; 34:34ff.; *Kyŏngguk taejŏn*, 4:63.

39. Professional and semi-professional soldiers served much longer periods. See ibid., 4:33b-47; *Chungjong sillok*, 22:36.

40. *Kyŏngguk taejŏn*, 4:63b; *Yejong sillok*, 4:29bff. Often the reserves were charged far more than two *p'il*. See *Richō jidai no zaisei*, p. 198. At this time one *p'il* was 35 *ch'ŏk*. One *ch'ŏk* of cloth was around one foot long and 0.7 foot wide. *MHBG*, 160:4.

41. *MHBG*, 160:5b-6; *Taejŏn husongnok* (Late supplement to the great code; Keijo, 1935), 4:16.

42. For commentaries on the development of this military tax, see *MHBG*, 160:3; *Man'gi yoram chaeyong p'yŏn*, p. 365; Yu Hyŏng-wŏn, *Pan'gye surok* (Collected works; reprint, Seoul, 1958), 21:30ff.

43. *Hyŏnjong sillok*, 20:51b; *Sukchong sillok*, 38a:2-3; *Sŏnjo sillok*, 61:14. The military garrisons around Seoul, known as *oyŏng* ("five military camps"), were established after the war with Japan. For details, see *Man'gi yoram kunjŏng p'yŏn*. (Guide to royal administration, military section; Keijo, 1937).

44. For further reference, see ibid.

45. For instance, see *Sukchong sillok,* 50b:35; 62:2; *Yŏngjo sillok,* 4:15; 38:25b; 45:19b; 71:23; *MHBG,* 109:16b; Cho Ik, *P'ojŏ chip* (Collected works), in *Chōsen fūzoku kankei shiryō satsuyō* (A compendium of source materials on Korean manners and customs; Keijo, 1944), *kwŏn* 15, pp. 1716-17; Yu Kye, *Sinam chip* (Collected works), in ibid., *kwŏn* 14, p. 1696; Yi Kŏn-myŏng, *Hanp'ojae chip* (Posthumous works), in ibid., *kwŏn* 7, p. 1875; Yi Pyŏng-sŏng, *Sunam sŏnsaeng munjip* (Collected works), in ibid., *kwŏn* 13, p. 1864.

46. The records on this terrible practice are too many to cite. See, for instance, *Injo sillok,* 14:42b-43. (The military register of a small Chŏlla district included sixteen children between the ages of three and ten); *Hyojong sillok,* 21:12; *Sukchong sillok,* 36:15; 5:26; 6:63b-65; see also Yi I, *Yulgok chŏnsŏ* (Collected works), *kwŏn* 15; *Man'gi yoram chaeyong p'yŏn,* p. 366.

47. Ibid., pp. 365-373; *Yŏngjo sillok,* 75:7b-10; *MHBG,* 156:6b-11, 16b-17.

48. The composition of the total number of households in six provinces, exclusive of P'yŏngan and Hamgyŏng, is given as follows: 720,000 with only one male adult per household *(chan tokho);* 520,000 households of yangban, officials, clerks, couriers, Buddhist monks; and 100,000 peasant households with more than one adult of military age per household. See *Yŏngjo sillok,* 75:7b-8. For an interpretation of *chan tokho,* see ibid., 71:25b; Pak Si-hyŏng, p. 257.

49. According to various sources one *kyŏl* seems to have been the normal average tilled by one household throughout the eighteenth and nineteenth centuries when the population remained around 7 million. In many localities, however, the average holding ranged between 0.5 and 0.6 *kyŏl* (less than two acres). See, for example, *P'yŏngsan kunji* (The P'yŏngsan gazetteer), comp. Ku Haeng, rev. and enlarged ed. (1802), 1:5b-6b; *Yŏngch'ŏn chŏnji* (The Yŏngch'ŏn gazetteer), new and enlarged ed. (1940), 1:5-7. According to the *Yŏngjo sillok* cited above the average income of a household did not exceed ten *sŏk.* This sum seems low to me. See also *Yŏngjo sillok,* 75:7b-8.

50. *Man'gi yoram chaeyong p'yŏn,* pp. 373, 417-418; *PBTN,* 236:62, 64; 241:638; 243:856.

II. *Reformist Thought in Yi Korea*

1. The term *sirhak (shih-hsüeh),* which may have derived from the words *shih-shih-ch'iu-shih* of the *Han-shu,* seems to have been first used by men like Yi Che-hyŏn (1287-1367), a scholar-official of the Koryŏ, and Kwŏn Kŭn (1352-1409), one

of the original supporters of King T'aejo. They used *sirhak* as a slogan for promoting the study of the Confucian classics as opposed to poetry and prose. The
later reformers, however, used the term to refer to the study of practical subjects
such as economics, government, agriculture, mathematics, and archaeology. See
Ch'ien Han-shu (History of the early Han dynasty), 53:1; Han U-gǔn, "Yijo
sirhak ǔi kaenyǒm e tae hayǒ" (On the concept of the Sirhak in the Yi dynasty),
Chindan hakpo (Journal of the Chindan Society), 19:27-46 (May 1958). For a
general study on the Sirhak, see *Chosǒn t'ongsa* (A general history of Korea),
comp. Kwahagwǒn yǒksa yǒn'guso (Institute of History of the Academy of
Sciences), new ed. (P'yǒngyang, 1962), pp. 677-687, 737-752; Chǒng Chin-sǒk
et al., *Chosǒn ch'ǒrhak sa* (A history of Korean philosophy; P'yǒngyang, 1962),
I, 189-271.

2. Ch'ien Mu, *Chung-kuo chin-san-pai-nien hsüeh-shu shih* (Chinese intellectual
    history in the last three hundred years; Taiwan, 1957), I, 19; Ku Yen-wu,
    Jih-chih lu (Notes on the daily accumulation of knowledge), comp. and anno-
    tated by Huang Ju-ch'eng (Hupeh, 1872),7:6b; *Hu Shih wen-ts'un san-chi*
    (Collected works of Hu Shih; Shanghai, 1930), 3:53-54.

3. Pak Che-ga was the first to urge Korea to learn from the Manchus; he coined the
    work *pukhak* (learning from the north). Other reformers used such slogans as
    "puguk kangbyǒng" (Enrich the nation and strengthen the military) and *"iyong
    husaeng"* (Utility and the enhancement of livelihood).

4. Hwang Hyǒn, *Maech'ǒn yarok* (Collected works), Han'guk saryo ch'ongsǒ, No.
    1 (Seoul, 1955), p. 6.

5. Kim's collected works contain a few of his letters to the Taewǒn'gun; unfortu-
    nately, they are mainly concerned with personal matters and painting. See Kim
    Chǒng-hǔi, *Wandang sǒnsaeng chǒnjip* (Collected works; 1934), 1:25b-26b;
    2:29-30b.

6. Pak Kyu-su, *Hwanjae chip* (Collected works; 1911), preface, pp. 2a-b; 1:9b;
    4:25b.

7. Ibid., preface, p. 3; Kikuchi Kenjō, *Taiinkun den tsuki ōhi no isshō* (A biography
    of the Taewǒn'gun and the life of the queen; Keijo, 1910), pp. 19-24.

8. *ISN*, 4.4.29.

9. For details, see Yu Hyǒng-wǒn, *Pan'gye surok* (Collected works; repr. Seoul,
    1958), 1:1-57.

10.   Ibid., 1:3a-b, 8b, 11, 44-45, 55a-b.

11.   Yi Ik, *Sŏngho saesŏl* (Collected works; Seoul, 1929), 4b:20.

12.   Ibid., 3a:19; 4b:34.

13.   Hyŏn Sang-yun, *Chosŏn yuhak sa* (A history of Korean Confucianism; Seoul, 1954), p. 346; Pak Chi-wŏn, *Yŏnam chip* (Collected works; Seoul, 1932), 17: 59-64b.

14.   *Yŏ (lü* in Chinese) designated a village consisting of twenty-five households in the Chou period. The significant feature of this system was the communal (village) ownership of land. For details, see Chŏng Yag-yong, *Yŏyudang chŏnsŏ* (Collected works; Seoul, 1934), *chip* 1, 16:3-6b. For further studies on Chŏng, see Kim Kwang-jin, *Chŏng Tasan ŭi kyŏngje sasang* (A study on the economic thought of Chŏng Yag-yong; P'yŏngyang, 1962); Hong I-sŏp, *Chŏng Yag-yong ŭi chŏngch'i kyŏngje sasang yŏn'gu* (A study on the politico-economic thought of Chŏng Yag-yong), Han'guk yŏn'gu ch'ongsŏ, No. 3 (Seoul, 1959); *Chŏng Tasan* (A collection of studies on Chŏng Yag-yong in commemoration of the two hundredth anniversary of his birth), comp. Kwahagwŏn ch'ŏrhak yŏn'guso (Institute of Philosophy of the Academy of Sciences; P'yŏngyang, 1962).

15.   For his proposals concerning the grain-loan and the stabilization granaries, see Yu Hyŏng-wŏn, 3:49b-55.

16.   For his views on the village granary system, see ibid., 3:55b-56b.

17.   Ibid., 1:22-24; 2:3-8b; 21:29b-34b; 26:2-3.

18.   Ibid., 10:26b-28b.

19.   Ibid., 10:15-18.

20.   Yi Ik, 3b:43.

21.   Ibid., 3b:22; 4a:40; 3b:52; 8b:22; Han U-gŭn, "Sŏngho Yi Ik yŏn'gu ŭi iltan: kŭ ŭi kwagŏje sibi rŭl chungsim hayŏ" (A study on Yi Ik with emphasis on his criticism of the civil service examination), *Yŏksa hakpo* (Journal of history), 7:326-350 (1954); Han U-gŭn, "Sŏngho Yi Ik yŏn'gu: kŭ ŭi saron kwa pungdang non" (A study on Yi Ik: His views on history and factionalism), *Sahoe kwahak* (Social science journal), 1:33-52 (1957).

22.   Yi Ik, 4a:43.

23.   Hong Tae-yong, "Imha kyŏng yun," in his *Tamhŏnsŏ* (Collected works; Seoul, 1939).

24.   For his criticism of the examination system, see Pak Che-ga, *Pukhak ŭi* (Discourse on "northern learning"; 1821), 2:8, 14, 29b. Also see Kim Yong-dŏk, "Chŏngyu Pak Che-ga yŏn'gu" (A study on Pak Che-ga), *Sahak yŏn'gu* (The study of history), 10:8-10 (1961).

25.   For his essays on government organization, see Yu Hyŏng-wŏn, *kwŏn* 15-16.

26.   Ibid., 15:46b; 16:1b-22.

27.   Ibid., 16:3b-4b.

28.   Ibid., 19:1-3.

29.   Yi Ik, 4b:39-40.

30.   Pak Chi-wŏn, *Yŏrha ilgi* (Diary of Jehol; reprint, Taiwan, 1956), 3:7a-b.

31.   Ibid., 21:3-7b; *Kukcho inmulchi* (Eminent Koreans of the Yi dynasty; 1909), III, 158-160.

32.   Pak Che-ga, 1:30b-31b.

33.   Ibid., 1:32; 2:30b.

34.   Ibid., 2:19-20.

35.   Chŏng Yag-yong, *Yŏyudang chŏnsŏ, chip* 1, 11:11a-b.

36.   Ibid., 11:10b-12.

37.   Ibid.

III. *Social Unrest On the Eve of the Taewŏn'gun's Rise to Power*

1.   For various opinions on the corruption of provincial and local governments, see *Kukcho pogam* (The comprehensive history of the Yi dynasty; 1909), 87:7bff.; *kwŏn* 88-89; 90:8b-9.

2. *Ch'ŏlchong sillok,* 3:3a-b, 4b; *CS,* ser. 6, vol. 3, p. 302.

3. In January 1856 Right Councillor Pak Hoe-su memorialized that in choosing officials the qualifications of the candidates were never considered, and that it was the fashion to say that so-and-so had been so poor that he should be given a "district," or that so-and-so had been obscure and therefore had to be given a "district." See *Kukcho pogam,* 88:18b-19.

4. *ISN,* Ch'ŏlchong 9.1.2, 9.12.4; *CS,* ser. 6, vol. 3, pp. 517, 543.

5. Ibid., p. 601.

6. This biographical note is based on *Chōsen no ruiji shūkyō* (Pseudo-religions of Korea), Chōsen sōtokufu chōsa shiryō, no. 42 (Keijo: Chōsen sōtokufu, 1935), pp. 18-22; *PBTN,* 250:120-122b; *KS,* 1:9b-11 *(ch'ongsŏ),* 23b-25b. For other versions of Ch'oe's biography, see Shinobu Jumpei, *Kan hantō* (The Korean peninsula; Tokyo, 1901), pp. 72-74; Yoshikawa Buntarō, *Chōsen no shūkyō* (Religions of Korea; Keijo, 1921), pp. 307-312; Matsushita Yoshio, *Nisshin senyō zengo* (Before and after the Sino-Japanese war, 1894-1895; Tokyo, 1939), p. 43; Tabohashi Kiyoshi, *Nisshin sen'eki gaikō shi no kenkyū* (A diplomatic history of the Sino-Japanese war, 1894-1895), Tōyō Bunko ronsō, no. 32 (Tokyo, 1951), p. 49; and Yi Pyŏng-do, *Tugye chapp'il* (Essays; Seoul, 1956), pp. 82-86. See also Yi Ton-hwa, *Ch'ŏndo 'gyo ch'anggŏn rok* (A history of the founding of the Tonghak; Keijo, 1934).

7. It has been popularly believed that Ch'oe's name as a child and as an adult was Pok-sul. According to Kim Mun-gyŏng, however, this was not the name Ch'oe himself used. Unsympathetic people called him that to insult him, for Pok-sul has the meaning of "fortune-teller." His original name was Che-sŏn. At the age of thirty-five Ch'oe changed it to Che-u; the new name means "save the ignorant." The change in name paralleled an important change in his personal ambition—from a selfish or personal motive to a greater, social motive, the salvation of the poor. See Kim Mun-gyŏng, "Yongdam yusa" (The posthumous poems of Ch'oe Che-u), *Seikyū gakusō* (Korean studies quarterly), no. 7:128, 134 (February 1932).

8. These feelings are vividly expressed in many of his poems with social and religious themes. For an annotated Japanese translation of these poems, see ibid., 7:123-139, 8:145-165 (May 1932). See also, *Tonggyŏng taejŏn pu yongdam yusa* (The scripture of the Tonghak and the posthumous poems of Ch'oe Che-u; Seoul, 1955).

9. According to the official Tonghak view, Ch'oe then resolved to discover a common truth in Confucianism, Buddhism, and Taoism so that he could found a new syncretic religion. See *Tonghak kyŏngŭi* (An interpretation of the Tonghak tenets), ed. Pak Chŏng-dong (Seoul, 1914), 1:52-53.

10. It is commonly said that the book was on Taoism or Taoist-Buddhism. See Yi Pyŏng-do, p. 83; Yoshikawa, p. 309.

11. For Ch'oe's attitude toward Catholicism and its Korean converts, see Kim Mun-gyŏng, 8:151; also *KS*, 1:23bff., 27.

12. For the official Tonghak account of Ch'oe's "communication," see *Tonghak kyŏngŭi*, 1:15-19b; also Yi Pyŏng-do, p. 79; Charles A. Clark, *Religions of Old Korea* (New York, 1932), p. 260.

13. For further study of Tonghak doctrine and its religious practices, see Ching Young Choe, "The Decade of the Taewŏn'gun," Ph.D. thesis (Harvard University, 1960), Pt. 1, pp. 70-85.

14. Kim Mun-gyŏng, 7:129; 8:150.

15. Ibid.

16. Ibid., 8:161, 163.

17. The poor and lowly would not automatically become rich and rise to high posts. They would have to have some good deed to their credit, either performed by themselves (such as becoming Tonghak men) or by their ancestors. In Ch'oe's case, he believed that his divine mandate was the result of the "deeds accumulated by his ancestors." See ibid., 7:128-129; 8:160-161, 163; and *Tonghak kyŏngŭi*, 1:14b, 36a-b.

18. Kim Mun-gyŏng, 8:163.

19. *KS*, 1:9b-10b, 11.

20. *Ch'ŏlchong sillok*, 14:2a-b; *PBTN*, 249:753b-754, 756b-757b. For detailed accounts of the peasant uprisings in Chinju and other areas, see *Imsullok* (Collected documents concerning the uprisings of 1862), Han'guk saryo ch'ongsŏ, No. 8 (Seoul, 1958).

21. *ISN*, Ch'ŏlchong 13.3.25; *PBTN*, 249:761b-762.

22. *Ch'ŏlchong sillok,* 14:4b; *CS,* ser. 6, vol. 3, p. 632.

23. *Ch'ŏlchong sillok,* 14:5b; *PBTN,* 249:781b.

24. *Ch'ŏlchong sillok,* 14:5b; *PBTN,* 249:784b.

25. *PBTN,* 249:789.

26. *Ch'ŏlchong sillok,* 14:6b-7; *PBTN,* 249:792b.

27. *Ch'ŏlchong sillok,* 14:6, 7, 10a-b, 20b; *PBTN,* 249:787-788, 794-795, 820b-821, 884-885.

28. Most of those sentenced to banishment were released by September 1863. See *Ch'ŏlchong sillok,* 15:9.

29. The localities which apparently suffered most from the grain system were Tansŏng, a small district in Kyŏngsang with 1,000 households, and Chŏngyangjin, a tiny garrison settlement in Kyŏngsang with 100 households. The former was indebted to the government in the amount of 90,000 *sŏk* of grain, while the latter owed the government more than 108,900 *sŏk.* See ibid., 14:8; *CS,* ser. 6, vol. 3, pp. 630-640.

30. *Ch'ŏlchong sillok,* 14:9.

31. Ibid. For the official (selected) record of this committee, see *Imsullok,* pp. 297-362.

32. *Ch'ŏlchong sillok,* 14:9a-b, 12b.

33. Ibid., 14:11b-12.

34. Ibid., 14:13b-14; *Kyŏngguk taejŏn,* 1:58b-63b; *Sok taejŏn,* 1:24b-28b; 4:21-22.

35. *Ch'ŏlchong sillok,* 14:17b, 18b; *Imsullok,* pp. 322, 324.

36. For the details of their arguments, see *Ch'ŏlchong sillok,* 14:18a-b; Chŏng Wŏn-yong, *Kyŏngsan chip* (Collected works; 1895), *kwŏn* 1: appendix; *CS,* ser. 6, vol. 3, pp. 660-661.

37. *Ch'ŏlchong sillok,* 14:18b; *CS,* ser. 6, vol. 3, p. 661.

38. *PBTN*, 249:854b.

39. *Ch'ŏlchong sillok*, 14:20.

40. Ibid., 15:10.

41. *ISN*, Ch'ŏlchong, 14.12.4; *PBTN*, 250:115b.

IV. *The Taewŏn'gun and Economic Reconstruction*

1. Ikchong (Munjo) was the temple name of Sunjo's son, Yi Yŏng, who was desig-
    nated heir to the throne in 1812 and took over certain of his father's functions
    in 1827. He died before Sunjo, however, and after his son Hŏnjong succeeded to
    the throne he was posthumously elevated to the status of king and his wife to
    that of queen.

2. *Ch'ŏlchong sillok*, 15:13; *KS*, 1:1. According to the "order of generation" Yi
    Myŏng-bok was one degree lower than Munjo. In fact, Yi was adopted as Munjo's
    son.

3. *KS*, 1:1, 2b, 3. There are several reasons why Yi Myŏng-bok was chosen to
    succeed King Ch'ŏlchong. Neither the Andong Kim nor the P'ungyang Cho
    had a suitable male heir. Since the Cho clan was relatively weak, Dowager Cho
    may have preferred a child king to secure her own regency. Moreover, the
    Andong Kim may have considered their position at court as secure enough to
    tolerate the choice of a boy whose father had hitherto been rather obscure.

4. Hwang Hyŏn, p. 2; Tabohashi Kiyoshi, *Kindai Nissen kankei no kenkyū* (A
    study of modern Korean-Japanese relations; Keijo, 1940), I, 23-25. Also Hosoi
    Hajime, *Koku taikō no manajiri* (A biography of the Taewŏn'gun; Tokyo,
    1929), pp. 50-51.

5. *ISN*, 3.2.13.

6. *KS*, 1:27b, 28.

7. For the edict of October 7, 1864, see *KS*, 1:76b.

8. *KS*, 1:79, 83; 2:13.

9. *KS*, 2:12, 22.

10.   *KS,* 2:24b, 25. For other provinces, see *KS,* 1:77; 2:14b, 44b; 3:52b.

11.   *KS,* 4:21a-b, 28a-b, 32b-33, 41a-b; 5:45a-b, 46b-49, 50b-51, 54a-b, 55b-56.

12.   *KS,* 4:30b-31, 33b-34, 43a-b; 8:47.

13.   *KS,* 4:21b, 33.

14.   *KS,* 1:10, 11a-b, 12b, 51b-52; 2:18a-b, 47, 50; 3:43, 50, 96; 4:10b, 17; 7:17; 8:40a-b, 53b.

15.   *KS,* 10:6a-b.

16.   *KS,* 1:18b-19; 3:32a-b, 33a-b, 55; 6:32a-b; 7:6b-7.

17.   Four districts completed the survey; they recovered a total of some 1,700 *kyŏl* of land. See *KS,* 6:11b, 36b; 7:35b; 8:56b.

18.   The figure of 30,000 *kyŏl* is a rough estimate based upon the Pibyŏnsa record of 1860. See *PBTN,* 247:476-482. See also Pak Si-hyŏng, II, 302. The total amount of palace land in 1864 was 34,999 *kyŏl.*

19.   The *tojang* were the general managers of the palace estates. Their primary function was to collect and deliver rents and taxes to their respective owners. Although the post was hereditary, it was openly sold. The *tojang* had the right to change the tenants. It is easy to see the evils inherent in this system. For instance, the *tojang* could and did extort more rent or tax than the sum officially stipulated. Unfortunately, this system was widely adopted by other absentee landlords. See Moritani Katsumi, "Kyūrai no Chōsen nōgyō shakai ni tsuite no kenkyū no tame ni" (A study of the agrarian society of old Korea), *Chōsen shakai keizai shi kenkyū* (Studies of the socio-economic history of Korea; Tokyo, 1933), pp. 504-505; Ōuchi Takeji, "Richō makki no nōson" (Agrarian villages in the late Yi dynasty), ibid., pp. 227-295; *KS,* 1:34. The tax agents, commonly called *kyŏngch'ain,* who were sent into the provinces to collect taxes for certain government agencies, thereby circumventing the local governments, were also abolished. See *KS,* 1:45b-46; 4:42b; 6:22a-b; 9:28.

20.   *KS,* 1:2, 18, 21b, 34, 53b-54.

21.   *KS,* 2:34b; 3:49, 52b; 5:21b, 22; 7:2a-b; 8:67; 9:31b.

22.   The "village tax" *(tongp'o)* system seems to have been introduced between 1866 and 1867. See *KS,* 3:33a-b; 4:23, 41b, 43a-b; *PBTN,* 251:186b.

23. *KS*, 8:21; 9:38a-b; *MHBG*, 156:17b; *PBTN*, 253:444b; 254:612b-613. When the *hop'o* was first introduced, commoners fulfilled their share by active military service.

24. Earlier, P'yŏngan had been allowed to use the military grain as capital; no specific allocation of funds was made at this time for Hamgyŏng. See *KS*, 3:30b-31.

25. *KS*, 4:27b-28.

26. *KS*, 7:34b; 9:38b; 10:4b.

27. It seems that the price of rice during this period was three *yang* per *sŏk*. The legal interest on grain loans was 10 per cent of the original loan. See *KS*, 9:39-40.

28. For the general rules of the *sach'ang* and related documents, see *KS*, 4:28b-29, 29b-30; *MHBG*, 167:33-34; *Richō jidai no zaisei*, p. 369.

29. *KS*, 4:14; 10:3b.

30. *KS*, 4:19; 5:45; 8:56.

31. *KS*, 8:35. Besides the *p'oryangmi*, another surtax on land, commonly called *kyŏltujŏn*, was introduced on November 19, 1868. The exact nature of this tax is not clear; it seems to have been a temporary emergency measure issued to meet the financial problems caused by the construction of the Kyŏngbok palace. The tax seems to have been one *yang* per *kyŏl*, or perhaps more. See Yi Nŭng-hwa, *Chosŏn kidokkyo kŭp oegyo sa* (A history of Christianity and diplomacy in Korea; Seoul, 1928), pt.2, p. 5; Chŏng Kyo, *Taehan kyenyŏn sa* (A chronological record of the latter part of the Yi dynasty), Han'guk saryo ch'ongsŏ, no. 5 (Seoul, 1957), 1:1; *KS*, 5:45.

32. *KS*, 3:44, 87; 7:15b; *PBTN*, 251:278.

33. For the traditional policy on the taxation of the fishing and salt industries, see *Kyŏngguk taejŏn*, 2:14; *Sok taejŏn*, 2:12b-13; Chŏng To-jŏn, *Sambong chip* (Collected works), Han'guk saryo ch'ongsŏ, no. 13 (Seoul, 1961), pp. 217-218; *MHBG*, 158:1b-24; *Man'gi yoram chaeyong p'yŏn*, pp. 381-404; *Yŏngjo sillok*, 75:9; *Chŏngjo sillok*, 36:57-58; and *ISN*, Chŏngjo, 10.1.22, 10.10.4, 16.11.25, 16.12.24, 23.6.22. See also *PBTN*, 236:55b-56; *Imsullok*, pp. 309-310.

34. *KS*, 1:10b-11; 3:87; 4:14; 8:6b; *PBTN*, 251:277b-278; *Richō jidai no zaisei*,
    p. 299. Once before the export quota had reached some 40,000 *kŭn*, but the
    tax had been much lower. For detailed regulations, see *PBTN*, 234:836-837;
    238:321b-323b.

35. *KS*, 8:6b. At times, the number of commissioned merchants *(p'osam pyŏlchang)*
    seems to have been much lower. See *PBTN*, 238:322.

36. Coin money was used briefly during the reigns of Sejong (r. 1418-1450) and
    Sejo (r. 1455-1468). During the reign of Injo (r. 1623-1649) coin money called
    sangp'yŏng t'ongbo was introduced in 1633, but soon fell into disuse. During
    the reign of Hyojong (r. 1649-1659) efforts were made to put it back into
    circulation without much success. In 1678 the minting of the *sangp'yŏng
    t'ongbo* was resumed; from then until the time of the Taewŏn'gun it was the
    only coin circulated in Korea. *MHBG*, 159:6-9.

37. For instance, in 1829 it cost the government 533,600 *yang* to mint 730,360
    yang. See *MHBG*, 150:20b.

38. *Ch'ŏlchong sillok*, 4:6; *PBTN*, 242:842; *CS*, ser. 6, vol. 3, pp. 461, 513.

39. *KS*, 3:85b; *PBTN*, 251:271b.

40. *KS*, 3:88b; 4:24; *PBTN*, 251:278-282b.

41. *KS*, 3:93; *PBTN*, 251:294b.

42. *ISN*, 4.3.2; *KS*, 4:14b.

43. *ISN*, 4.6.3; *KS*, 4:27b-28. The peasants refused to use the new coin; see *Imsullok*,
    pp. 290-291.

44. *KS*, 5:6b-7.

45. *KS*, 11:5b, 7.

46. *ISN*, 2.+5.10; *KS*, 2:29; *MHBG*, 131:15b-16; Yi Nŭng-hwa, 2:11; Pak Ŭn-sik,
    Han'guk t'ongsa (A tragic history of Korea; Hansŏng, 1946), p. 5.

47. *KS*, 9:40, 10:7b-8; *PBTN*, 255:640.

48. *PBTN*, 256:735.

49. *Richō jidai no zaisei*, p. 374.

V. *The Taewŏn'gun and Government Reform*

1. The Supreme Council was renamed the Ŭijŏngbu on April 30, 1400. The Board
    of Civil Affairs was incorporated into the new council of state on August 22,
    1401. See *Chŏngjong sillok*, 4:5; *T'aejong sillok*, 2:1b. For the establishment of
    the Ŭijŏngbu and related matters see Suematsu Yasukazu, "Chōsen Giseifu kō"
    (A study on the council of state of Yi Korea), *Chōsen gakuhō*, no. 9:1-35 (1956);
    Asō Takekame, "Richō no kenkoku to seiken no suii" (The founding of the Yi
    dynasty and change in political power), *Seikyū gakusō*, no. 5:118-134 (August
    1931).

2. For the traditional structure of the Ŭijŏngbu, see *Kyŏngguk taejŏn*, 1:7-9b;
    4:18; 5:19b-20.

3. Ibid., 1:7.

4. Ibid., 1:65; 3:32b, 39b; 5:3. The Ŭijŏngbu was given these specific powers:
    (1) together with the senior members of the six administrative departments and
    the members of the Inspectorate and Censorate, it was entitled to recommend
    candidates for the offices of provincial governor and military commander; (2) it
    was allowed to participate in the inspection of diplomatic papers carried by
    missions to the court of China, and it was given complete control over the
    appointment of attendants to officials associated with the missions; (3) no legis-
    lation of new laws or revision of old laws could be undertaken without consult-
    ing the council; and (4) the Department of Punishment was not authorized to
    enter upon trial of criminal cases subject to capital punishment until the council
    was notified.

5. Compare the provisions given above with the following powers and rights, given
    to the council and its predecessors by royal decrees between 1392 and 1404:
    (1) supervisory power over all civil officials; (2) the right to remonstrate the
    throne; (3) veto power in the appointment of officials; (4) the right to transmit
    official communications from government departments to the throne; (5) the
    right to discuss memorials presented by the censoring bodies in the presence of
    the throne; (6) the right to issue permits to use troops; (7) the right to discuss the
    revision of the criminal code; (8) the right to approve new laws legislated by
    other departments; and (9) the right to enact new laws subject, of course, to
    royal approval. See *T'aejong sillok*, 8:4b-8b, 11b-15, 25b, 26.

6. King T'aejong attempted to curtail the power of the council after 1405, but he did not succeed. See ibid., 9:1b, 7; 15:2, 26:52.

7. Ibid., 27:24-25. The censoring bodies shared King T'aejong's views and even suggested the abolition of the council.

8. *Sejong sillok,* 72:3. Under the new decree the government operated as follows: When a department wished to carry out a program it would submit the plan to the council for examination and approval. If the council approved, the program was submitted to the throne for royal sanction. If the king approved the program he sent it back to the council and the council then authorized the said department to put the program into effect.

9. *Sejo sillok,* 2:2b.

10. *Chungjong sillok,* 25:41b. For the interesting debates which led to the restoration of *sŏsa* power, see ibid., 24:49b-51; 25:1a-b. The weakening of the council did not have much effect on the working of the government as long as strong kings like T'aejong and Sejo were on the throne. If the ruling monarch was weak, however, his power could be abused by ambitious members of the royal family or by government offices that were close to the sovereign. For instance, the power of the Censorate grew rapidly when the *sŏsa* power of the Ŭijŏngbu was abolished after Sejo's reign. The tragic political events known as *sahwa* (literati purges) may be attributed largely to the growth of the Censorate's power. See Edward W. Wagner, "The Literati Purges," Ph.D. thesis (Harvard University, 1959).

11. *T'aejo sillok,* 1:46a-b. The duties of the Department of War were largely related to personnel matters such as the selection and appointment of officers and the administration of the military register. The Chungch'uwŏn was in charge of weapons, military units, defense, and troop movements. The early Board of Military Command also acted as royal secretariat, a function later transferred to the Royal Secretariat (Sŭngjŏngwŏn). See ibid., 1:16b.

12. The Ŭihŭng samgunbu established in 1393 succeeded the older Samgun toch'ongjebu, which King T'aejo had organized in the last years of the Koryŏ. Each of the three corps in the new army had military jurisdiction over a number of regions in addition to guard duty about the capital. Each corps consisted of three or four divisions, and each division was in turn subdivided into five units. Besides this centralized army, there were private armies under the control of provincial military commanders. The private armies were dissolved and integrated into the royal army, the Samgun, in 1400. For the internal organization of the royal army, see ibid., 1:46a-b; 4:7b; 5:12-14; 7:4.

13. *Chŏngjong sillok,* 4:5.

14. In 1404 T'aejong subordinated the Samgunbu to the Ŭijŏngbu whose power was still intact. In 1405 the Samgunbu was completely absorbed into the Department of War. In 1409, to avoid the growing concentration of military power in a single department, T'aejong restored the Samgunbu under a different name, and placed it under the direct surveillance of the king. This situation lasted until 1422, when T'aejong died. Although T'aejong abdicated in 1418, the army had remained under his control. *T'aejong sillok,* 2:1b; 8:11b; 9:1b-2; 14:48; 16:31b, 36b; 18:11a-b, 16b, 39a-b, 40; 36:20a-b; *Sejong sillok,* 1:19b-20.

15. Ibid., 55:24.

16. The general organization of the new system was as follows: Each corps consisted of five divisions, and each division was divided into four sections. Besides the regular army *(chŏnggun),* each division commanded five units of a kind of partisan army known as the *yugun.* The provinces and the capital were divided into five military districts, each assigned to one of the five corps, which had headquarters located in the capital. For further information on the new military organization, see *Munjong sillok,* 8:2-3, 5b-8, 16b-23; *Man'gi yoram kunjŏng p'yŏn,* pp. 1-30.

17. *Sejo sillok,* 38:7.

18. The Chungch'uwŏn (the degenerated form of which, the Chungch'ubu, I call the Board of Officials-without-Portfolio) lost the power to carry out its old function from this time on and became an office to which officials of high rank were appointed as a face-saving gesture on being removed from active duty, or when no appropriate portfolio was available. Because of its historical origin, however, the Chungch'uwŏn remained in the military class *(sŏban)* instead of the civil class *(tongban)* of government offices. In 1466 it was re-named Chungch'ubu.

19. Officials without active posts who were not eligible for appointment to the Chungch'uwŏn were given military titles and were assigned to this office.

20. It is difficult to determine whether the Pibyŏnsa existed prior to 1517. The *Sillok* merely shows that the name was used for the first time in 1510. The office was abolished for a short time, probably between 1518 and 1520. See *Chungjong sillok,* 11:5b-7; 39:39. Also, Shigeyoshi Manji, "Bihenshi no setchi ni tsukite" (On the establishment of the Pibyŏnsa), *Seikyū gakusō,* no. 23:23-81 (February 1936).

21. All three state councillors soon held concurrent appointments as commissioners. See *Chungjong sillok*, 28:65; 29:1, 8, 12a-b, 13b.

22. *Myŏngjong sillok*, 14:55b; 18:60; 24:72b. These recommendations were presented to the throne either at the command of the king issued through his secretariat, or on the Pibyŏnsa's initiative, or occasionally in joint memorials with the department concerned.

23. *Chungjong sillok*, 45:22a-23, 36b-37, 51b-53, 55b-56b, 57a-b; 61:25b-26b, 27, 33-34; 95:61b; *Myŏngjong sillok*, 14:55b, 70; 16:10b-11; 18:45b-47, 49a-b, 60; 19:28b; 21:18b; 22:55-57b; 23:23b; 24:11b-12b, 24b-25, 25b, 72b; 25:21, 35b-36, 67b-69; 29:16b, 18, 40-41; *Sŏnjo sillok*, 7:9b-10, 10b-11b, 25, 26; 9: 20b, 22b; 17:4a-b, 7b, 9a-b, 10, 13b; 21:2a-b, 3b-4; 23:5a-b.

24. Ibid., 7:25; 9:20b; 17:9a-b, 10; 21:2a-b, 3b-4; 23:5a-b. See also *CS*, ser. 4, vol. 9, pp. 243, 246. As a result of the Pibyŏnsa's growing powers, civil magistrates of important districts in the southwestern regions were replaced by military men at the Pibyŏnsa's request. A policy of social mobility was initiated and maintained for the first time on a grand scale. Slaves and sons of concubines were permitted to leave their class, provided they pay a given amount of grain or join the army, and criminals could be pardoned on the same conditions. See *Sŏnjo sillok*, 17:7b, 13b.

25. For the internal organization of the Pibyŏnsa, see *Man'gi yoram kunjŏng p'yŏn*, pp. 102-104. In the course of changing the internal structure of the Pibyŏnsa former state councillors were added to the ruling body as commissioners. An unlimited number of officials whose rank was above the senior 3A grade, and who were conversant with frontier and coastal affairs, might sit as deputy commissioners (holding either single or concurrent appointment). The ministers of appointment, finance, rites, and war, and the magistrate of Kanghwa also received concurrent appointments as deputy commissioners. Three of the deputy commissioners were especially appointed *yusa tangsanggwan* (senior executive officers); most official business was conducted by these executive officers. They were assisted by a body of twelve administrative secretaries—four civil officials and eight military men.

26. In 1592 the post of *pujejo* (assistant commissioner) was created and reserved for civil officials who held the rank of senior 3A grade and who had mastered the arts of frontier and coastal defense. The number of senior executive officers was increased to four. The number of deputy commissioners was increased radically with the inclusion of the commanders of the five military regiments (Hullyŏndogam, Ch'ongsulch'ŏng, Suŏch'ong, Ŏyŏngch'ŏng, and Kŭmwiyŏng)

established between 1594 and 1682 and located around the capital, the magistrate of Kaesŏng, Kwangju, and Suwŏn, the chief academician of the Academy of Literature (Hongmun'gwan), and the ministers of punishment and works.

27. For instance, it directly administered matters related to tributes, markets (in Seoul), grain transportation by sea, and water conservation. For various aspects of the Pibyŏnsa's power and functions, see *Man'gi yoram kunjŏng p'yŏn*, pp. 104, 108-123; *Sok taejŏn*, 1:29; *MHBG*, 199:4b-34b; *Hyŏnjong sillok*, 4:35; *Sukchong sillok*, 53:25b; *Yŏngjo sillok*, 29:26a-b, 35b-36, 42; 32:18; 37:9b; and later volumes of *PBTN*.

28. These posts were: magistrates of Kaesŏng, Suwŏn, Kwangju, Kanghwa, Ŭiju, Tongnae, and Cheju (Kanggye and Hoeryŏng were later included), governors and military commanders of P'yŏngan and Hamgyŏng; the *t'ongjesa* (naval commander-in-chief) of the southern provinces, the ministers of appointment, war and revenue; commanders of the five military regiments, and almost all the *ad hoc* officials who were assigned special duties such as secret investigation, pacification of local disturbances, and administration of relief goods. In addition, Pibyŏnsa members had the privilege of recommending candidates for many other important posts. Their recommendations carried more weight than those by other officials. See *Man'gi yoram kunjŏng p'yŏn*, pp. 108-113; *Sok taejŏn*, 1:29.

In connection with recommendation practices, a brief explanation of the procedure of appointing officials may be needed. Generally, candidates for the post of councillor and department head were recommended by the remaining councillors or councillor and then appointed by the king. On the other hand, candidates for minor positions were recommended by officials who held a given rank; these candidates received formal appointment through a variety of procedures. For example, to fill a minor post (i.e. junior 4 grade and below) a number of candidates had to be recommended (by qualified officials) to the Department of Appointment, or, in the case of military posts, to the Department of War. The department then chose three candidates and presented their names to the throne for final selection. This process may be loosely called *ŭimang*. Next, the department sent the names of the appointee, his father, his paternal and maternal grandfathers, and his great-grandfather to the Inspectorate and Censorate for investigation. If the appointee passed this investigation successfully, the censoring bodies would jointly notify the department that the appointee was qualified for the post. This process is sometimes known as *sŏgyŏng*. Lastly, the appointee received from the department the official writ or warrant of appointment called *kosin* or *chikch'ŏp*, signed by the members of the department. For general rules on recommendation and appointment, see *Kyŏngguk taejŏn*, 1:65-66; *Sok taejŏn*, 1:29-31; *MHBG*, kwŏn 193-196. For more on the Pibyŏnsa's powers of appointment and recommendation, see *MHBG*, 199:4b-34b.

29. In addition to the Kim family, which had provided queens for Sunjo, Hŏnjong, and Ch'ŏlchong, the in-law group consisted of relatives of Sunjo's mother (the Pak family with their clan seat at Pannam), relatives of Munjo's consort (the Cho family of P'ungyang), and those of Hŏnjong's second consort (the Hong family of Namyang). The composition of the Pibyŏnsa is given at the beginning of the entries of each month in the *PBTN*.

30. *KS*, 1:7b, 19a-b. Editor's note: The author obviously interprets royal edicts as commands from the Taewŏn'gun. This, to be sure, cannot be evidenced from the documents. The edicts were issued by either Dowager Regent Cho or King Kojong. This is true for the following chapters as well.

31. *KS*, 1:20. For instance, royal trips, royal tombs and shrines, ceremonies, sacrifices, diplomatic missions, audiences, service examinations, tributes, flood and drought control, schools, seals, population, land, taxation, grain-loan, markets, relief, storage, grain transportation, change of residence, water conservation, *corvée* labor, appointment of officials, crimes, prohibition, finance, the fishing and salt industries, and payment of salaries. For details, see *KS*, 1:20.

32. In the classification of Yi officials, *tangsang* usually refers to officials of senior 3A grade and above. The head of a department was customarily excluded from this category and was addressed with a title signifying "head." In the case of the Pibyŏnsa, all members, except the commissioners, were known as *tangsang*.

33. *KS*, 2:14b, 15b.

34. It seems that the title *kongsagwan* did not come into use until 1870. See *PBTN*, 252:358b-359, 364, 368b-369.

35. In the absence of the senior councillors, the four junior councillors and other members of the committee were made to act according to their ranks. See *KS*, 5:21b.

36. *KS*, 8:20a-b, 43, 53; *MHBG*, 216:12b, 28-29.

37. The post of *kŏmsang*, which had been abolished for some time, was restored on August 21, 1868. See *KS*, 5:32.

38. Ibid.

39. *KS*, 2:25b.

40. *KS*, 5:9a-b.

41. These were: the posts of military commander of the northern and southern
    sections of Hamgyŏng, military commander of P'yŏngan, naval commander of
    the left section of Kyŏngsang, commander of the Chinmu regiment in Kanghwa,
    t'ongjesa of the southern provinces, and magistrates of Hoeryŏng, Cheju, and
    Kanggye. See *KS*, 5:32b; 7:29; *PBTN*, 252:387b.

42. *KS*, 5:26.

43. *KS*, 5:9a-b, 26a-b. In addition to this body the Samgunbu had what could be
    called a supervisory board. It consisted of a number of directors, all of whom
    were present or former state councillors, and three assistant directors *(chejo)*–
    the minister of war and the two metropolitan police commanders. See *KS*, 5:26;
    6:13b; 5:27b; 8:43; *PBTN*, 253:476b; *MHBG*, 216:22.

44. The Chinmu regiment was first established in 1700, primarily to defend Kanghwa
    Island. For detailed accounts of the reorganization, see *PBTN*, 251:272a-b, 277b,
    287-289.

45. *PBTN*, 251:299b-300.

46. *KS*, 8:5, 7, 8b, 9, 13b, 14, 15b, 18, 24, 24b, 26b, 27b-28, 30b-31, 39, 39b, 42,
    46b, 50b-51b, 54b-55, 60b-61, 65; 9:3b-4, 15, 20b, 27b, 29b, 36b, 46; 10:6b,
    13, 17b, 19b, 23.

47. He urged this in a memorial in March 1867. He also proposed the establishment
    of a fortification system which would be supported by a militia. The system
    was to have the inhabitants of the coastal districts build their own defense
    fortresses, and introduce the old five-household system as a basic defense unit.
    The text of his memorial may be found in *KS*, 4:5-10b. See also *KS*, 4:8a-b;

48. The weapon depots in Taegu, the capital of Kyŏngsang, were said to have been
    locked up for nearly sixty years. See Yi Ch'am-hyŏn, "Chongsan chipch'o,"
    Imsullok, p. 287.

49. *KS*, 4:25b, 36.

50. *KS*, 4:40.

51. Apparently Kang Yun had been in charge of manufacturing weapons at the
    Hullyŏn regiment. See *KS*, 10:12b; see also Yi Nŭng-hwa, 2:123-124.

52. *KS*, 10:2b.

53. *KS,* 4:5-6, 9a-b.

VI. *The Taewŏn'gun and the Officialdom*

1. The recruiting system, including the examinations and recommendations, is extensively treated in the sections on appointments and rites of the *Kyŏngguk taejŏn, Sok taejŏn,* and *Taejŏn t'ongp'yŏn* (Comprehensive code of administration; Keijo, 1937). The most revealing criticism of the degeneration of the recruiting system can be found in two memorials: one was submitted to King Sunjo in 1804 by Right Councillor Yi Kyŏng-il, who said that the front yards of the officials in charge of appointments had become "trading markets"; the other was submitted in 1815 by Chief Councillor Kim Chae-ch'an, who attacked the influence of the in-laws on appointments. See *PBTN,* 195:669b-770; *Sunjo sillok,* 18:9b-10.

2. The origins of factionalism in Yi Korea can probably be traced back to the *sahwa* (literati purges). Factionalism first began as a struggle between two groups of officials, and became "institutionalized" political strife in the latter part of the sixteenth century. After many subdivisions and realignments four factions remained in 1683: the Noron, Soron, Namin, and Pugin. The Pugin and Namin were out of power from 1623 and 1694, respectively. For a study of the literati purges, see Wagner. For an outline of the history of factional strife, see Yi Kŏn-ch'ang, *Tangŭi t'ongnyak* (A general history of factional strife; Seoul, 1948); Shidehara Hiroshi, *Kankoku seisō shi* (A history of Korean factional strife; Tokyo, 1907); Oda Shōgo, "Richō seisō ryaku shi" (An outline history of political strife in the Yi dynasty), *Chōsen shi kōza, bunrui shi* (Selected articles on Korean history; Keijo, 1924).

3. *PBTN,* 234:796b-797.

4. *PBTN,* 244:73b-74b.

5. *PBTN,* 251:136-137b.

6. *PBTN,* 255:621b-623.

7. *PBTN,* 239:415; 241:727; 244:65b; 245:227; 247:493; 249:734b.

8. *PBTN,* 232:571; 234:780b; 238:308b; 240:592; 242:810a-b; 245:255; 246:387, 431b; 247:448b; *KS,* 1:1, 35; 3:26b.

9. *PBTN*, 235:928b; 240:617; 245:184, 304, 311b; *KS*, 1:36b; 2:10.

10. *PBTN*, 233:726; 237:109, 153b, 162b; 238:271b; 245:280; 246:311b; 247:494; 248:611b, 732; 249:912; *KS*, 1:36b; 2:10; 5:21, 22b.

11. *PBTN*, 235:927; 236:58; 246:327b; 248:665b; 249:881b; *KS*, 5:21, 22b.

12. *PBTN*, 240:566a-b, 575b; 244:88b, 109b, 117, 124b, 155; 245:195b, 213b, 255b; 246:315b, 431b; 249:849b; *KS*, 1:13, 15b, 74; 2:11; 4:16b, 17, 24a-b, 25, 26; 5:21, 22b; *CS*, ser. 6, vol. 4, p. 510.

13. *Ch'ŏlchong sillok*, 10:6b; *PBTN*, 250:81; 247:473b, 517b; *KS*, 1:90b; 2:51b; 3:1-2; 4:26; *CS*, ser. 6, vol. 4, p. 390.

14. *PBTN*, 247:500b; *KS*, 1:9; 3:28b, 41, 95b; 4:35b; 6:4, 4b; 9:32a-b, 34b-35, 35b-36, 37b-40.

15. *PBTN*, 226:47; 228:266b; 229:366; 234:799; 240:575b; 247:565b, 571b; 249:770b, 851b; *KS*, 1:34b; 2:36; 3:31, 35b, 54; 4:24; 5:8, 37; 6:10, 12b; 8:4b; 9:32b, 36b-37.

16. *PBTN*, 238:285b; 244:63b; 250:24b; *KS*, 2:29; 3:93b; 4:20, 31b; 7:3b-4, 16b; 8:21a-b; 9:32a-b, 33b; *CS*, ser. 6, vol. 4, p. 480.

17. For specific cases, see *PBTN*, 251:192a-b; 252:316-320b, 326b-327b, 386b-387b; *KS*, 1:10, 46, 85; 2:34a-b; 3:34b-35; 5:8a-b, 13b, 60; 7:6b, 8b, 9b, 12, 18b, 22b; 8:20a-b, 39, 44, 53; 10:10b. For examples of recommendations which were made by the ruling members of the Pibyŏnsa, but which were seldom effected, see *PBTN*, 252:354a-b, 360b-361, 366a-b, 401b; 253:412a-b, 503b; 254:532, 550b-551, 591b, 593a-b, 605a-b, 619a-b; 255:624a-b.

18. For an interesting critique on the traditional rules on promotion, see the memorial presented to King Sunjo by Ki Hak-kyŏng on September 21, 1802 (*PBTN*, 193:481). In this memorial Ki urged that officials be promoted according to their ability, without going through the conventional order of promotions.

19. The most prominent of those who had held high positions were Kang Si-yŏng (Pugin; once minister of rites), Im T'ae-yŏng (Pugin; commander of the Kŭmwi regiment), Im Paeng-nŭng (Pugin; royal secretary), Hŏ Kye (Namin; commander of the Kŭmwi regiment), and Yi Ŭi-ik (Namin; magistrate of Kanghwa). Since their appointments were changed frequently, see *PBTN*, ch'aek 236-249 for the composition of the Pibyŏnsa and appointments.

20. Yi Chung-hwan, *T'aengni chi* (A geography of Korea; Seoul, 1912), p. 8. During the early days of the Yi dynasty a number of people from the Northwest obtained prominent positions. Their descendants, however, resided in Seoul and never returned to the north. See ibid., p. 9.

21. Tagawa Kōzō, "Kindai Hokusen nōson shakai to ryūmin mondai" (The agrarian society of northern Korea in the modern era and the problems of migration), *Kindai Chōsen shi kenkyū* (Studies in modern Korean history; Keijo, 1944), p. 420.

22. See *Kyŏngguk taejŏn*, 3:2-4b for the examination quotas.

23. Tagawa, "Kindai Hokusen nōson shakai to ryūmin mondai," pp. 418-419.

24. Yi Chung-hwan, pp. 6-7.

25. The Yŏ P'il-hŭi incident illustrates the traditional ill will between the northerners and the southern yangban. In November 1714 a number of students from P'yŏngan came to Seoul to take the lower civil service examination. During the examination a proctor named Yŏ P'il-hŭi called the P'yŏngan students "barbarians" and "beasts." As a result, the students returned home without finishing the examination. See *Sukchong sillok*, 55:34b.

26. *Hŏnjong sillok*, 3:2a-b.

27. For specific measures introduced to bring the northerners into the government, see *Injo sillok*, 10:23b; 28:59; *Sukchong sillok*, 16:23b-24; 17:63; 33:39; 36:10a-b; 38:24b-25, 54; 39:65a-b; *Yŏngjo sillok*, 30:5b-6; *Chŏngjo sillok*, 1:60a-b; 11:74b-75; 12:56b-57b; 13:41b-42b; and *Sunjo sillok*, 16:9b-10b; 18:10b-11; 27:33b.

28. *Sukchong sillok*, 17:21b-22.

29. For a study of the Hong Kyŏng-nae uprising, see Oda Shōgo, "Kō Kei-rai hanran no gairyaku to sono dōki ni tsuite" (A general description of the Hong Kyŏng-nae rebellion and its motives), *Seikyū gakusō*, no. 8:1-18 (May 1932); no. 11:88-107 (February 1933).

30. The text of the proclamation can be found in *Sunjo sillok*, 14:59b-60 and *CS*, ser. 6, vol. 1, pp. 383-384.

31. It is almost impossible to ascertain how many people from the northwest held

government posts after 1812. One record shows that one man was appointed a royal secretary *(u pusŭngji)*. See *Hŏnjong sillok*, 3:2a-b, 4a-b.

32. *KS*, 1:44b.

33. *KS*, 1:71b-72.

34. Yi Chung-hwan, pp. 40-41.

35. *KS*, 3:73.

36. *KS*, 6:10a-b, 18.

37. *KS*, 7:15.

38. *KS*, 8:65.

39. *KS*, 9:7b.

40. *KS*, 9:8.

41. *KS*, 9:9a-b; *PBTN*, 254:616.

42. *KS*, 4:52; 9:20b-21, 26, 28; *PBTN*, 254:563, 574a-b; and *Chōsen jimmei jisho* (Korean biographical dictionary; Keijo, 1937), *kukcho pangmok* (examination roster).

43. Hwang Hyŏn, p. 14; *KS*, 6:3b-4.

44. *ISN*, 9.3.19; *KS*, 4:4; 9:9.

45. *KS*, 9:7b, 9.

46. On July 5, 1872, Chief Councillor Kim Pyŏng-hak complained that clerks had been taking the examinations in violation of the old law. He proposed that no clerk in active clerical service be allowed to take the examination. See *KS*, 9:17b.

47. Ma Haeng-il, a magistrate, and Cho Nŭng-jo, the son of a Chŏngju clerk, who became a liaison officer *(sŏnjŏn'gwan)*, are outstanding examples. See *KS*, 9:20b.

48. It appears that some of these clerks were assigned to various government departments, provincial headquarters, and the royal palace to work as the personal

agents of the Taewŏn'gun. See Yi Nŭng-hwa, pp. 6-7; Hosoi, pp. 90-91; *Imsullok*, p. 273.

49.   *KS*, 3:89b. Another recorded case was that of Cho Chŏng-jo, whose mother was a public female slave. Cho became superintendent of a postal district. *KS*, 9:20b.

50.   *KS*, 1:9.

51.   *KS*, 4:13, 46; 5:33; 9:5b, 26b. See also Ŏ Yun-jung, *Chongjŏng yŏnp'yo* (Chronology of political events), Han'guk saryo ch'ongsŏ, no. 6 (Seoul, 1958), 1:1, 25, 27. All of the men mentioned in this paragraph, however, were of yangban origin.

VII. *The Consolidation of the Royal House*

1.   The "royal family" here includes those persons closely related to a reigning king by blood, members of close branch houses, and sons-in-law of the king and their immediate descendants.

2.   *Kyŏngguk taejŏn*, 1:2-7; *Sok taejŏn*, 1:1. For the early system of ennoblement, see *T'aejong sillok*, 22:43b-44; 23:31b, 37b.

3.   Ibid., 27:7. For the later elaborated organization of this council, see *Sŏngjong sillok*, 4:30b; *Kyŏngguk taejŏn*, 1:7-9b; *MHBG*, 217:2-4b.

4.   The Ŭibinbu was called the Pumabu until 1466. *Sejo sillok*, 38:4b.

5.   *Kyŏngguk taejŏn*, 1:7-8b; *MHBG*, 217:4b-5.

6.   *MHBG*, 222:14b-16.

7.   *MHBG*, 222:17a-b. The school ceased to exist, probably from 1514 on.

8.   *Sŏngjong sillok*, 10:17b; 34:6-7b; *MHBG*, 186:12b. A similar action against sons-in-law of kings was taken in 1400. *MHBG*, 186:15.

9.   For a roster of individual cases, see *MHBG*, 43:14b-23b.

10.   *KS*, 1:43a-b, 2:9a-b, 36a-b; 6:4b-6b; *MHBG*, 216:4b-6; *Taejŏn hoet'ong*, pp. 7-8. There were also some minor changes in the organization of the two other councils. See *KS*, 6:6b.

11. *KS*, 6:1-2; *ISN*, 6.1.2.

12. Yi Se-bo was the adopted heir of Prince P'unggye. For criticizing two of
     Ch'ŏlchong's in-laws, Kim Mun-gŭn and Kim Chwa-gŭn, on December 15, 1860,
     he was stripped of his rank and title, severed from the house of the prince and
     banished to a southern island. *Ch'ŏlchong sillok*, 12:8b; *ISN*, 0.12.20; *KS*, 1:9.
     Lady Sŏ was the wife of Yi Ha-jŏn, a descendant of Chungjong (1506-1544).
     Ha-jŏn, who had been considered a likely successor to Ch'ŏlchong, was suddenly
     charged on August 13, 1862 with plotting usurpation, and subsequently banished
     to Cheju. On September 4 he was ordered to commit suicide. Then four days
     later his mother and wife were sent into exile on Kŏje island. *Ch'ŏlchong sillok*,
     14:14b-16, 16-17; *KS*, 1:22b.

13. *KS*, 1:50b, 51a-b, 56b-57, 61b-62, 62b, 63.

14. *KS*, 1:68, 70, 74a-b; 9:27a-b, 37b.

15. For instance, see *ISN*, 9.11.29, 9.12.3; *KS*, 9:37b.

16. *KS*, 1:46, 56b; 2:2a-b; 4:10b; 5:9; 6:3; 7:10b, 14; 8:5, 19; 9:2b; 10:5, 11b.
     The special examinations were called *chongch'inkwa* (the examination for the
     royal clansmen) or *sŏnp'a ŭngje* (the special examination for the royal clansmen).

17. *ISN*, 2.9.10, 2.10.12, 10.2.12; *KS*, 2:46, 51; 10:5a-b.

18. *KS*, 5:33a-b. Previously, illegitimate granddaughters were appointed to junior
     second grade and legitimate ones to senior second grade. *Kyŏngguk taejŏn*, 1:2b.

19. *KS*, 7:37a-b, 38a-b, 39a-b.

20. *KS*, 1:44, 45b; 8:5, 18b, 19; *ISN*, 1.4.21, 8.1.15, 8.3.30; *MHBG*, 216:4b, 6.

21. For a general description of the palace, see *Keijō-fu shi* (A history of Seoul;
     Keijo, 1934-1941), I, 45-52; *Sinjŭng Tongguk yŏji sŭngnam* (The new and en-
     larged gazetteer of Korea; Keijo, 1930), I, 13ff.

22. *Keijō-fu shi*, I, 45; *Kukcho pogam*, 1:19b-20; and *Sinjŭng Tongguk yŏji sŭngnam*,
     I, 13.

23. *KS*, 2:15b-16, 16b, 17b-18; *Keijō-fu shi*, I, 453-454.

24. *KS*, 2:20b-21, 23b; 3:72b; *ISN*, 2.5.12, 3.10.1.

25. The king moved to the new palace on August 19, 1868, before its completion. *KS*, 5:29b.

26. *KS*, 9:29b; *ISN*, 9.9.15, 9.9.16.

27. *ISN*, 2.5.5.

28. *Keijō-fu shi*, I, 466.

VIII. *The Taewŏn'gun's Cultural Policies*

1. The rise of the *sŏwŏn* was closely related to the influence of Chu Hsi's teaching on the literati class of the late fifteenth and early sixteenth centuries, and the decline of the traditional educational system. The *sŏwŏn* were first introduced in Korea in 1543 by an enthusiastic patron of Neo-Confucianism, Chu Se-bung, as a means of promoting education. For a study of the early *sŏwŏn* system, see Yu Hong-nyŏl, "Chōsen ni okeru shoin no seiritsu" (On the establishment of *sŏwŏn* in Korea), *Seikyū gakusō*, no. 29:24-90 (August 1937); no. 30:63-116 (October 1939). The decline of the early educational system based upon the public schools may be attributed to the anti-Confucian and anti-literati policy of Sejo (1455-1468) and Yŏnsan-gun (1495-1506). See Yu Hong-nyŏl, "Raimatsu Sensho no shigaku" (Private schools in late Koryŏ and early Yi Korea), ibid., no. 24:97-100 (May 1936). For the date of the first name-grant *sŏwŏn*, see *Chukkye chi* (The recordings of the Sosu Academy), comp. Chu Se-bung (1863), *ponsŏ* (original preface). The name was formally granted in 1550. See *MHBG*, 210:1a-b.

2. The *sŏwŏn* resembled the Sŏnggyun'gwan in Seoul, the major difference being that the Sŏnggyun'gwan was a national institution and the *sŏwŏn* were not.

3. The majority of the academies were dedicated to more than one patron-hero, and it was not uncommon for one person to be enshrined at several academies. See *MHBG*, *kwŏn* 211-213.

4. The administrative personnel generally consisted of a president *(wŏnjang)*, two executive secretaries *(yusa)*, and two treasurers *(chŏn'gok)*.

5. All figures appearing in this study are based upon *MHBG*, *kwŏn* 211-213.

6. *Injo sillok*, 45:41a-b.

7. *Sukchong sillok,* 6:29a-b.

8. *Hyojong sillok,* 19:29a-b.

9. *Sukchong sillok,* 6:29a-b.

10. Ibid., 7:40; 10:28a-b; 20:46a-b; 22:25b-26; 36:25a-b.

11. Hwang Hyŏn, 1:5; *CS,* ser.6, vol. 3, p. 533, 629; *Chŏngjo sillok,* 38:26b; *Hŏnjong sillok,* 12:7b; *PBTN,* 245:258; 249:761b. For a more detailed study of traditional criticism of the academies, see *MHBG,* 210:4b-26b.

12. *Yŏngjo sillok,* 47:38a-b.

13. During Yŏngjo's reign some effort was made to curtail the construction of the *sŏwŏn.* In 1741 some 300 miscellaneous local shrines were reportedly destroyed. *MHBG,* 210:18b-19.

14. *KS,* 1:45b. The majority of the "attached people" usually settled outside the *sŏwŏn* area; they paid taxes or were called up when their labor was needed.

15. *KS,* 1:54b.

16. *KS,* 1:68.

17. *KS,* 1:72-73.

18. *KS,* 2:15a-b. The name plate of the shrine and the tablets were transferred to Hwangdan in Seoul, which was the government shrine for the two emperors as well as for T'ai-tsung. For a detailed account of the Mandongmyo, which was built in Hwayang-dong, Ch'ungch'ŏng, by the disciples of Song Si-yŏl, see *Sukchong sillok,* 39:2b-5b; *Yŏngjo sillok,* 62:12b; *Chŏngjo sillok,* 1:22b-24; *Hwayang chi* (Recordings of the Hwayang Academy; 1807) with a preface by Song Chu-sang.

19. *KS,* 2:27a-b, 38b, 57a-b; *Chonhwa rok* (Records of the Revere-China School), comp. Song Pyŏng-jik (1900), 3:31b-34.

20. *KS,* 5:40a-b.

21. *KS,* 7:23b-24.

22. *KS*, 8:15. The criteria for the screening were somewhat changed on May 7. Only the *sŏwŏn* dedicated to worthies enshrined at the State Confucian Shrine (Munmyo) and to men of exceptional loyalty, virtue, and principle were allowed to remain, one *sŏwŏn* for each man. *KS*, 8:17b-18.

23. *KS*, 8:13b.

24. *KS*, 8:16a-b.

25. *KS*, 8:18b-19.

26. For the edict of September 30, 1871, see *KS*, 8:49b.

27. This figure and the following one are the results of my own calculations. *MHBG* lists some 700 *sŏwŏn* and shrines, a number which seems to be too low. An investigation of a number of local gazetteers available at present shows that the average number of *sŏwŏn* and shrines was probably no less than ten per district. This means that in approximately 310 districts in the country there were some 3,000 *sŏwŏn* and shrines. Some districts had as many as forty *sŏwŏn*. As for the figure 100,000, it is based upon the assumption that the average number of students and "attached people" per *sŏwŏn* or shrine ranged between thirty and thirty-five. The majority of the *sŏwŏn* were officially eligible to keep as many as sixty or seventy men. In actuality they far exceeded that number. The local shrines may have had a smaller number. See, for instance, the sections on *sŏwŏn* and shrines in *Yŏngju kunji* (Gazetteer of Yŏngju; 1957); *P'yŏngsan kunji* (Gazetteer of P'yŏngsan; 1802); *Kangdo chi* (Gazetteer of Kanghwa; 1932); *Koksŏng kunji* (Gazetteer of Koksŏng; 1918); *Kyonam chi* (Gazetteer of Kyŏngsang; 1940); and *Pukkwan ŭpchi* (Gazetteer of North Hamgyŏng; 1871).

28. The lack of source material makes it impossible to determine the actual average amount of land held by the *sŏwŏn* and the local shrines. It is very probable that they owned as much as ten *kyŏl* and as little as one *kyŏl*.

29. In the edict of September 30, 1871, the Taewŏn'gun suggested for the first time that the students study at the local Confucian shrines. *KS*, 8:49b.

30. *KS*, 3:43b-44.

31. *KS*, 6:24a-b; 8:13b.

32. For the text of the reform plan, see *KS*, 6:26b-28.

33. For the general rules of the various examinations, see *Taejŏn hoet'ong* (New comprehensive code of administration; Keijo, 1912), *kwŏn* 3: examinations.

34. The *Ta-Ming lü* was used as a supplement to this section.

35. The dates given here indicate completion of compilation rather than publication.

36. During the reign of King Sunjo (1800-1834), two monumental works called the *Man'gi yoram* (Guide to royal administration) had been published. The *Yoram* was divided into the financial section and the military section. The financial section consisted of six chapters dealing with various economic institutions and their operations. The military section dealt with general military organization and the operation of each military unit.

37. *ISN*, 2.3.16, 2.9.25; *KS*, 2:13b, 48a-b, 57b; Maema Kyōsaku, *Kosen sappu* (Bibliographical notes on old Korean works; Tokyo, 1957), III, 1299.

38. The term *samban* refers to the three classes that constitute the principal body of Yi officialdom: the *tongban* (civil class), the *sŏban* (military class), and the *ŭmban* (favorite class).

39. *ISN*, 2.9.26, 2.11.30; *KS*, 2:49a-b, 57b; Maema, III, 1928.

40. *ISN*, 2.12.17; 4.5.16, 4.5.17; *KS*, 2:58b, 59; 4:25b-26; Maema, III, 2023-24.

41. *Samban yesik* (Rules of etiquette for the three classes), comp. Yi Ha-ŭng (1866), 11:4b. The following are typical rules of conduct included in this work: "The secret inspector *(ŏsa)* and the provincial governor shall treat each other as equals . . . without observing any special ceremony. A *yŏngjang* (commander of a military base) . . . shall refer to himself as *hagwan* (inferior officer) [in speaking] to the inspector. The inspector shall receive the officer sitting, and treat him cordially."

42. *KS*, 7:13b-14, 27; 10:14b, 21a-b; Maema, II, 832-833.

43. In addition to these codes, several other significant works were published: a supplementary volume to the *Chŭngjŏng kyorinji*, a revised and enlarged history of Korean-Japanese relations, was brought out in 1864; the *Tongmun hwigo* was revised in 1864 and 1871; the *Hongmun'gwan chi* (Records of the Academy of Literature) was revised and enlarged in 1870; the *Sŏnwŏn sokpo* (Supplement to the Register of the Royal Clan) was revised; the *Chongbu chorye* (Regulations of the Council of the Royal House) was codified; and the *Kinyŏn aram*, written

in 1777 by Yi Man-un, which treated the important historical events of China and Korea from ancient times and which also contained valuable geographical notes on Korea, was supplemented. See *KS*, 1:43b, 86b; 8:14; 9:13a-b, 15; *ISN*, 1.4.13, 1.11.15, 8.2.28, 10.9.3; Maema, II, 832-833, 1192; III, 1533.

IX. *The Northern Frontier and Emigration*

1. *Kolonizaciya sibiri: v svyazi s obščim peresellenčeskim voprosom*, ed. Kancelyariya komiteta ministrov (St. Petersburg, 1900), p. 291; *Sibirskaya sovetskaya enciklopediya*, ed. M.K. Azadovskii et al. (1931), II, 950-951. These two sources say that Korean immigrants numbered 1,400 in 1868; 6,500 in 1870; 13,998 in 1897; 64,000 in 1914, and 178,009 in 1926.

2. *KS*, 1:23a-b.

3. *KS*, 1:27, 50; *ISN*, 1.3.2, 1.5.15; Yi Nŭng-hwa, 2:169-170.

4. Ibid., 2:171; *ISN*, 2.11.10, 2.10.11; *KS*, 2:55b-56.

5. *IWSM*, 47:27a-b; *KS*, 3:93a-b; *PBTN*, 251:254b-259b.

6. *IWSM*, 47:26; *KS*, 3:94a-b, 96b; *PBTN*, 251:296a-b.

7. *IWSM*, 47:32b-33; *ISN*, 4.13.14; *KS*, 4:3b-4.

8. *Sunjo sillok*, 27:34a-b; *Hŏnjong sillok*, 4:4; 14:11b-12; *Ch'ŏlchong sillok*, 8:7b; 10:1b, 6; 11:11a-b; *ISN*, Ch'ŏlchong 7.6.30.

9. The populace was required to provide maintenance for the Chinese officials who supervised the trade with the Korean authorities at Hoeryŏng and Kyŏngwŏn and their horses. See *Yŏngjo sillok*, 84:8a-b; also *Sunjo sillok*, 23:8-10b.

10. The land tax in Hamgyŏng and P'yŏngan was originally less than that in other regions. However, owing to negligence in land surveys, the actual amount of the land tax was usually far higher than the national average. Even wasteland that was potentially arable but had been abandoned was taxed. In addition, Hamgyŏng suffered severely from maladministration of the grain-loan system. See *Chŏngjo sillok*, 10:27; 26:21; *Sunjo sillok*, 25:27b-29b.

11. Because of the fear of a flow of money from Korea to China, the use of money was persistently prohibited in the border region, particularly in the Yukchin area.

Nevertheless, it seems that money did at times find its way there. Ibid., 25:27b-29b; 32:13b; *Hŏnjong sillok,* 7:4b.

12. Prior to 1686, when the Korean government issued a severe law prohibiting wild ginseng as a result of Chinese protests, gathering ginseng was the major source of livelihood. See *Sukchong sillok,* 17:1b-2; 22:42a-b; 25:31b-32.

13. *Yŏngjo sillok,* 93:1a-b; *Hŏnjong sillok,* 10:4b; *Ch'ŏlchong sillok,* 5:4; *PBTN,* 240:543b-544.

14. *IWSM,* 47:25b-28, 32b-33b; 77:15b-18; 78:1-3.

15. For instance, in 1842, 98 Chinese houses and some 3,300 *mu (mou)* of farm land located across from Sangt'ojin and Manp'ojin on the far bank of the Yalu were destroyed by the Chinese government at the request of the Korean government. Furthermore, 200 Chinese houses and 5,000 *mu* of land were destroyed in 1846. Then, in 1848, confirming the old agreement, China and Korea decided to send border investigators to the Yalu region four times a year. See *T'ongmun kwan chi* (Record of the Bureau of Interpreters; Keijo, 1944), 11:363; *Hŏnjong sillok,* 13:6; *CS,* ser. 6, vol. 3, pp. 145-146, 206, 225.

16. *CS,* ser. 6, vol. 4, p. 251; *KS,* 7:18; 8:7b, 37, 42b.

17. *ISN,* 1.7.22.

18. *ISN,* 4.1.20; 4.1.21; 4.6.7; *KS,* 4:8a-b, 29. As a rule, the commander stayed at his regular headquarters in Kyŏngsŏng from the third month of the year to the ninth, and at his temporary headquarters for the rest of the year.

19. *KS,* 4:20b-21, 53; 8:24a-b, 46b, 50b-51b, 60b-61; *Pukkwan ŭpchi,* as cited in Tagawa, "Kindai Hokusen nōson shakai to ryūmin mondai," pp. 596-597. The rifle units were also established in other parts of the country, as has been mentioned elsewhere.

20. Ibid., p. 596.

21. The old "Four Districts"—Much'ang, Uye, Yŏyŏn, and Chasŏng—had been established for the most part during Sejong's reign (1418-1450) as the result of his active colonization of the wild northern region. These districts were abolished, however, during Sejo's reign (1455-1468), primarily because it was difficult to defend them against the Jurchen tribes of Chien-chou. At the same time, the inhabitants were all moved far to the west, to Kusŏng. For centuries, the

"re-establishment" of the defunct districts remained an important subject of debate, though a number of garrisons were indeed established there in later years and a few villages rose around them. Most of the area, a rare oasis of fertile land in the north, had remained practically a wasteland for almost 400 years. See *Man'gi yoram kunjŏng p'yŏn* (Keijo, 1937), military section, pp. 507-509, 631-679.

22. *KS*, 6:16b, 20b, 30, 34b, 36; 7:38b; 9:4b; *ISN*, 6.10.13, 6.10.16; 7.12.9, 9.1.25; Yi Nŭng-hwa, 2:8.

23. Under the "roll-call" system the provincial governor and military commander were ordered to send officials to the various districts, without advance notice, to make sure that no one was missing. This was done by summoning all the inhabitants before the offices of the magistrates or garrison commanders for a roll-call. *ISN*, 3.1.21; *KS*, 5:54a-b; Tagawa, "Kindai Hokusen nōson shakai to ryūmin mondai," p. 597.

24. *ISN*, 6.11.23; *KS*, 6:34.

25. *KS*, 4:17a-b; 6:16b, 20b, 30, 34a-b, 36; 7:8, 17b, 40b; 8:7b, 48-49; 9:3; 10:4b; *MHBG*, 151:31, 32b.

26. Tagawa, "Kindai Hokusen nōson shakai no ryūmin mondai," pp. 600-602; *ISN*, 8.5.28; *KS*, 8:37a-b.

X. *The French Invasion*

1. Yi Su-gwang, *Chibong yusŏl* (Collected works; Keijo, 1915), vol. II; Yu Mong-in, *Ŏu yadam* (Collected essays), *kwangsa* 4, *chip* 1; Yamaguchi Masayuki, "Kinsei Chōsen ni okeru seigaku shisō no tōzen to sono hatten" (The coming of Christian thought to Korea and its development), *Oda sensei shōju kinen Chōsen ronshū* (A collection of studies on Korea in commemoration of Oda Shōgo's sixtieth birthday; Keijo, 1934), pp. 1005-40; Charles Dallet, *Histoire de l'Église de Corée* (Paris, 1874), I, 11; see also Yu Hong-nyŏl, *Han'guk ch'ŏnju kyohoe sa* (A history of the Catholic church in Korea; Seoul, 1962), pp. 52-54.

2. These, together with one of Ricci's world maps *(La Descrittione Universale di Tutta Terra?)* and many books on astronomy and mathematics, were gifts from Johann Adam Schall (1591-1666) to the crown prince. While in Peking as a hostage (June 27, 1644 [?]-Jan. 23, 1645), the prince had cultivated a warm friendship with the Jesuit missionary and had manifested profound interest in

the doctrine of Catholicism. Thinking that the prince was Korea's king, Schall apparently had great expectations of opening up a new field for missionary work. This dream was shattered by the sudden and mysterious death of the prince on May 21, 1645, shortly after his return to Seoul on March 15. See *Injo sillok*, 46:1, 2b, 4b-6, 23a-b; Yamaguchi Masayuki, "Shōken seishi to Tō Jaku-bō" (Sohyŏn Sejo and Johann Adam Schall), *Seikyū gakusō*, no. 5:101-117 (August 1931); Johann Adam Schall von Bell, *Historica relation de ortu et progressu fidei orthodoxae in Regno Chinensi per missionarios societatis Jesu ab anno 1581 usque ad annum 1669* (Ratisbon, 1672), pp. 139-142; *Sinica Franciscana*, Relationes et epistolas Fratrum Minorum Saeculi XVII, ed. and annotated by P. Anastasius van den Wyngaert (Florence, 1936), III, 307-309. For the best short account of the early Catholic movement in Korea, see Alexandre de Govéa, "Etablissement du Christianisme en Corée," *Revue d'Histoire des Missions*, no. 3:387-415 (1931).

3. Urakawa Wasaburō, *Chōsen junkyō shi* (A history of Korean martyrdom; Osaka, 1944), pp. 36-43.

4. *Chŏngjo sillok*, 17:20a-b; *CS*, ser.6, vol. 1, pp. 27, 32; *PBTN*, 192:303b-304b; Urakawa, pp. 43-44; Dallet, I, 16-18. Yi was not the first Korean to be converted and baptized. During the Hideyoshi invasion, many Koreans were taken to Japan as prisoners, and many of them are known to have been converted. It is not known, however, whether any of them returned. See Yamaguchi Masayuki, "Yasokai senkyōshi no Chōsen furyo kyūzai oyobi kyōka" (The relief and evangelization of Korean prisoners of war by Christian missionaries), *Seikyū gakusō*, no. 4:38-50 (May 1931).

5. For some of the earlier criticisms, see *Chŏngjo sillok*, 19:67b (a memorial by Yu Ha-wŏn); 26:6a-b (a remark by Ch'ae Che-gong); and 33:54b (a memorial by Song To-jŏng).

6. Ibid., 21:6, 7a-b (memorials by O Chae-sun, Kim I-so, and Sim P'ung-ji); 24:33b-34b (new regulations on import goods from China); 26:7a-b; *Ch'ugwan chi* (Records on punishments; Keijo, 1937), p. 874.

7. *Chŏngjo sillok*, 25:44b-45 (a memorial by Chŏng Man-si). For an outline of the interrelationship between Christian persecution and factional strife, see Oda Shōgo, "Richō no hōtō wo ryakujo shite tenshukyō hakugai ni oyobu" (An outline of factionalism in the Yi dynasty and notes on Catholic persecution), *Seikyū gakusō*, no. 1:1-26 (August 1930).

8. Yi Nŭng-hwa, 1:44-46, 60-71; 2:60.

9. Oda, "Richō no hōtō wo ryakujo shite tenshukyō hakugai ni oyobu," 1:17; Dallet, I, 69-74.

10. Urakawa, p. 90; G. Mutel, *The Catholic Church in Korea* (Hongkong, 1924), p. 21; *CS*, ser. 6, vol. 1, p. 22.

11. At least two non-Namin members were also executed. They were Yi Chung-bae, a Soron, and Kim Kŏn-sun, a Noron; both of them seem to have belonged to the Sip'a. See Urakawa, pp. 100, 121.

12. *CS*, ser. 6, vol. 1, pp. 33, 40.

13. For further study of the Hwang Sa-yŏng letter, see Yamaguchi Masayuki, *Kō Shi-ei hakusho no kenkyū* (A study of Hwang Sa-yŏng's *paeksŏ;* Osaka, 1946), pp. 1-179; and his "Yakuchū Kō Shi-ei hakusho" (The letter of Hwang Sa-yŏng on silk cloth) tr. and annotated, in *Chōsen gakuhō* (Journal of the Academic Association of Koreanology in Japan), no. 2:121-154 (1951).

14. *CS*, ser. 6, vol. 2, p. 650; *Hŏnjong sillok,* 6:14b; Urakawa, pp. 602-603, 616, 620.

15. Ibid., pp. 475, 482-483, 486-487; Dallet, II, 85-130, 183-184.

16. *PBTN*, 227:113; *ISN*, Hŏnjong 5.8.3/4; Yi Kyu-gyŏng, *Oju yŏnmun changjŏn san'go* (Collected works; Seoul, 1959), 53:701-712; Yi Man-ch'ae, *Pyŏgwi p'yŏn* (A study of Catholicism; Seoul, 1931), 7:1-6b; *Hŏnjong sillok,* 6:14b.

17. Ibid., 13:11b-12b; Urakawa, pp. 709-710; Dallet, II, 280-320.

18. Urakawa, pp. 711-720, 730-734, 743-744.

19. *Hŏnjong sillok,* 13:6, 12a-b.

20. Dallet, II, 452; Mutel, *The Catholic Church in Korea,* pp. 38-40.

21. Ibid., pp. 38-39.

22. Hwang Hyŏn, p. 7; Kikuchi Kenjō, *Kindai Chōsen shi* (A history of modern Korea; Tokyo, 1940), I, 98.

23. This summary of the episode is based on the following sources: *ISN*, 3.1.20; *KS*, 3:5-6; Yi Nŭng-hwa, 2:33-39; and *Pyŏngin choein Chong-sam Pong-ju*

tǔng kugan (The trial-records of the 1866 convicts, Nam Chong-sam and Hong
Pong-ju); Kikuchi, *Kindai Chōsen shi,* I, 92-100; Dallet, II, 501-505, 524; Mutel,
The Catholic Church in Korea, pp. 40-41; John R. Shortland, *The Corean
Martyrs* (London, 1869), pp. 79-80; see also Yu Hong-nyŏl, *Kojong ch'iha sŏhak
sunan ŭi yŏn'gu* (Studies on Catholic persecutions during King Kojong's reign,
1863-1907; Seoul, 1962).

24.   *ISN,* 3.1.5, 3.1.11, 3.1.15, 3.1.20, 3.1.25; 3.2.7; *KS,* 3:1b-6b, 7-8b; G. Mutel,
      Documents relatifs aux martyrs de Corée de 1866 (Hongkong, 1925).

25.   *ISN,* 5.4.19, 5.4.20, 5.4.25, 5.4.26, 5.4.27, 5.4.28; *Up'och'ŏng tǔngnok* (Records
      of the right metropolitan police headquarters, 1807-1881), 5.4.2, 5.4.6, 5.4.18,
      5.4.19, 5.4.26, 5.4.27, 5.4.29; Dallet, II, 568-570.

26.   Ibid., II, 568-570, 572.

27.   See *IWSM,* 42:54a-b, for the Chinese version; *FRUS, 1867,* pt. 1, p. 420 (M.
      de Bellonet to Prince Kung, enclosed in No. 122, Burlingame to Seward, Peking,
      Dec. 12, 1866).

28.   See Chinese extraction in *IWSM,* 42:54b-55; *FRUS, 1867,* pt. 1, p. 421 (Prince
      Kung to M. de Bellonet, enclosed in No. 122, Burlingame to Seward, Peking,
      Dec. 12, 1866).

29.   *ISN,* 3.7.8; *IWSM,* 44:12b-14; *KS,* 3:37a-b.

30.   *ISN,* 3.7.8, 3.7.11, 3.7.30; 3.8.2, 3.8.3; *KS,* 3:37a-b, 46a-b.

31.   *ISN,* 3.8.13; *Kyŏnggi suyŏng kyerok* (Dispatches from Kyŏnggi naval headquar-
      ters), T'ung-chih 5.8.13, 5.8.16; *KS,* 3:50; Dallet, II, 572-573; A. Piacentini,
      Mgr. Ridel, d'après sa correspondence (Lyon, 1890), pp. 110-111.

32.   *ISN,* 3.8.17, 3.8.18, 3.8.20, 3.8.21, 3.8.24; *Kyŏnggi suyŏng kyerok,* T'ung-chih
      5.8.16, 5.8.17, 5.8.18, 5.8.19, 5.8.22, 5.8.23, 5.8.24, 5.8.25; *KS,* 3:50-52b, 54;
      Dallet, II, 572-573, 574.

33.   *KS,* 3:52a-b.

34.   *ISN,* 3.8.18; *SMTN,* 3.8.18; *KS,* 3:52; *PBTN,* 251:219.

35.   *ISN,* 3.9.1, 3.9.2; *KS,* 3:54a-b.

36. Dallet, II, 573-574.

37. *FRUS, 1867*, pt. 1, p. 417, 421 (enclosed in No. 44, Williams to Seward, Peking, Oct. 24, 1866).

38. *ISN*, 3.9.12; *Kyŏnggi suyŏng kyerok*, T'ung-chih 5.9.6; *KS*, 3:62b-63b; Dallet, II, 576-577; Piacentini, pp. 114-115.

39. *ISN*, 3.9.7, 3.9.8, 3.9.9; *Kyŏnggi suyŏng kyerok*, T'ung-chih 5.9.8, 5.9.10; *SMTN*, 3.9.7; *KS*, 3:55b-57, 58b.

40. *ISN*, 3.9.7; *KS*, 3:55b-56.

41. *ISN*, 3.9.7; *SMTN*, 3.9.7; *PBTN*, 251:226a-b; *KS*, 3:56 (a memorial by the Ŭijŏngbu and a royal edict).

42. *ISN*, 3.9.8, 3.9.9; *SMTN*, 3.9.8, 3.9.10, 3.9.12; *KS*, 3:57a-b.

43. *ISN*, 3.9.8; *KS*, 3:57.

44. *KS*, 3:57a-b.

45. *ISN*, 3.9.10; *KS*, 3:59, 60b; *Chōsen shiryō shūshin kaisetsu* (Annotated historical documents of Korea; Keijo, 1936), p. 28; see also *PBTN*, 251:263 ff. for the list of volunteer *p'osu* rewarded after the war.

46. *SMTN*, 3.9.10, 3.9.12; *KS*, 3:82b; *PBTN*, 251:265b. For an historical survey of the peddlers' guild and its organization, see Yu Cha-hu, *Chosŏn pobusang ko* (A study of Korean peddlers; Seoul, 1948), pp. 5-123.

47. *ISN*, 3.9.9, 3.9.10; *SMTN*, 3.9.10, 3.9.11, 3.9.12, 3.9.13, 3.9.14; *KS*, 3:59, 60; *PBTN*, 251:227b, 229.

48. *ISN*, 3.9.9, 3.9.12; *KS*, 3:60b-61.

49. *ISN*, 3.9.12; *KS*, 3:61a-b, 62b; *SMTN*, 3.9.12.

50. Ibid.; *KS*, 3:61b-62; *PBTN*, 251:231; Dallet, II, 577, 581.

51. Tabohashi, *Kindai Nissen kankei no kenkyū*, I, 71-72; *CS*, ser. 6, vol. 4, p. 111; *KS*, 3:62.

52. *ISN*, 3.9.13, 3.9.16; *SMTN*, 3.9.14, 3.9.16, 3.9.19, 3.9.22; *KS*, 3:63b; see also the royal edicts in *KS*, 3:65-66.

53. *ISN*, 3.9.19, 3.9.21; *SMTN*, 3.9.17, 3.9.19; *KS*, 3:66a-b, 67.

54. *ISN*, 3.9.26; *SMTN*, 3.9.26; *KS*, 3:68, 69a-b.

55. *ISN*, 3.9.24, 3.9.27, 3.9.28, 3.9.29; 3.10.2, 3.10.3, 3.10.4; *SMTN*, 3.9.28, 3.9.29; 3.10.1, 3.10.2, 3.10.3; *KS*, 3:66, 67, 68, 73a-b; *PBTN*, 251:238b, 239.

56. *ISN*, 3.10.4, 3.10.5; *SMTN*, 3.10.4, 3.10.5, 3.10.6; *KS*, 3:73, 76a-b; Dallet, II, 577, 582-584.

57. Ibid., II, 577-578, 585-586.

58. *ISN*, 3.10.4, 3.10.5, 3.10.6, 3.10.7; *SMTN*, 3.10.4, 3.10.5, 3.10.6, 3.10.7, 3.10.9; *KS*, 3:78a-b, 81.

59. *ISN*, 3.10.15, 3.10.18; *KS*, 3:79b, 81, 83.

XI. *The American Expedition*

1. *ISN*, 3.2.25; *KS*, 3:13-14. Earlier, two American ships (one in 1855 and another in 1865) were stranded off the east coast of Korea. On each occasion the survivors were turned over to the Chinese government and their nationality ascertained by the Peking authorities. See *PBTN*, 242:791b-792, 794a-b, 800b; *KS*, 2:38b-39, 42b, 45b-46; *T'ongmun kwan chi*, 11:55, 70b; *IWSM*, 12:24b-25.

2. *ISN*, 3.5.17, 3.5.22, 3.5.23; *PBTN*, 251:181b-182.

3. *FRUS, 1867*, pt. 1, pp. 414-415 (no. 44, Williams to Seward, Peking, Oct. 24, 1866).

4. Ibid., pp. 426-428 (no. 124, Burlingame to Seward, Peking, Dec. 15, 1866); William E. Griffis, *Corea, the Hermit Nation* (New York, 1882), p. 391.

5. *ISN*, 3.7.15, 3.7.18; *P'yŏngan kamyŏng kyerok* (Dispatches from the P'yŏngan provincial government), 3.7.8, 3.7.9, 3.7.10, 3.7.11, 3.7.15; *Hwanghae kamyŏng kyerok* (Dispatches from the Hwanghae provincial government), 3.7.9; *KS*, 3:39-42b.

6. *ISN*, 3.7.22, 3.7.23, 3.7.25; *SMTN*, 3.7.22, 3.7.25; *P'yŏngan kamyŏng kyerok*, 3.7.19; *KS*, 3:42a-b; *PBTN*, 251:203a-b.

7. *ISN*, 3.7.25, 3.7.27; *P'yŏngan kamyŏng kyerok*, 3.7.20, 3.7.21, 3.7.22, 3.7.23, 3.7.24; *SMTN*, 3.7.26, 3.7.28; Pak Kyu-su, 7:8-9b. A circumstantial report on the *Sherman* incident was soon sent to the Chinese Board of Rites. In his report to the government Governor Pak expressed his deep regret for having been compelled to take the lives of the crew, violating the "virtue of loving the living and being kind to strangers." See *ISN*, 3.7.27, 3.7.29; *IWSM*, 45:1-7; Pak Kyu-su, 7:8-10; *KS*, 3:43a-b.

8. The first voyage took him only to the coast of Ch'ungch'ŏng. On the second, he was able to go up as far as the mouth of the Han River. See Ernest Oppert, *A Forbidden Land: Voyages to the Corea* (London, 1880), pp. 178-289; *ISN*, 3.2. 18, 3.2.21, 3.2.22; 3.7.5, 3.7.6, 3.7.12; *Kyŏnggi suyŏng kyerok*, T'ung-chih 5.7.10, 5.7.11, 5.7.20; *PBTN*, 251:201a-b, 202a-b; *KS*, 3:12b-13, 35b-36b, 38a-b, 41a-b.

9. Oppert, pp. 291-301.

10. Ibid., p. 303; *FRUS, 1868*, pt. 1, pp. 547-549 (no. 19, Williams to Seward, Peking, Aug. 1, 1868).

11. It is not clear what "Pirimang" stands for. Perhaps, it is a faulty transliteration for "Prussia." In another version it is written "Arimang," which is probably a transliteration for "Russia." Russia was sometimes called "Arasa." See Oppert, pp. 304-310; *ISN*, 5.4.21, 5.4.23; 8.4.6, 8.4.9, 8.4.10, 8.4.11; *KS*, 5:14b-16b; *Up'och'ŏng tŭngnok*, 5.4.21; *CS*, ser. 6, vol. 4, pp. 167-168.

12. Tabohashi, *Kindai Nissen kankei no kenkyū*, I, 79; *KS*, 5:16.

13. Oppert, pp. 311-321; *ISN*, 5.4.22, 5.4.23, 5.4.26, 5.4.28; *KS*, 5:15b-17; *CS*, ser.6, vol. 4, pp. 169-170.

14. *ISN*, 5.4.19, 5.4.20, 5.4.21, 5.4.23, 5.4.25, 5.4.26, 5.4.27, 5.4.28; 5.6.19, 5.6. 20, 5.6.21, 5.6.25, 5.6.26, 5.6.28, 5.6.29; *KS*, 5:14b-17b.

15. Dallet, II, 574; *FRUS, 1867*, pt. 1, pp. 425-426 (no. 123, Burlingame to Seward, Peking, Dec. 15, 1866); *ISN*, 3.8.24.

16. *FRUS, 1867*, pt. 1, pp. 416-417 (no. 44, Williams to Seward, Peking, Oct. 24, 1866, enclosure B).

17. Ibid., pt. 1, p. 428 (no. 124, Burlingame to Seward, Peking, Dec. 15, 1866, enclosure B: Messrs. Meadows & Co. to Mr. Burlingame).

18. *IWSM*, 45:12b-13.

19. *IWSM*, 45:13a-b; 47:3.

20. *ISN*, 3.11.6; *KS*, 3:87-88b; *IWSM*, 47:3-5; *CS*, ser. 6, vol. 4, pp. 127-129.

21. *FRUS, 1867*, pt. 1, pp. 426-427 (no. 124, Burlingame to Seward, Peking, Dec. 15, 1866).

22. Ibid., p. 428, enclosure A; *ISN*, 3.12.25, 3.12.28; Charles O. Paullin, *Diplomatic Negotiations of American Naval Officers, 1778-1883* (Baltimore, 1912), pp. 284-286; Pak Kyu-su, 7:8-10; *KS*, 3:96.

23. *FRUS, 1868*, pt. 1, pp. 545-546 (no. 18, Williams to Seward, Peking, July 31, 1868); *IWSM*, 57:25-26.

24. *FRUS, 1868*, pt. 1, p. 546; *IWSM*, 57:26b-28.

25. For an account of the Febinger mission, see *IWSM*, 60:13-18; *FRUS, 1868*, pt. 1, p. 544 (no. 18, Williams to Seward, Peking, July 31, 1868); *ISN*, 5.3.23, 5.3.24, 5.3.25, 5.3.26, 5.3.28, 5.3.29, 5.3.30; 5.4.3, 5.4.8, 5.4.28; *P'yŏngan kamyŏng kyerok*, 5.3.21, 5.3.24, 5.3.25, 5.3.26, 5.3.27, 5.3.30; 5.4.1, 5.4.2, 5.4.4, 5.4.6, 5.4.9, 5.4.25, 5.4.27; Pak Kyu-su, 6:10-15b, 17-18b; *KS*, 5:9-12, 12-13b, 17b-18; Paullin, p. 286.

26. *FRUS, 1870*, p. 336 (no. 281, G.F. Seward to W.H. Seward, Shanghai, Apr. 24, 1868).

27. Ibid.

28. *IWSM*, 60:17b; *ISN*, 8.4.6; *KS*, 8:21b-22b, 23a-b.

29. *FRUS, 1870*, pp. 336-337 (no. 282, G.F. Seward to W.H. Seward, Shanghai, Apr. 24, 1868).

30. *Dispatches to Consuls* (Department of State), vol. 49, no. 171 (W.H. Seward to G.F. Seward, June 27, 1868).

31. Ibid.

32. *Credences* (Department of State), IV, 491.

33. *Dispatches to Consuls,* vol. 49, no. 171.

34. Ibid. (W.H. Seward to Wells, June 23, 1868).

35. *Instructions to Flag Officers* (Department of Navy), vol. 6 (Wells to Rowan, June 29, 1868).

36. *FRUS, 1870,* p. 337 (no. 292, G.F. Seward to W.H. Seward, Shanghai, May 25, 1868).

37. *Dispatches to Consuls,* vol. 49, no. 172 (W.H. Seward to G.F. Seward, July 22, 1868).

38. The three letters were dated Sept. 28 and Oct. 14, 1868, and Jan. 19, 1869. See *Consular Dispatches* (Department of State), vol. 9 (G.F. Seward to W.H. Seward, Yokohama, Sept. 28, 1868), and vol. 10, no. 335 (G.F. Seward to W.H. Seward, Jan. 19, 1869); *FRUS, 1870,* pp. 337-339 (no. 317, G.F. Seward to W.H. Seward, Shanghai, Oct. 14, 1868).

39. *Consular Dispatches,* vol. 11 (G.F. Seward to Davis, Washington, Feb. 28, 1970); *Asiatic Squadron Letters* (Department of the Navy), I, 4-7 (Rodgers to Robeson, Washington, Mar. 28, 1870).

40. *FRUS, 1870,* p. 333 (no. 220, Fish to Robeson, Washington, Apr. 4, 1870).

41. Ibid.

42. *Instructions to Flag Officers,* VI, 547 (Robeson to Rodgers, Apr. 16, 1870).

43. *FRUS, 1870,* pp. 334-335 (no. 222, Fish to Low, Washington, Apr. 20, 1870).

44. *FRUS, 1870,* pp. 362-363 (no. 225, Low to Fish, Peking, July 16, 1870).

45. *FRUS, 1871,* pp. 73-74 (no. 21, Low to Fish, Peking, Nov. 22, 1870).

46. *IWSM,* 80:12a-b.

47. *IWSM,* 80:13a-b.

48. *FRUS, 1871,* pp. 111-112 (no. 29, Low to Fish, Peking, Apr. 3, 1871).

49. *CS*, ser. 6, vol. 4, p. 234; *IWSM*, 80:14-15.

50. *ISN*, 8.2.21; *PBTN*, 253:429a-b; *KS*, 8:12b; *CS*, ser. 6, vol. 4, pp. 235-237.

51. For the original text of the letter, see *IWSM*, 80:9-12.

52. *FRUS, 1871*, p. 115 (no. 31, Low to Fish, on board the flagship *Colorado*, Harbor of Nagasaki, May 13, 1871); Paullin, p. 288.

53. *KS*, 8:22b.

54. *KS*, 8:22b-24.

55. These three interpreters should be identified with the "three officials of third rank" mentioned in Low's report to Fish. According to Korean sources the date of the meeting was May 28. See *KS*, 8:24a-b; *ISN*, 8.4.10; *CS*, ser. 6, vol. 4, pp. 242-243; *FRUS, 1871*, pp. 116-117 (no. 32, Low to Fish on board the flagship *Colorado* off Isle Boisée, Corea, May 31, 1871).

56. Ibid.; *KS*, 8:24b; *CS*, ser. 6, vol. 4, p. 243.

57. Ibid.; *ISN*, 8.4.14; *KS*, 8:25a-b.

58. Even before the formal announcement to the Korean government, explorations had been carried on for a few days. See *FRUS, 1871*, pp. 119-120 (no. 32, enclosure 4, John P. Cowles Jr. to Low, May 29, 1871).

59. Ibid.

60. *FRUS, 1871*, pp. 121-123 (no. 33, Low to Fish, on board the flagship *Colorado* off Isle Boisée, Corea, June 2, 1871).

61. *KS*, 8:25b.

62. *FRUS, 1871*, no. 33; *KS*, 8:26a-b.

63. *CS*, ser. 6, vol. 4, p. 244; *ISN*, 8.4.18, 8.4.19; *KS*, 8:25b-26.

64. *CS*, ser. 6, vol. 4, p. 245; *FRUS, 1871*, pp. 132-133 (no. 35, Low to Fish, on board the flagship *Colorado* off Isle Boisée, Corea, June 20, 1871, enclosure 4). According to the *KS*, this letter was dated June 4. See *KS*, 8:26b-27.

65. Ibid.

66. *FRUS, 1871*, pp. 121-122 (no. 33, Low to Fish, on board the flagship *Colorado* off Isle Boisée, Corea, June 2, 1871).

67. Ibid.

68. *CS*, ser. 6, vol. 4, p. 245; *KS*, 8:27.

69. *FRUS, 1871*, p. 135 (no. 35, Low to Fish, June 20, 1871, enclosure 7: Admiral Rodgers to Commander H.C. Blake on board the *Colorado*, Isle Boisée Anchorage, Corea, June 9, 1871).

70. Ibid.; *ISN*, 8.4.28; *KS*, 8:28. During the night, Korean Catholic converts made a secret visit to one of the American vessels and said that there was great discontent among the people as a result of the tyrannical conduct of the government and the exaction of local officials. Consequently, they said they desired the overthrow of the government, and they wanted to join "any movement foreign nations might make which would accomplish the result." *FRUS, 1871*, pp. 124-126 (no. 34, Low to Fish, on board the flagship *Colorado* off Isle Boisée, Corea, June 15, 1871).

71. Ibid., pp. 126-129 (no. 35, Low to Fish, June 20, 1871); *ISN*, 8.4.28; *KS*, 8:28a-b, 30a-b.

72. *FRUS, 1871*, p. 128 (no. 35, Low to Fish, June 20, 1871).

73. *ISN*, 8.4.28, 8.5.3; *KS*, 8:29b-30. The account of Korean dead and wounded given by American sources is different from that of the Korean records. According to the American record, "about 250 of the enemy's dead were counted lying on the field, 50 flags and several prisoners were captured and brought away." See *FRUS, 1871*, pp. 126-129 (no. 35, Low to Fish, June 20, 1871).

74. Ibid.; *CS*, ser. 6, vol. 4, p. 247; *ISN*, 8.4.28; *KS*, 8:29.

75. *ISN*, 8.4.20, 8.4.25, 8.5.7, 8.5.15.

76. *ISN*, 8.4.28, 8.5.3.

77. *CS*, ser. 6, vol. 4, pp. 248-249.

78. *FRUS, 1871*, p. 129 (no. 35, Low to Fish, June 20, 1871).

XII. *Korea and Japan*

1. The articles generally consisted of hot pepper, sapanwood, buffalo horn, copper, and swords.

2. Before 1502, it seems that five *kŭn* of Japanese copper were exchanged for one *p'il* of Korean cloth. Later, the official exchange rates between Japanese and Korean goods were set as follows: 10 *kŭn* of copper (and iron) to 6 *p'il* of cotton cloth; 1 *kŭn* of pewter *(napch'ŏl)* to 2 *p'il* of cotton cloth; 1 *kŭn* of hot pepper to 1 *p'il* of cotton cloth. See *Chŭngjŏng kyorinji*, appendix, p. 2.

3. This and another guest house for the Japanese, the West House (Sŏp'yŏnggwan), were built in 1409. See *T'aejong sillok*, 17:13.

4. The first voice against the free settlement of Japanese traders was raised in 1407, when the military commander of Kyŏngsang, Kang Sa-dŏk, proposed that Japanese trade ships be allowed to stay in only two places, Pusanp'o and Naeip'o. Ibid., 14:10-11.

5. *Sejong sillok*, 85:7.

6. *T'aejong sillok*, 27:26.

7. Ibid., 28:19b.

8. Ibid., 14:10-11; 35:19.

9. *Sejong sillok*, 11:1b-2; 19:24a-b; 80:21.

10. For other prohibited articles, see ibid., 44:24b-25.

11. Ibid., 82:23b-24; 83:6b-7; 84:15b; 85:21a-b, 33.

12. Ibid., 98:23b-34; 99:9, 12, 18b-19; 104:23b-24, 27b-28b; 105:22b-23. The main clauses of the Treaty of Kyehae were: (1) Tsushima could send fifty ships to Korea each year; (2) thirty shiploads of goods could be disposed of at the East House in Seoul, and their crews were to be allowed provisions for fifty days; (3) twenty shiploads of goods could be disposed of at the three ports, with their crews allowed provisions for thirty days; (4) the size of the crew of each ship was further defined as follows (except in the case of envoys): large ships forty men, medium ships thirty men, small ships twenty men; (5) provisions for fifty days were provided for the return voyage; (6) Sō Hikoshichi, brother of the lord of

Tsushima, was allowed to send seven ships independently (four for trade in Seoul, and three for trade at the ports). The full text can be found in *Sejong sillok,* 105:22b-23. Even after this treaty, which was reaffirmed with some minor changes in 1444, several other daimyo apparently were allowed to send a few ships each.

13. *Sŏngjong sillok,* 217:12a-b.

14. *CS,* ser. 4, vol. 4, p. 753; *Sŏngjong sillok,* 295:15b-16.

15. *Chungjong sillok,* 8:7-8, 9b, 10, 13b-14b, 17b-18b, 19b, 23-24.

16. Ibid., 10:43b-44.

17. For the immediate cause, see ibid., 10:47b, 48a-b, 57.

18. For details of the uprising, see the entries of the fourth and fifth month, in particular, ibid., 11:5b-6b, 8b-12, 33b, 39; 12:11b, 12b-13b.

19. For the main text of the Treaty of Imsin, see ibid., 16:55a-b. Some of these provisions were amended later. For instance, in 1523, Tsushima fief was allowed to send five additional ships. Thirteen ships out of the twenty-five were allowed to come to Pusanp'o, although in 1547 all ships were confined to Pusanp'o. See ibid., 42:59b; 49:8b-11b, 16b-17, 17b-18b; *Myŏngjong sillok,* 30:38b-39.

20. For the content of the treaty, see *Kwanghae-gun ilgi* (The annals of King Kwanghae), 17:10-11, 14a-b; *T'ongmun kwan chi,* 5:2b ff.; *CS,* ser. 5, vol. 1, p. 48.

21. During the Tokugawa period the actual number of ships was twenty-four. In addition to the original number, four "additional special ships" *(pu t'ŭksong sŏn)* were allowed: one by the Tsushima daimyo, one by the Iteian temple, one by the Bansōin temple and one by the houses of deceased former holders of Korean titles. For further reference, see *Chŭngjŏng kyorinji,* 1:6-25.

22. For further details, see ibid., 1:6-37b.

23. The primary objective of sending such envoys was still trade; they were able to bring as much merchandise as regular trade ships did. See ibid., 2:1.

24. There were fourteen other occasions on which envoys of the first class might be sent. See ibid., 2:1b-16b.

25. For other occasions, see ibid., 2:1b-25b.

26; Ibid., 2:1b-16b.

27. Ibid.

28. For an historical survey of the Japan House, see ibid., 3:1-6; *Nissen tsūkō shi* (A history of Korean-Japanese relations; Fusan, 1915), I, 510-514.

29. *Chŭngjŏng kyorinji*, 3:7-19b.

30. Ibid., 4:9-14b.

31. For an account of each of these missions, see ibid., 5:1-44; appendix, pp. 6-13.

32. It took the two countries nearly twenty years to agree upon a new site. See *Chŏngjo sillok*, 40:56b-58; *CS*, ser.6, vol. 1, pp. 343-344.

33. *Tokugawa Keiki-kō den* (A biography of Tokugawa Keiki), comp. Shibusawa Eiichi (Tokyo, 1913-1918), VII, 32-33; Tabohashi, *Kindai Nissen kankei no kenkyū*, I, 107-108.

34. After Roches's refusal, the shogun approached the American minister, Robert B. Van Valkenburgh, to the same end. This offer of good offices to the United States, which was then in trouble with Korea over the *General Sherman*, was enthusiastically supported by Van Valkenburgh, and was finally approved by Secretary of State Seward on January 27, 1868. See ibid., I, 108-109; *FRUS, 1867*, pt. 2, pp. 36-37 (no. 24, Van Valkenburgh to Seward, Osaka, May 18, 1867); *FRUS, 1868*, pt. 1, pp. 634-635 (no. 43, Seward to Van Valkenburgh, Jan. 27, 1868).

35. Tabohashi, *Kindai Nissen kankei no kenkyū*, I, 109-110.

36. Ibid., I, 110-111.

37. Ibid.

38. Ibid., I, 109-110.

39. Ibid., I, 111-112.

40. *ISN*, 4.10.1; according to Korean sources, however, the note from Tsushima was

sent to Seoul by the magistrate of Tongnae. See *KS*, 4:44-45.

41. The mission was to leave by December 25, 1867. See *NGB*, vol. *(kan)* 1, pt. *(satsu)* 1, no. 20, pp. 67-68; no. 31, pp. 104-105; Kikuchi, *Taiinkun den tsuki ōhi no isshō*, p. 58.

42. Tabohashi, *Kindai Nissen kankei no kenkyū*, I, 116-118.

43. Ibid.

44. Ibid., I, 119.

45. Ibid., I, 120.

46. *IWSM*, 47:22-23.

47. *IWSM*, 48:26b.

48. *IWSM*, 48:20b.

49. *IWSM*, 48:23a-b.

50. *IWSM*, 48:23b, 25b-26.

51. *ISN*, 4.3.7, 4.4.2.

52. *ISN*, 4.3.7; *KS*, 4:15a-b.

53. *IWSM*, 48:26-27; *KS*, 4:15b-16.

54. For the Korean note, see *NGB*, vol. 1, pt. 1, no. 21, appendix 2, pp. 74-75; *KS*, 4:16.

55. For the Japanese reply, which came near the end of October, see *NGB*, vol. 1, pt. 1, no. 21, appendix 4, pp. 76-78, and appendix 5, pp. 78-79.

56. *NGB*, vol. 1, pt. 1, no. 99, pp. 229-239; *Nissen tsūkō shi*, I, 654.

57. *NGB*, vol. 1, pt. 1, nos. 245-246, pp. 573-574.

58. Tabohashi, *Kindai Nissen kankei no kenkyū*, I, 137.

59.   For this paper and the accompanying memorandum, see *NGB*, vol. 1, pt. 1, no. 288, and appendices 1 and 2, pp. 657-671.

60.   Ibid., appendix 2, pp. 660-666.

61.   Ibid., no. 355, p. 791. The Osaka branch of the Foreign Office seems to have been headed by Komatsu Tachibaki of Satsuma and Date Muneki, Lord of Uwajima.

62.   This seal was later changed to read "Taira no Ason Yoshitatsu shō" (The seal of Taira no Yoshitatsu, courtier).

63.   *Nissen tsūkō shi*, I, 649-653.

64.   Tabohashi, *Kindai Nissen kankei no kenkyū*, I, 150.

65.   Ibid.

66.   *Nissen tsūkō shi*, I, 655.

67.   For the text of the letter, see *NGB*, vol. 1, pt. 2, no. 705, pp. 690-691; *Nissen tsūkō shi*, I, 690-691. *Iwakura-kō jikki* (Accounts of Iwakura Tomomi), comp. Tada Yoshito (Tokyo, 1927), has a slightly different version of the text.

68.   For the texts of these letters and an illustration of the new seal, see *NGB*, vol. 1, pt. 2, no. 706, pp. 692-697, and vol. 2, pt. 2, no. 320, p. 224.

69.   *Tongnaebu kyerok* (Dispatches from the Tongnae district government), T'ung-chih 8.12.3; *Nissen tsūkō shi*, I, 657; *CS*, ser. 6, vol. 4, p. 208-209.

70.   Tabohashi, *Kindai Nissen kankei no kenkyū*, I, 156.

71.   *NGB*, vol. 2, pt. 2, no. 320, pp. 235-237.

72.   Ibid.

73.   Tabohashi, *Kindai Nissen kankei no kenkyū*, I, 171-172; *KS*, 6:36.

74.   *Nissen tsūkō shi*, I, 668-671; *NGB*, vol. 2, pt. 3, no. 615, pp. 410-412, and no. 616, p. 413.

75.   *NGB*, vol. 2, pt. 2, no. 320, pp. 229-230.

76. *ISN*, 6.12.13; see also *KS*, 6:36.

77. For the official instructions to Urase, see *NGB*, vol. 3, no. 95, pp. 151-153. In retrospect, it is probable that if the Ōshima plan had been adopted earlier, Korea-Japanese relations would have proceeded more smoothly. During the Tokugawa period, no part of a treaty and no aspect of established diplomatic procedure had been revised by arbitrary means; it had always been done by formal negotiations between the two countries. An outstanding example of this was the selection of a title to designate the shogun in diplomatic notes. The shogun was called "Ilbon kuk wang" (King of Japan) until 1695, when the title was changed to *taegun* (*taikun* in Japanese). Then in 1711, the Bakufu wanted to change it back to "King of Japan." The Bakufu's proposal was finally settled by formal negotiations. See *Sukchong sillok*, 50a:27a-b, 28a-b.

78. For a summary of the An-Urase negotiations, see *NGB*, vol. 3, no. 95, appendix 1, pp. 154-155. During these negotiations An Tong-jun pointed out that the use of the characters "imperial" and "imperial edict" would never be permitted by the Chinese government. Therefore, Urase's proposal that the two countries maintain their relations not in the names of *wang* (king) and *kō*, but in the names of the governments, and on an equal basis, seems to have satisfied An Tong-jun.

79. *NGB*, vol. 3, no. 95, appendix 1, p. 155.

80. Tabohashi, *Kindai Nissen kankei no kenkyū*, I, 235; *Dajōkan nikki* (The daily record of the Dajōkan), Meiji 3.4.13, 3.4.14; *NGB*, vol. 3, no. 96, p. 158; *FRUS, 1871*, p. 74 (enclosure in No. 21, Low to Fish, Peking, Nov. 22, 1870).

81. Ibid., pp. 74-75.

82. *Tongnaebu kyerok*, T'ung-chih 11.5.4, 11.5.5; *ISN*, 7.5.11, 7.5.12; also *KS*, 7:12b-13.

83. *PBTN*, 252:339b; *ISN*, 7.5.12.

84. Ibid.

85. *ISN*, 7.8.25. This was proposed by Chief Councillor Kim Pyŏng-hak. See *PBTN*, 252:362b, 363.

86. *NGB*, vol. 3, no. 95, appendix 2, pp. 156-157; and nos. 99-100, pp. 165-170.

87. The foremost advocates of the "conquest of Korea" were Ōshima Masatomo and his old friend, Kido Kōin. As early as the Bunkyu-Kanji period (1861-1865), Ōshima proposed that Japan make Korea a Japanese protectorate and annex China. Kido followed Ōshima's line. On March 13, 1869, Kido presented his Korea policy to Sanjō Sanetomi and Iwakura Tomomi and voiced the urgent necessity of conquering Korea. See *Nissen tsūkō shi*, I, 640-647; *NGB*, vol. 2, pt. 2, no. 51, pp. 205-208; and *Kido Takayoshi nikki* (Diary of Kido Kōin; Tokyo, 1932-1933), Meiji 1.12.14.

88. *NGB*, vol. 2, pt. 3, no. 486, pp. 849-850.

89. Ibid., no. 539, p. 95; no. 543, p. 102.

90. Ibid., no. 559, pp. 154-157.

91. *NGB*, vol. 3, no. 522, pp. 59-60; nos. 629-630, pp. 457-458; Sada Hakuchi, "Seikanron no kyūmudan" (Old dreams of the conquest of Korea), *Meiji bunka zenshū* (Complete works of Meiji culture), no. 22:38-39.

92. For details, see *NGB*, vol. 2, pt. 3, no. 574, pp. 265-269.

93. Ibid., no. 634, pp. 471-472; vol. 3, nos. 84-85, p. 127; Sada, p. 43.

94. For this report, see *NGB*, vol. 3, no. 87, pp. 131-138.

95. For the original text, see *NGB*, vol. 3, no. 88, appendix 1, pp. 138-140.

96. For the Korea policy proposed by Saitō and Moriyama, see ibid., appendices 2-3, pp. 140-143.

97. Yanagihara, then assistant minister of foreign affairs, and Kido were advocates of an "armed diplomacy." They argued that Korea had to be placed in Japan's sphere of influence before Britain, Russia, France, or America annexed her. For their Korea policy, see *NGB*, vol. 3, no. 90, pp. 145-146; no. 94, pp. 149-150; *Kido Takayoshi nikki*, Meiji 3.6.24, 3.6.26; and *Iwakura-kō jikki*, Meiji 3.7.18.

98. For Urase's report, see *NGB*, vol. 3, no. 95, pp. 151-158.

99. Ibid., appendix 1, pp. 154-155.

100. Ibid., no. 96, p. 158.

101.   Ibid., pp. 158-159; *Dajōkan nikki,* Meiji 3.9.18.

102.   Ibid., no. 98, pp. 160-161.

103.   For the texts of these letters, see ibid., appendix 1, pp. 162-165.

104.   Ibid., no. 101, pp. 170-171.

105.   Koma had been dismissed because of his alleged dishonesty and corruption. Ibid., nos. 102-103, pp. 171-173.

106.   Ibid.

107.   *NGB,* vol. 4, no. 166, pp. 267-268; no. 167, pp. 268-270.

108.   Ibid., no. 169, pp. 271-272.

109.   Ibid., no. 202, p. 317; no. 203, pp. 319-321.

110.   Ibid., no. 179, appendix, pp. 285-288.

111.   Ibid., no. 212, p. 329. This time the magistrate acknowledged Sō Shigemasa's earlier promotion and title, although the latter was no longer in use in his own country.

112.   Ibid., no. 197, p. 313 n. 1; no. 200, pp. 314-315.

113.   Ibid., no. 219, pp. 339-340.

114.   Ibid., p. 340; nos. 222-223, pp. 341-344.

115.   *NGB,* vol. 5, no. 135, pp. 305-306.

116.   Tabohashi, *Kindai Nissen kankei no kenkyū,* I, 270-271; ibid., pp. 305-307.

117.   Ibid., no. 217, pp. 336-339.

118.   Ibid., no. 140, pp. 311-312.

119.   Ibid., no. 141, p. 313.

120.   This time the letters again contained a few controversial words such as "Dai Nippon" and "Tenshi" (Son of Heaven).

121.   *NGB,* vol. 5, no. 141, pp. 313-314.

122.   Ibid., no. 146, pp. 318-319; *KS,* 9:15a-b; *PBTN,* 254:555b. These Korean
       sources do not mention this oral report. An's dispatch to Pusan, proposed by
       Chief Councillor Kim Pyŏng-hak, was related to the fact that he was well
       experienced in Japanese affairs.

123.   *Nissen tsūkō shi,* I, 685; *NGB,* vol. 5, no. 151, p. 330; no. 156, pp. 341-342;
       Tabohashi, *Kindai Nissen kankei no kenkyū,* I, 282.

124.   *ISN,* 9.8.6; *Tongnaebu kyerok,* T'ung-chih 11.5.27; 11.6.1, 11.6.6; *KS,* 9:21b;
       PBTN, 254:566b, 567a-b; *NGB,* vol. 5, no. 151, pp. 330, 331-332; pp. 332-334
       n. 2; no. 156, p. 342.

125.   Ibid., no. 157, p. 344.

126.   Ibid., no. 158, p. 345.

127.   Ibid., no. 157, pp. 344-345.

128.   Ibid., no. 162, p. 347; Tabohashi, *Kindai Nissen kankei no kenkyū,* I, 215.

129.   *NGB,* vol. 5, no. 162, pp. 348-350.

130.   *Tongnaebu kyerok,* T'ung-chih 11.9.20; Tabohashi, *Kindai Nissen kankei no
       kenkyū,* I, 217-218; *NGB,* vol. 5, no. 164, pp. 351-352; no. 167, p. 356.

131.   Tabohashi, *Kindai Nissen kankei no kenkyū,* I, 218-219; *NGB,* vol. 5, no. 150,
       pp. 327-329; no. 167, p. 356.

132.   Tabohashi Kiyoshi, *Kindai Nissen kankei no kenkyū,* I, 220-221; *NGB,* vol. 5,
       no. 162, p. 348.

133.   Ibid., no. 167, pp. 356-357.

134.   Tabohashi, *Kindai Nissen kankei no kenkyū,* I, 221.

135.   *NGB,* vol. 6, no. 105, pp. 238-240; no. 108, pp. 244-245; no. 114, p. 262.

136.   Ibid., no. 109, p. 246; no. 111, p. 252; no. 112, pp. 256-258; no. 115, p. 268;
       no. 118, pp. 276-277.

137.   Ibid., no. 119, pp. 280, 282-283.

138.   Sada, pp. 44-45.

139.   Sada, p. 45; *NGB*, vol. 6, no. 141, pp. 316-319.

XIII. *The Opposition Movement and the Fall of the Taewŏn'gun*

1.   The Taewŏn'gun wanted to prevent the reemergence of the in-law faction. For
     instance, he annulled a much rumored agreement with Kim Pyŏng-hak whereby
     his son was to marry one of Kim's daughters, provided that Kim would support
     the appointment of the son to the kingship. The primary reason for the king's
     marriage to Queen Min in May 1866 was that she had no living parents and
     belonged to the same clan as that of the Taewŏn'gun's wife. This marriage was
     strongly advocated by the Taewŏn'gun's wife, whose blood brother, Min Sŭng-ho,
     had earlier been adopted into the house of the queen. Both the Taewŏn'gun and
     his wife failed to discern the true character of Queen Min and the potential
     political rivalries among her kinsmen. Kikuchi, in his biography of Queen Min,
     noted that she possessed unusual intelligence, was a gifted political intriguer,
     and an enthusiastic reader of the *Tso chuan.* And, perhaps because she was an
     orphan, she was keenly aware of her insecure position in the face of the
     Taewŏn'gun's constant interference in the affairs of the royal house. A number
     of her kinsmen, such as Min Sŭng-ho, her adopted brother, and Min Kyŏm-ho,
     Sung-ho's blood brother, proved to be her close political associates. See Kikuchi,
     Taiinkun den tsuki ōhi no isshō, pp. 17, 80-85; Hwang Hyŏn, p. 22.

2.   Yi Ch'oe-ŭng, the Taewŏn'gun's brother, and Yi Yu-wŏn, a prominent Soron who
     once served as left councillor, actively sided with the queen's faction. See ibid.,,
     pp. 22, 24-25.

3.   For example, working with them were Yi Chae-myŏn (eldest son of the
     Taewŏn'gun), Cho Kyŏng-ho (the Taewŏn'gun's son-in-law), Cho Sŏng-ha
     (nephew of the ex-regent, Dowager Queen Cho), and Sŏng-ha's brother, Yŏng-ha.
     The Taewŏn'gun had consistently blocked their promotion to higher posts in the
     government because he felt they were not capable. See ibid., pp. 17, 26, 55-56;
     Kikuchi, *Taiinkun den tsuki ōhi no isshō,* p. 80.

4.   *ISN,* 3.8.9.

5.   For brief biographical notes, see *Chōsen jimmei jisho,* pp. 547-548; Chang
     Chi-yŏn, *Yugyo yŏnwŏn* (The origins of Confucianism; Seoul, 1922), pp. 145-
     147; Yi Hang-no, *Hwasŏ chip* (Collected works), vol. 9, appendix.

6. *Hŏnjong sillok,* 7:3.

7. *Chōsen jimmei jisho,* pp. 547-548.

8. Hwang Hyŏn, pp. 51-52, 402; Hong Hŭi, "Richō matsu jugaku keitō taiyo" (A general outline of Confucian schools in the late Yi dynasty), *Seikyū gakusō,* no. 19:205 (February 1935).

9. Here he means the China that was not ruled by barbarians, especially ancient China and Ming China, referred to as Chunghwa (Chung-hua), the true China. It is interesting to draw a parallel between the ideology of this school and that of Confucian scholars of the Sung period, such as Sun Ming-fu, Yeh Meng-te, Hu An-kuo, and Chu Hsi; these scholars wanted to deliver China from barbarian oppression (under the Liao and the Chin) or strike back at the barbarians through the study and reinterpretation of Confucius' *Spring and Autumn Annals,* kindling animosity against the foe and loyalty to their native Chinese dynasty. See Taki Kumanosuke, *Shina keigaku shi gaisetsu* (A general outline of Chinese Confucianism; Tokyo, 1934), p. 269; Takada Shinji et al., *Jukyō no shiteki gaikan* (A historical outline of Confucianism; Tokyo, 1937), pp. 127-128. For a general study of the philosophy of Hwasŏ's school, see *Chonhwa rok, kwŏn* 3-6; Yu In-sŏk, *Chaegyŏk paekkwan mun* (1896).

10. *Chonhwa rok,* preface by Ch'oe Ik-hyŏn, p. 1a-b.

11. Ibid., p. 2b.

12. Although the memorial was officially addressed to the king, it was understood that the Taewŏn'gun was its primary target. For the text, see *ISN,* 3.9.12; Yi Hang-no, vol. 3 (memorials), 3.9.12.

13. *ISN,* 3.9.14; Yi Hang-no, vol. 9, appendix (1866); Chang Chi-yŏn, *Yugyo yŏnwŏn,* p. 147.

14. In this memorial, he also called for the prescription of Western goods. See *ISN,* 3.9.19; *Meng-tzu,* bk. 7A *(chin-shin, shang),* chap. 14.

15. *Chonhwa rok,* 4:6b.

16. *ISN,* 3.10.7; Yi Hang-no, vol. 3; *KS,* 3:77b; *CS,* ser. 6, vol. 4, p. 121.

17. Yi Hang-no, vol. 9, appendix (1868).

18. One of Ch'oe Tae's sons, Ch'oe Ik-hyŏn, was born in 1833 in P'och'ŏn, Kyŏnggi. In addition to his key role in the downfall of the Taewŏn'gun, Ch'oe is remembered as a leading founder of the militia force (ŭibyŏng or "righteous army") that fought the Japanese regulars during the last years of Korea's independence. Many of the militia leaders, such as Yu In-sŏk and Yu Chung-gyo, were Hwasŏ's disciples. Ch'oe's own unit was formed in June 1906 after he sent his famous open letter to the Japanese government charging Japan with "sixteen crimes" committed against Korea. However, he was captured on June 11 at Sunch'ang, and removed to Tsushima for imprisonment, on July 28. He died there on December 2 at the age of seventy-three. He entrusted to Im Pyŏng-ch'an, another captured militia leader, his moving posthumous memorial. For biographical and other accounts, see Hwang Hyŏn, pp. 198, 326-329, 331-333, 359-363, 366, 376-381, 386, 402; Yi Ki, *Haehak yusŏ* (Posthumous collection of works), Han'guk saryo ch'ongsŏ, no. 3 (1955), pp. 150-157; Chang Chi-yŏn, *Wiam mun'go* (Collected works), Han'guk saryo ch'ongsŏ, no. 4 (1956), pp. 46, 90-91.

19. Ch'oe passed the civil service examination in 1855. Between 1855 and 1863 he held several minor posts: vice-inspector, vice-censor, first assistant secretary of appointment, and magistrate of Sinch'ang, resigned from the last of these in 1863 after a quarrel with the provincial authorities. Yi Ki, p. 150; Ch'oe Ik-hyŏn, *Myŏnam chip* (Collected works; 1933), vol. 6 *(yŏnbo)*: 1855-1863.

20. Ibid., vol. 6 *(yŏnbo)*: 1868.

21. Ibid., vol. 3: *so* (memorial of the tenth month of 1868); *ISN*, 5.10.10; *KS*, 5:46a-b.

22. *ISN*, 5.10.14 5.4.18; Yi T'ae-wang, *Chuyŏn sŏnjip* (Selected works of King Kojong), ed. Aoyanagi Kōtarō (Keijo, 1919), p. 389; *KS*, 5:47a-b, 48.

23. *ISN*, 9.11.17.

24. *ISN*, 10.4.5; *KS*, 10:9.

25. *ISN*, 10.9.10; *KS*, 10:22.

26. *ISN*, 10.10.10; Chŏng Kyo, p. 8.

27. *ISN*, 10.10.25; *KS*, 10:24a-b.

28. *ISN*, 10.10.25; Ch'oe Ik-hyŏn, appendix: *yŏnbo* (tenth month of 1873); *KS*, 10:24b.

29. *ISN,* 10.10.26, 10.10.27; *KS,* 10:24b-25.

30. *ISN,* 10.10.28, 10.10.29; *KS,* 10:25, 26b-27b, 29b.

31. *ISN,* 10.10.28; *KS,* 10:25-26.

32. *ISN,* 10.10.29; 10.11.1, 10.11.2, 10.11.5; *KS,* 10:27, 29b, 30a-b, 39b.

33. *ISN,* 10.10.29; Ŏ Yun-jung, pp. 44-45; *KS,* 10:28-29.

34. *ISN,* 10.11.3; for the text of the memorial, see Ch'oe Ik-hyŏn, vol. 3
     (memorials): 11.3. kyeyu (1873); *KS,* 10:31-35.

35. For the quotation, see *Lun-yü,* "Pa-i." For the background and significance of
     this passage, see Akaike Atsushi, *Seikyō yori mitaru Rongo shin shaku* (A new
     political and educational interpretation of the *Analects;* Tokyo, 1930), pp. 100-
     101.

36. On August 12, 1864, over one hundred former "traitors," most of them victims
     of factional strife, were posthumously pardoned. See *ISN,* 1.7.7, 1.7.10, 1.7.11,
     1.7.12, 1.7.14, 1.7.18.

37. Han Hyo-sun (?-1621), a member of the Taebuk faction, was responsible for
     demoting Queen Dowager Kim, Sŏnjo's second consort, in 1618. This action
     was instigated by the Taebuk faction which was then in power. At the time, Han
     was the right councillor. In 1623, when Kwanghae was deposed and Injo
     installed by the Sŏin (the predecessor of the Noron and Soron), Han was
     stripped of rank and title, and was banished. See Yi Man-un, *Kinyŏn aram*
     (Keijo, 1911), p. 352; *Kukcho inmulchi,* II, 298; *Kwanghae-gun ilgi,* 123:3b, 28.

38. Mok Nae-sŏn (1617?-1704) and Yi Hyŏn-il (1627?-1704), both of whom
     belonged to the Namin, took part in deposing Queen Min, King Sukchong's
     consort, in 1689 when the Namin were in power. Mok and Yi were then respec-
     tively left councillor and assistant minister of works. In 1694, when the Namin
     lost power to the Noron and Soron and the queen was reinstated, Mok and Yi,
     like Han Hyo-sun, were stripped of rank and title, and banished. See *Kukcho
     inmulchi,* III, 174, 183; *Sukchong sillok,* 20:44b, 51b-52b, 53-61; 21:1a-b,
     4a-b; 26:12-13, 18b-19b, 27a-b; 40:32a-b, 36.

39. *ISN,* 10.11.3; *KS,* 10:35.

40. *ISN,* 10.11.4; Ŏ Yun-jung, p. 45; *KS,* 10:35b-38.

41. Ch'oe Ik-hyŏn, vol. 16 (miscellaneous): "Circumstantial Account of the 1873 Exile"; *ISN*, 10.11.5; *KS*, 10:39b.

42. *ISN*, 10.11.5; *KS*, 10:38-39.

43. Ch'oe Ik-hyŏn, vol. 16.

44. *KS*, 10:41a-b. During the night of December 27, while Myŏnam was imprisoned at the Tribunal, a secret messenger delivered a letter said to have come from a man named Yun, a personal secretary to the queen. The author of the letter advised Myŏnam not to mention the restoration of the Mandongmyo at the trial on the following day, because it had been abolished by the edict of the Queen Dowager Cho while she was regent, but urged him not to be afraid to criticize other matters. The messenger told Myŏnam that the court (the queen?) would help him, if he answered the letter, but Myŏnam returned the letter to its author and ignored the request. This episode shows that Myŏnam was not really politically in league with the queen's faction. See Ch'oe Ik-hyŏn, vol. 16.

45. *ISN*, 10.11.9, 10.11.10, 10.11.12; 12.2.8; *KS*, 10:41b-44b.

46. The public announcement of this decision was canceled on the following day because such a decision had already been officially announced on March 10, 1865, when Queen Dowager Cho terminated her regency. See *ISN*, 10.11.5; 3.2.13; *KS*, 10:38.

47. *ISN*, 10.11.10, 10.11.11, 10.11.13; *KS*, 10:44b, 45b.

48. *ISN*, 10.12.2; *KS*, 10:50a-b.

49. *ISN*, 10.11.7, 10.12.10; *KS*, 10:40b-41, 45b-46b, 52b-53.

50. *ISN*, 11.8.29; 12.3.4; *KS*, 11:74b; 12:15a-b.

51. *ISN*, 10.12.14, 10.12.15, 10.12.18; *KS*, 10:53-54b, 55a-b.

52. *ISN*, 11.10.20, 11.10.21, 11.10.22, 11.10.23; *KS*, 11:87-88.

53. *ISN*, 12.3.5, 12.3.6; *KS*, 12:15b.

54. *ISN*, 12.5.17, 12.6.17, 12.6.18; *KS*, 12:20b-21, 23a-b.

55. In 1882, as the result of a mutiny among the military, the Taewŏn'gun returned to power. He was soon abducted, however, and brought to China by Chinese

troops that had been called to Korea to quell the mutiny. He was kept in custody
at Paoting for nearly three years. In 1894 the Japanese asked him to carry out
political reforms, but he apparently worked with the Tonghak rebels against the
Japanese. In 1895, after the Tonghak rebellion was crushed, he was again briefly
supported by the Japanese, who assassinated Queen Min that same year.

BIBLIOGRAPHY

Akaike Atsushi 赤池濃. *Seikyō yori mitaru Rongo shin shaku* 政教 より觀たる 論語新釋 (A new political and educational interpretation of the *Analects*). Tokyo, 1930.

Asō Takekame 麻生武龜 . "Richō no kenkoku to seiken no suii" 李朝の建國と政權の推移 (The founding of the Yi dynasty and change in political power), *Seikyū gakusō* 青丘學叢 (Korean studies quarterly), 5:118-134 (August 1931).

Cable, E.M. "United States-Korean Relations, 1866-1871," *Transactions of the Korea Branch of the Royal Asiatic Society,* 28:1-230 (1938).

Ch'a Mun-sŏp 車文燮 . "Imnan ihu ŭi yangyŏk kwa kyunyŏkpŏp ŭi sŏngnip" 壬亂以後의良役과均役法의成立 (On the *ryang-yeok* and *gyun-yeok* assize in the late Yi dynasty), *Sahak yŏn'gu* 史學研究 (The study of history), 10:115-130 (April 1961); 11: 83-146 (July 1961).

Chang Chi-yŏn 張志淵 . *Yugyo yŏnwŏn* 儒教淵源 (The origins of Confucianism). Seoul, 1922.

———*Wiam mun'go* 韋庵文稿 (Collected works). Han'guk saryo ch'ongsŏ 韓國史料叢書 (Series of historical material on Korea), no. 4. Seoul, 1956.

Ch'ien Mu 錢穆. *Chung-kuo chin-san-pai-nien hsüeh-shu shih* 中國近三百年學術史(Chinese intellectual history in the last three hundred years). 2 vols. Taiwan, 1957.

Cho Ik 趙翼 . *P'ojŏ chip* 浦渚集 (Collected works), in *Chōsen fūzoku kankei shiryō satsuyō,* pp. 1713-17.

Choe Ching Young. "The Decade of the Taewŏn'gun: Reform, Seclusion, and Disaster." 2 vols. Ph.D. thesis, Harvard University, 1960.

Ch'oe Ik-hyŏn 崔益鉉 . *Myŏnam chip* 勉菴集 (Collected works). 24 vols. (40 *kwŏn,* 4 *kwŏn,* and 4 *kwŏn*). 1933.

Ch'ŏlchong sillok 哲宗實錄 (The annals of King Ch'ŏlchong). 16 *kwŏn.*

Chŏng Chin-sŏk 鄭鎮石 et al. *Chosŏn ch'ŏrhak sa* 朝鮮哲学 (A history of Korean philosophy), vol. 1. P'yŏngyang, 1962.

Chǒng Kyo 鄭喬 . *Taehan kyenyǒ sa* 大韓季年史 (Chronological record of the latter part of the Yi dynasty). Han'guk saryo ch'ongsǒ, no. 5. Seoul, 1957.

Chǒng Tasan 丁茶山 (A collection of studies on Chǒng Yag-yong in commemoration of the two hundredth anniversary of his birth), comp. Kwahagwǒn ch'ǒrhak yǒn'guso 科學院哲學研究所 (Institute of Philosophy of the Academy of Sciences). P'yǒngyang, 1962.

Chǒng To-jǒn 鄭道傳 . *Sambong chip* 三峯集 (Collected works). Han'guk saryo ch'ongsǒ, no. 13. Seoul, 1961.

Chǒng Wǒn-yong 鄭元容 . *Kyǒngsan chip* 經山集 (Collected works). 26 *kwǒn*. 1895.

Chǒng Yag-yong 丁若鏞 . *Mongmin simsǒ* 牧民心書 .48 *kwǒn*. 1901.

———*Kyǒngse yup'yo* 經世遺表 . 44 *kwǒn*. 1914.

———*Yǒyudang chǒnsǒ* 與猶堂全書 (Collected works), comp. Kim Sǒng-jin 金誠鎮 . 152 *kwǒn*. Kyǒngsǒng, 1934.

Chǒngjo sillok 正祖實錄 (The annals of King Chǒngjo). 56 *kwǒn*.

Chǒngjong sillok 定宗實錄 (The annals of King Chǒngjong). 6 *kwǒn*.

Chonhwa rok 尊華錄 (Records of the Revere-China school), comp. Song Pyǒng-jik 宋秉櫻 , with prefaces by Ch'oe Ik-hyǒn 崔益鉉 , Hong Sǔng-un 洪承運 et al. 6 *kwǒn*. 1900.

Chōsen fūzoku kankei shiryō satsuyō 朝鮮風俗關係資料撮要 (A compendium of source materials on Korean manners and customs). Keijo, Chōsen sōtokufu chūsū in, 1944.

Chōsen jimmei jisho 朝鮮人名辭書 (Korean biographical dictionary). Keijo, Chōsen sōtokufu chūsū in, 1937.

Chōsen no ruiji shūkyō 朝鮮の類似宗教 (Pseudo-religions of Korea), Chōsen sōtokufu chōsa shiryō 朝鮮總督府調査資料 (Series of research materials of the government general of Korea), no. 42. Keijo, Chōsen sōtokufu, 1935.

Chōsen no senboku to yogen 朝鮮の占卜と豫言 (The divinations and prophecies of Korea). Chōsen sōtokufu chōsa shiryō, no. 37. Keijo, Chōsen sōtokufu, 1933.

Chōsen shi 朝鮮史 (Chronological abstracts of historical documents on Korea), comp. Chōsen sōtokufu. 37 vols. Keijo, 1932-1940.

Chōsen shiryō shūshin kaisetsu 朝鮮史料集真解説 (Annotated historical documents of Korea). Chōsen shi henshū kai 朝鮮史編修會 (Committee on the Compilation of Korean History Series), no. 6. Keijo, Chōsen sōtokufu, 1936.

Chosŏn t'ongsa 朝鮮通史 (A general history of Korea), comp. Kwahagwŏn yŏksa yŏn'guso 科學院歷史研究所 (Institute of History of the Academy of Sciences). New ed. P'yŏngyang, 1962.

Chosŏn ŭi myŏngin 朝鮮의名人 (Famous Koreans), ed. Kim Il-sŏng chonghap taehak yŏksa yŏn'guso 金日成綜合大學歷史研究会 (Kim Il-sŏng University, Institute of History). P'yŏngyang, 1962.

Ch'ou-pan i-wu shih-mo 籌辦夷務始末 (A complete account of our management of barbarian affairs). 100 *chüan* for the T'ung-chih period. Peking, The Palace Museum, 1929-1930.

Ch'ugwan chi 秋官志 (Records on punishments). Reprint. Keijo, Chōsen sōtokufu chūsū in, 1937.

Chukkye chi 竹溪誌 (The recordings of the Sosu Academy), comp. Chu Se-bung. 3 *kwŏn*. 1863 ed.

Chŭngbo munhŏnbigo 增補文獻備考 (The enlarged and supplemented encyclopedia). Reprint. 250 *kwŏn*. Seoul, 1957.

Chŭngjŏng kyorinji 增正交隣志 (A revised and enlarged history of Korean-Japanese relations). Reprint. 6 *kwŏn* and *chŭngbo* 增補. Keijo, 1940.

Chungjong sillok 中宗實錄 (The annals of King Chungjong). 105 *kwŏn*.

Clark, Charles A. *Religions of Old Korea.* New York, 1932.

Courant, Maurice. *Bibliographie Coréenne.* 3 vols. Paris, 1894-1896.

Dai Nippon gaikō bunsho 大日本外交文書 (Diplomatic documents of Japan), comp. Gaimushō chōsabu 外務省調査部 (Research division of the foreign ministry). 11 vols. (1867-1875). Tokyo, 1936-1940.

Dajōkan nikki 太政官日記 (The daily record of the Dajōkan).

Dallet, Charles. *Histoire de l'Eglise de Corée.* 2 vols. Paris, 1874.

Fonti Ricciane; Documenti originali concernenti Matteo Ricci e la storia delle prime relazioni tra l'Europa e la Cina (1579-1615), ed. with comments by Pasquale M. d'Elia, S.J. 3 vols. Rome, 1942-1949.

Fukaya Toshitetsu 深谷 敏鉄 . "Sensho no tochi seido ippan: iwayuru kadenhō wo chūshin to shite" 鮮初の土地制度一班： いわゆる科田法を中心として (A study of the land system of the early Yi dynasty with special emphasis on the so-called degree land system), *Shigaku zasshi* 史學雜誌 (Journal of history), 50.5:47-82 (May 1939); 50.6:32-78 (June 1939).

———"Kadenhō kara shokudenhō e" 科田法から職田法へ (A study of the rank land system and the service land system), *Shigaku zasshi,* 51.9:1-42 (September 1940); 51.10:1-29 (October 1940).

Govéa, Alexandre de. "Etablissement du Christianisme en Corée," *Revue d'Histoire des Missions,* 8.3:415-432 (September 1931).

Griffis, William Elliot. *Corea, the Hermit Nation.* New York, 1882.

Hamgyŏng kamyŏng kyerok 咸鏡監營啓錄 (Dispatches from Hamgyŏng provincial government), comp. Pibyŏnsa and Ŭijŏngbu after 1865.

Han U-gŭn (Han Woo-keun) 韓沽劤 . "Sŏngho Yi Ik yŏn'gu ŭi iltan: kŭ ŭi kwagŏje sibi rŭl chungsim hayŏ" 星湖李瀷研究의一端： 그의科學制是非을中心하여 (A study on Yi Ik: With emphasis on his criticism of the civil service examination), *Yŏksa hakpo* 歷史學報 (Journal of history), 7:326-350 (1954).

———"Sŏngho Yi Ik yŏn'gu: kŭ ŭi saron kwa pungdang non" 星湖李瀷研究, 그의史論과朋黨論 (A study on Yi Ik: His views on history and factionalism), *Sahoe kwahak* 社會科學 (Social science journal), 1:33-52 (1957).

———"Yijo sirhak ŭi kaenyŏm e tae hayŏ" 李朝實學의概念에對하여 (On the concept of the Sirhak of the Yi dynasty), *Chindan hakpo* 震檀學報 (Journal of the Chindan Society), no. 19:25-46 (May 1958).

———*Yijo hugi ŭi sahoe wa sasang* 李朝後期의社會와思想 (Society and culture: Eighteenth-century Korea). Han'guk munhwa ch'ongsŏ 韓國文化叢書 (Korean culture series), no. 16. Seoul, 1961.

Hong Hŭi 洪熹 . "Richō matsu jugaku keitō taiyo" 李朝末儒學系統 (A general outline of Confucian schools in the late Yi dynasty), *Seikyū gakusō*, no. 19:205-206 (February 1935).

Hong I-sŏp 洪以燮 . *Chŏng Yag-yong ŭi chŏngch'i kyŏngje sasang yŏn'gu* 丁若鏞의政治經濟思想研究 (A study on the politico-economic thought of Chŏng Yag-yong). Han'guk yŏn'gu ch'ongsŏ 韓國研究叢書 (Series on Korean studies), no. 3. Seoul, 1959.

Hong Tae-yong 洪大容 . "Imha kyŏng yun", in his *Tamhŏnsŏ* 湛軒書 (Collected works). 10 *kwŏn*. Seoul, 1939.

Hŏnjong sillok 憲宗實錄 (The annals of King Hŏnjong). 17 *kwŏn*.

Hosoi Hajime 細井肇 . *Koku taikō no manajiri* 國太公の眦 (A biography of the Taewŏn'gun). Tokyo, 1929.

Hu Shih wen-ts'un san-chi 胡適文存三集 (Collected works of Hu Shih). 4 *ts'e*. Shanghai, 1930.

Hwanghae kamyŏng kyerok 黃海監營啓錄 (Dispatches from the Hwanghae provincial government), comp. Pibyŏnsa and Ŭijŏngbu.

Hwang Hyŏn 黃玹 . *Maech'ŏn yarok* 梅泉野錄 (Collected works). Han'guk saryo ch'ongsŏ, no. 1. Seoul, 1955.

Hwayang chi 華陽誌, (Recordings of the Hwayang Academy), with a preface by Song Chu-sang 宋周相 . 2 *kwŏn*. 1807.

Hyojong sillok 孝宗實錄 (The annals of King Hyojong). 22 *kwŏn*.

Hyŏn Sang-yun 玄相允 . *Chosŏn yuhak sa* 朝鮮儒學史 (A history of Korean Confucianism). Seoul, 1954.

Hyŏnjong sillok 顯宗實錄 (The annals of King Hyŏnjong). 23 *kwŏn*.

Ilsŏngnok 日省錄 (The daily records concerning national affairs), comp. Kyujanggak 奎章閣 . 2294 *kwŏn*.

Imsullok 壬戌錄 (Collected documents concerning the uprisings of 1862). Han'guk saryo ch'ongsŏ, no. 8. Seoul, 1958.

Injo sillok 仁祖實錄 (The annals of King Injo). 50 *kwŏn*.

Iwakura-kō jikki 岩倉公實記 (Accounts of Iwakura Tomomi), comp. Tada Yoshito 多田好問 . 3 vols. Tokyo, 1927.

Junkin, William M. "The Tong Hak," *The Korean Repository*, 2:56-61 (January 1895).

Kangdo chi 江都誌 (Gazetteer of Kanghwa), ed. Pak Hŏn-yong 朴憲用. 2 vols. 1932.

Keijō-fu shi 京城府史 (A history of Seoul). 3 vols. Keijo, 1934-1941.

Kido Takayoshi nikki 木戸孝允日記 (Diary of Kido Kōin). 3 vols. Tokyo, 1932-1933.

Kikuchi Kenjō 菊池謙讓. *Taiinkun den tsuki ōhi no isshō* 大院君傳付王妃の一生 (A biography of the Taewŏn'gun and the life of the queen). Keijo, 1910.

———*Kindai Chōsen shi* 近代朝鮮史 (A history of modern Korea). 2 vols. Tokyo, 1940.

Kim Chŏng-hŭi 金正喜. *Wandang sŏnsaeng chŏnjip* 阮堂先生全集 (Collected works), with a preface by Kim Yŏng-han 金甯漢. 10 *kwŏn*. 1934.

Kim Ki-dong 金起東. *Yijo sidae sosŏllon* 李朝時代小説論 (Studies on the novels of the Yi period). 2nd ed. Seoul, 1964.

Kim Kwang-jin 김 광 진. *Chŏng Tasan ŭi kyŏngje sasang* 丁茶山의 經濟思想 (A study on the economic thought of Chŏng Yag-yong). P'yŏngyang, 1962.

Kim Mun-gyŏng 金文卿. "Yongdam yusa" 龍潭遺詞 (The posthumous poems of Ch'oe Che-u), *Seikyū gakusō*, 7:123-139 (February 1932); 8:145-165 (May 1932).

Kim Tŭk-hwang 金得榥. *Han'guk sasang sa* 韓國思想史 (A history of Korean thought). Rev. ed. Seoul, 1963.

Kim Yong-dŏk 金龍德. "Chŏngyu Pak Che-ga yŏn'gu" 貞蕤朴齊家研究 (A study on Pak Che-ga). *Sahak yŏn'gu*, 10:1-24 (April 1961).

Kojong sillok 高宗實錄 (The annals of King Kojong). 52 *kwŏn*.

Koksŏng kunji 谷城郡誌 (Gazetteer of Koksŏng), ed. Chŏng Su-t'ae 丁秀泰 et al. 1918.

Kolonizaciya sibiri: v svyazi s obščim pereselenčeskim voprosom (The colonization of Siberia and its relationship to general immigration problems), ed. Kancelyariya komiteta ministrov. St. Petersburg, 1900.

Koryŏsa 高麗史 (The history of Koryŏ). Reprint. Seoul, 1955.

Ku Yen-wu 顧炎武 . *Jih-chih lu* 日知錄 (Notes on daily accumulation of knowledge), comp. and annotated by Huang Ju-ch'eng 黃汝成 . Hupeh, 1872.

Kukcho inmulchi 國朝人物誌 (Eminent Koreans of the Yi dynasty), comp. An Chong-hwa 安鍾和 . 3 vols. 1909.

Kukcho pogam 國朝寶鑑 (The comprehensive history of the Yi dynasty). 90 *kwŏn.* 1909.

Kuksa taesajŏn 國史大事典 (A dictionary of Korean history), comp. Yi Hong-jik 李弘植 . 2 vols. Seoul, 1962-1963.

Kwanghae-gun ilgi 光海君日記 (The annals of King Kwanghae). The Mt. Chŏngjok-san pon 鼎足山本 text. 187 *kwŏn.*

Kyonam chi 嶠南誌 (Gazetteer of Kyŏngsang). 76 *kwŏn.* 1940.

Kyŏnggi suyŏng kyerok 京畿水營啓錄 (Dispatches from Kyŏnggi naval headquarters), comp. Pibyŏnsa and Ŭijŏngbu.

Kyŏngguk taejŏn 經國大典 (The great code of administration). Collated and reprinted by Chōsen sōtokufu chūsū in. Keijo, 1934.

Lanunay, Adrien. *La Corée et les Missionnaires Français.* Tours, 1901.

———*Martyrs Français et Coréens, 1838-1846.* Paris, 1925.

Maema Kyōsaku 前間恭作 . *Kosen sappu* 古鮮冊譜 (Bibliographical notes on old Korean works). 3 vols. Tokyo, 1957.

Man'gi yoram chaeyong p'yŏn 萬機要覽財用編 (Guide to royal administration, section on finance). Collated and reprinted by Chōsen sōtokufu chūsū in. Keijo, 1937.

Man'gi yoram kunjŏng p'yŏn 萬機要覽軍政編 (Guide to royal administration, section on the military). Collated and reprinted by Chōsen sōtokufu chūsū in. Keijo, 1937.

Matsushita Yoshio 松下芳男 . *Nisshin sensō zengo* 日清戰爭前後 (Before and after the Sino-Japanese war, 1894-1895). Tokyo, 1939.

Moritani Katsumi 森谷克己 . "Kyūrai no Chōsen nōgyō shakai ni tsuite no kenkyū no tame ni" 舊來の朝鮮農業社會についての研究のために (A study of the agrarian society in old Korea), in *Chōsen shakai keizai shi kenkyū* 朝鮮社會經濟史研究 (Studies of the socio-economic history of Korea), pp. 297-520. Tokyo, 1933.

Munjong sillok 文宗實錄 (The annals of King Munjong). 13 *kwŏn.*

Mutel, G. *The Catholic Church in Korea.* Hongkong, 1924.

———*Documents relatifs aux martyrs de Corée de 1839 et 1848.* Hongkong, 1924.

———*Documents relatifs aux martyrs de Corée de 1866.* Hongkong, 1925.

Myŏngjong sillok 明宗實錄 (The annals of King Myŏngjong). 34 *kwŏn.*

Nissen tsūkō shi 日鮮通交史 (A history of Korean-Japanese relations). 2 vols. Fusan, 1915.

Ŏ Yun-jung 魚允中 . *Chongjŏng yŏnp'yo* 從政年表 (Chronology of political events). Han'guk saryo ch'ongsŏ, no. 6. Seoul, 1958.

Oda Shōgo 小田省吾 . "Richō seisō ryaku shi" 李朝政爭略 (An outline history of political strife in the Yi dynasty), in *Chōsen shi kōza, bunrui shi* 朝鮮史講座, 分類史 (Selected articles on Korean history). Keijo, Chōsen shi gakkai, 1924.

———"Richō no hōtō wo ryakujo shite tenshukyō hakugai ni oyobu" 李朝 の朋黨を略叙して天主敎迫害に及ぶ (An outline of factionalism in the Yi dynasty and notes on Catholic persecution), *Seikyū gakusō,* 1:1-26 (August 1930).

———"Kō Kei-rai hanran no gairyaku to sono dōki ni tsuite" 洪景來 叛亂の概略と其の動機に就いて (A general description of the Hong Kyŏng-nae rebellion and its motives), *Seikyū gakusō,* 8:1-18 (May 1932); 11:88-107 (February 1933).

Oppert, Ernest. *A Forbidden Land: Voyages to the Corea.* London, 1880.

Ōuchi Takeji 大内武次 . "Richō makki no nōson" 李朝末期の 農村 (Agrarian villages in the late Yi dynasty), in *Chōsen shakai keizai shi kenkyū,* pp. 227-295.

Pak Che-ga 朴齊家 . *Pukhak ŭi* 北學議 (Discourse on "northern learning"), transcribed by Pak Kŭng-sŏng 朴兢性 . 2 *kwŏn.* 1821.

Pak Chi-wŏn 朴趾源. *Yŏnam chip* 燕岩集 (Collected works), comp. Pak Yŏng-ch'ŏl 朴榮喆 . 17 *kwŏn*. Kyŏngsŏng, 1932.

——*Yŏrha ilgi* 熱河日記 (Diary of Jehol). Reprint. Taiwan, 1956.

Pak Kyu-su 朴珪壽 . *Hwanjae chip* 瓛齋集 (Collected works), with preface by Kim Yun-sik 金允植. 11 *kwŏn*. 1911.

Pak Si-hyŏng 朴時亨 . *Chosŏn t'oji chedo sa* 朝鮮土地制度史 (Studies on the Korean land system), vol. 2. P'yŏngyang, 1961.

Pak Ŭn-sik 朴殷植 . *Han'guk t'ongsa* 韓國痛史 (The tragic history of Korea). Hansŏng, 1946.

Pak Wŏn-sŏn 朴元善 . *Pubosang* 負裸商 (A study on Korean native merchants). Han'guk yŏn'gu ch'ongsŏ, no. 16. Seoul, 1965.

Paullin, Charles O. *Diplomatic Negotiations of American Naval Officers, 1778-1883*. Baltimore, 1912.

Piacentini, Arthur. *Mgr. Ridel, évêque de Philippolis, vicaire apostolique de Corée, d'après sa correspondence.* Lyon, 1890.

Pibyŏnsa tŭngnok 備邊司謄錄 (The records of the Pibyŏnsa), comp. Pibyŏnsa and Ŭijŏngbu after 1866. Reprinted by Kuksa p'yŏnch'an wiwŏnhoe. 28 vols. Seoul, 1959-1960.

Pukkwan ŭpchi 北關邑誌 (Gazetteer of North Hamgyŏng). 5 vols. 1871.

Puyŏ chi 扶餘誌 (Gazetteer of Puyŏ), with preface by Hong Han-p'yo 洪漢杓 . 1929.

P'yŏngan kamyŏng kyerok 平安監營啓錄 (Dispatches from the P'yŏngan provincial government), comp. Pibyŏnsa and Ŭijŏngbu. 37 *kwŏn*. 1830-1884.

Pyŏngin choein Chong-sam Pong-ju tŭng kugan 丙寅罪人鍾三鳳周等鞫案 (The trial records of the 1866 convicts, Nam Chong-sam and Hong Pong-ju), comp. Ŭigŭmbu. 1 *kwŏn*.

P'yŏngsan kunji 平山郡誌 (Gazetteer of P'yŏngsan), originally comp. Ku Haeng 具縇 . New and enlarged ed. 1802.

Richō jidai no zaisei 李朝時代の財政 (A study of Yi finance). Keijo, Chōsen sōtokufu, 1936.

Rodgers, John, Rear Admiral, USN. "Partial Report on the Military Expedition to Corea," *Transactions of the Korea Branch of the Royal Asiatic Society,* 28:189-191 (1938).

Sada Hakuchi 佐田白茅 . "Seikanron no kyūmudan" 征韓論の
舊夢談 (Old dreams of the conquest of Korea), in *Meiji bunka
zenshū* 明治文化全集 (Complete works of Meiji culture), 22:
35-52 (1929).

Samban yesik 三班禮式 (Rules of etiquette for the three classes),
comp. Yi Ha-ŭng 李昰應 . 2 *kwŏn*. 1866.

Schall von Bell, Johann Adam. *Historica relation de ortu et progressu fidei
orthodoxae in Regno Chinensi per missionarios societatis Jesu ab anno
1581 usque ad annum 1669*. Ratisbon, 1672.

Schley, Winfield Scott, Rear-Admiral, USN. "Partial Report of the Engagement of the June 10-11th, 1871," *Transactions of the Korea Branch of
the Royal Asiatic Society*, 28:192-197 (1938).

Sejo sillok 世祖實錄 (The annals of King Sejo). 49 *kwŏn*.

Sejong sillok 世宗實錄 (The annals of King Sejong). 163 *kwŏn*.

Shakanmai seido 社還米制度 (Studies on the grain-loan system). Keijo,
Chōsen sōtokufu, 1933.

Shidehara Hiroshi 幣原坦 . *Kankoku seisō shi* 韓國政爭志. (A
history of Korean factional strife). Tokyo, 1907.

Shigeyoshi Manji 重吉万治 . "Bihenshi no setchi ni tsukite" 備邊司
の設置に就きて (On the establishment of the Pibyŏnsa),
Seikyū gakusō, 23:23-81 (February 1936).

Shinobu Jumpei 信夫淳平 . *Kan hantō* 韓半島 (The Korean
peninsula). Tokyo, 1901.

Shortland, John R. *The Corean Martyrs*. London, 1869.

Sibirskaya sovetskaya enciklopediya (The encyclopedia of Soviet Siberia),
ed. M.K. Azadovskii et al., vol. 2. Zapadnosibirskoe otdelenie ogis, 1931.

Sinica Franciscana, vol. 3: *Relationes et epistolas Fratrum Minorum Saeculi
XVII*, comp., ed., and annotated by P. Anastasius van den Wyngaert,
O.F.M. Florence, 1936.

Sinjŭng Tongguk yŏji sŭngnam 新增東國與地勝覽 (The new and
enlarged gazetteer of Korea). Reprint. 55 *kwŏn*. Keijo, 1930.

Sok taejŏn 續大典 (Supplementary great code). Collated and reprinted
by Chōsen sōtokufu chūsū in. 2nd ed. Keijo, 1938.

Sŏngjong sillok 成宗實錄 (The annals of King Sŏngjong). 297 *kwŏn*.

Sŏnjo sillok 宣祖實錄 (The annals of King Sŏnjo). 221 *kwŏn.*

Sudō Yoshiyuki 周藤吉之 . "Raimatsu Sensho ni okeru nōsō ni tsuite" 麗末鮮初に於ヶる農莊に就いて (On the estates of the late Koryŏ and early Yi dynasties), *Seikyū gakusō,* 17:1-80 (August 1934).

———"Kōraichō yori Richō shoki ni itaru densei no kaikaku" 高麗朝より李朝初期に致る田制の改革(The reform of the land system from the Koryŏ dynasty to the early Yi dynasty), *Tōa gaku* 東亞學 (Orientalica), 3:115-191 (1940).

Suematsu Yasukazu 末松保和 . "Chōsen Giseifu kō" 朝鮮議政府考 (Study on the council of state of Yi Korea), *Chōsen gakuhō* 朝鮮學報 (Journal of the Academic Association of Koreanology in Japan), 9:1-35 (1956).

Sukchong sillok 肅宗實錄 (The annals of King Sukchong). 65 *kwŏn.*

Sŭngjŏngwŏn ilgi 承政院日記 (The diary of the royal secretariat), comp. Sŭngjŏngwŏn. 1,674 *kwŏn.*

Sunjo sillok 純祖實錄 (The annals of King Sunjo). 36 *kwŏn.*

Sunmuyŏng tŭngnok 巡撫營謄錄 (Records of the Kiboyŏnhae sunmuyŏng). 5 *kwŏn.* 1866.

Suzuki Yoshijirō 鈴木由次郎 . *Tōyō tetsugaku shisō shi* 東洋哲學思想史 (A history of Oriental philosophy and thought). Tokyo, 1950.

Tabohashi Kiyoshi 田保橋潔 . *Kindai Nissen kankei no kenkyū* 近代日鮮關係の研究 (A study of modern Korean-Japanese relations). 2 vols. Keijo, Chōsen sōtokufu chūsū in, 1940.

———*Nisshin sen'eki gaikō shi no kenkyū* 日清戰役外交史研究 (A diplomatic history of the Sino-Japanese war, 1894-1895). Tōyō Bunko ronsō 東洋文庫論叢 (Tōyō Bunko Publication Series), no. 32. Tokyo, 1951.

T'aejo sillok 太祖實錄 (The annals of King T'aejo). 15 *kwŏn.*

Taejŏn hoet'ong 大典會通 (New comprehensive code of administration). Reprint. Keijo, 1912.

Taejŏn husongnok 大典後續錄(Late supplement to the great code). Reprint. Keijo, Chōsen sōtokufu chūsū in, 1935.

Taejŏn songnok 大典續錄 (Early supplement to the great code). Reprint. Keijo, Chōsen sōtokufu chūsū in, 1935.

Taejŏn t'ongp'yŏn 大典通編 (Comprehensive code of administration). Reprint. Keijo, Chōsen sōtokufu, 1937.

T'aejong sillok 太宗實錄 (The annals of King T'aejong). 36 *kwŏn*.

Tagawa Kōzō 田川孝三 . "Kindai Hokusen nōson shakai to ryūmin mondai" 近代北鮮農村社會と流民問題 (The agrarian society of Northern Korea in the modern era and the problems of migration), in *Kindai Chōsen shi kenkyū* 近代朝鮮史研究 (Studies in the history of modern Korea), comp. Chōsen shi henshū kai, pp. 407-625. Keijo, 1944.

———*Richō kōnōsei no kenkyū* 李朝貢納制の研究 (A study on the tribute system of the Ri dynasty). Tōyō Bunko ronsō, no. 47. Tokyo, 1964.

Takada Shinji 高田真治 et al. *Jukyō no shiteki gaikan* 儒教の史的概觀 (A historical outline of Confucianism). Tokyo, 1937.

Taki Kumanosuke 瀧熊之助 . *Shina keigaku shi gaisetsu* 支那經學史概說 (A general outline of Chinese Confucianism). Tokyo, 1934.

Tanjong sillok 端宗實錄 (The annals of King Tanjong). 14 *kwŏn*.

Tochi seido chizei seido chōsa hōkokusho 土地制度地税制度調査報告書 (Reports on the findings about the land and tax system). Keijo, Chōsen sōtokufu, 1920.

Tokugawa Keiki-kō den 德川慶喜公傳 (Biography of Tokugawa Keiki), comp. Shibusawa Eiichi 澁澤榮一 . 8 vols. Tokyo, 1913-1918.

Tonggyŏng taejŏn pu yongdam yusa 東經大典附龍潭遺詞 (The scripture of the Tonghak and the posthumous poems of Ch'oe Che-u). Seoul, 1955.

Tonghak kyŏngŭi 東學經義 (An interpretation of the Tonghak tenets), ed. Pak Chŏng-dong 朴晶東 . 2 *p'yŏn*. Seoul, 1914.

Tongmun hwigo wŏnp'yŏn 同文彙考原編 (Historical records of Korea's relations with China and Japan), rev. Tabohashi Kiyoshi. 2 vols. Keijo, 1936 and 1937.

T'ongmun kwan chi 通文館志 (Record of the Bureau of Interpreters), rev. and enlarged by Sayŏgwŏn in 1862. Reprint. 12 *kwŏn*. Keijo, Chōsen sōtokufu, 1944.

Tongnaebu kyerok 東萊府啓錄 (Dispatches from the Tongnae district government), comp. Pibyŏnsa and Ŭijŏngbu. 9 *kwŏn*. 1849-1889.

Up'och'ŏng tŭngnok 右捕廳謄錄 (Records of the right metropolitan police headquarters), comp. Up'och'ŏng. 26 *kwŏn*. 1807-1881.

Urakawa Wasaburō 浦川和三郎. *Chōsen junkyō shi* 朝鮮殉教史 (A history of Korean martyrdom). Osaka, 1944.

U.S. Department of Navy, *Asiatic Squadron Letters,* vol. 1.

———*Instructions to Flag Officers,* vol. 6.

U.S. Department of State. *Dispatches to Consuls,* vol. 49.

———*Credences,* vol. 4.

———*Consular Dispatches,* vols, 9-11.

———*Papers Relating to Foreign Relations, 1867-1871.*

Wagner, Edward W. "The Literati Purges." Ph.D. thesis, Harvard University, 1959.

Yamaguchi Masayuki 山口正之. "Yasokai senkyōshi no Chōsen furyo kyūzai oyobi kyōka" 耶蘇會宣教師の朝鮮俘虜救濟及び教化 (The relief and evangelization of Korean prisoners of war by Christian missionaries), *Seikyū gakusō,* 4:38-50 (May 1931).

———"Shōken seishi to Tō Jaku-bō" 昭顯世子と湯若望 (Sohyŏn Seja and Johann Adam Schall), *Seikyū gakusō,* 5:101-117 (August 1931).

———"Kinsei Chōsen ni okeru seigaku shisō no tōzen to sono hatten" 近世朝鮮に於ける西學思想の東漸と其の發展(The coming of Christian thought to Korea and its development), in *Oda sensei shōju kinen Chōsen ronshū* 小田先生頌壽記念朝鮮論集 (Collection of studies on Korea in commemoration of Oda Shōgo's sixtieth birthday), pp. 1005-40. Keijo, 1934.

———"Kō Shi-ei hakusho no kenkyū" 黄嗣永帛書の研究 (A study of Hwang Sa-yŏng's *paeksŏ*). Osaka, 1946.

———"Yakuchū Kō Shi-ei hakusho" 譯註黄嗣永帛書 (The letter of Hwang Sa-yŏng on silk cloth), tr. and annotated, *Chōsen gakuhō,* 2:121-154 (1951).

Yangjŏn p'yŏn'go 兩銓便攷 (Manual for the departments of Appointment and War), preface by Nam Pyŏng-gil 南秉吉 . 2 vols. 1865.

Yejong sillok 睿宗實錄 (The annals of King Yejong). 8 *kwŏn.*

Yi Chung-hwan 李重煥. *T'aengni chi* 擇里誌 (A geography of Korea), ed. Ch'oe Nam-sŏn 崔南善 . Seoul, 1912.

Yi Hang-no 李恒老 . *Hwasŏ chip* 華西集 (Collected works). 22 vols. 1899.

Yi Hyŏn-jong 李鉉淙. *Chosŏn chŏn'gi taeil kyosŏpsa yŏn'gu* 朝鮮前期對日交涉史研究 (A study of Korean-Japanese relations in the early Yi dynasty). Han'guk yŏn'gu ch'ongsŏ, no. 10. Seoul, 1964.

Yi I 李珥 . *Yulgok chŏnsŏ* 栗谷全書 (Collected works). Reprint. Seoul, 1958.

Yi Ik 李瀷 . *Sŏngho saesŏl* 星湖僿說 (Collected works), collated by Chŏng In-bo 鄭寅普 . 10 *kwŏn.* Seoul, 1929.

Yi Ki 李沂 . *Haehak yusŏ* 海鶴遺書 (Posthumous collection of works). Han'guk saryo ch'ongsŏ, no. 3. Seoul, 1955.

Yi Kŏn-ch'ang 李建昌 . *Tangŭi t'ongnyak* 黨議通略 (A general history of factional strife), rendered in modern Korean by Yi Pyŏng-sik 李丙植 and Yi Min-su 李民樹. Seoul, 1948.

Yi Kŏn-myŏng 李健命 . *Hanp'ojae chip* 寒圃齋集 (Posthumous works), in *Chōsen fūzoku kankei shiryō satsuyō,* pp. 1874-75.

Yi Kyu-gyŏng 李圭景 . *Oju yŏnmun changjŏn san'go* 五洲衍文長箋散稿 (Collected works). Reprint. 60 *kwŏn.* Seoul, 1959.

Yi Man-ch'ae 李晩采 . *Pyŏgwi p'yŏn* 闢衛編 (A study of Catholicism). 7 *kwŏn.* Seoul, 1931.

Yi Man-un 李萬運 . *Kinyŏn aram* 紀年兒覽 . Reprint. 7 *kwŏn.* Keijo, 1911.

Yi Nŭng-hwa 李能和 . *Chosŏn kidokkyo kŭp oegyo sa* 朝鮮基督教及外交史 (A history of Christianity and diplomacy in Korea). 2 pts. Seoul, 1928.

Yi Pyŏng-do 李丙燾 . *Tugye chapp'il* 斗溪雜筆 (Essays). Seoul, 1956.

Yi Pyŏng-sŏng 李秉成 . *Sunam sŏnsaeng munjip* 順菴先生文集 (Collected works), in *Chōsen fūzoku kankei shiryō satsuyō,* pp. 1862-66.

Yi Sang-baek 李相佰 . *Han'guk sa: kŭnse chŏn'gi p'yŏn* 韓國史 近世前期篇 (A history of Korea: Early pre-modern part). Seoul, 1962.

———*Han'guk sa, kŭnse hugi p'yŏn* 韓國史近世後期篇 (A history of Korea: Later pre-modern part). Seoul, 1965.

Yi Sŏn-gŭn 李瑄根. *Han'guk sa, ch'oegŭnse p'yŏn* 韓國史最近世篇 (A history of Korea: Modern part). Seoul, 1961.

Yi Su-gwang 李晬光 . *Chibong yusŏl* 芝峰類説 (Collected works). Reprint. 2 vols. Keijo, 1915.

Yi T'ae-wang 李太王 . *Chuyŏn sŏnjip* 珠淵選集 (Selected works of King Kojong), ed. Aoyanagi Kōtarō. Keijo, 1919.

Yi Ton-hwa 李敦化 . *Ch'ŏndo'gyo ch'anggŏn rok* 天道教創建錄 (A history of the founding of the Tonghak). Keijo, 1934.

Yŏngch'ŏn chŏnji 永川全誌 (Gazetteer of Yŏngch'ŏn). New and enlarged ed. 2 *kwŏn*. 1940.

Yongho kannok 龍湖間錄. 25 *kwŏn*.

Yŏngjo sillok 英祖實錄 (The annals of King Yŏngjo). 127 *kwŏn*.

Yŏngju kunji 榮州郡誌 (Gazetteer of Yŏngju). New and enlarged ed. 4 *kwŏn*. 1957.

Yŏnsan-gun ilgi 燕山君日記 (The annals of King Yŏnsan). 63 *kwŏn*.

Yoshikawa Buntarō 吉川文太郎 . *Chōsen no shūkyō* 朝鮮の宗教 (Religions of Korea). Keijo, 1921.

Yu Cha-hu 柳子厚 . *Chosŏn pobusang ko* 朝鮮褓負商攷 (A study of Korean peddlers). Seoul, 1948.

Yu Hong-nyŏl 柳洪烈 . "Raimatsu Sensho no shigaku" 麗末鮮初の私學 (Private schools in late Koryŏ and early Yi Korea), *Seikyū gakusō*, 24:64-119 (May 1936).

———"Chōsen ni okeru shoin no seiritsu" 朝鮮に於ける書院の成立 (On the establishment of *sŏwŏn* in Korea), *Seikyū gakusō*, 29:24-90 (August 1937); 30:63-116 (October 1939).

———*Han'guk ch'ŏnju kyohoe sa* 韓國天主教會史 (A history of the Catholic Church in Korea). Seoul, 1962.

———*Kojong ch'iha sŏhak sunan ŭi yŏn'gu* 高宗治下西學受難의研究 (Studies on Catholic persecution during King Kojong's reign [1863-1907]). Seoul, 1962.

Yu Hyŏng-wŏn 柳馨遠. *Pan'gye surok* 磻溪隨錄 (Collected works). Reprint. 27 *kwŏn*. Seoul, 1958.

Yu In-sŏk 柳麟錫. *Chaegyŏk paekkwan mun* 再檄百官文. 1896.

Yu Kye 俞棨. *Sinam chip* 市南集 (Collected works), in *Chōsen fūzoku kankei shiryō satsuyō*, pp. 1693-96.

Yu Mong-in 柳夢寅. *Ŏu yadam* 於于野談 (Collected essays).

GLOSSARY

amhaeng ǒsa 暗行御史
An Tong-jun 安東晙
anhaeksa 按覈使

ch'abigwan 差備官
Ch'ae Che-gong 蔡濟恭
chejo 提調
chikchǒn 職田
Chinmuyǒng 鎮撫營
chinsang 進上
Cho Kwang-sun 趙光淳
Cho Tu-sun 趙斗淳
chǒbwigwan 接慰官
Ch'oe Che-sǒn 崔濟宣
Ch'oe Che-u 崔濟愚
Ch'oe Ik-hyǒn 崔益鉉
Ch'oe Ok 崔沃
chojǒk 糶糴
ch'ǒmwi 僉尉
Chǒng Hyǒn-dǒk 鄭顯德
Chǒng Kae-ch'ǒng 鄭介清
Chǒng Ki-wǒn 鄭岐源
Chǒng Wǒn-yong 鄭元容
Chǒng Yag-yong 丁若鏞
Chǒng Yǒ-rip 鄭汝立
Chongbusi 宗簿寺
Chonghak 宗學
Chonhwap'a 尊華派
Chu Se-bung 周世鵬
Ch'uksǒngsa 築城司
Chungch'ubu 中樞府

Chwap'och'ǒng 左捕廳

Han Kye-wǒn 韓啓源
Hanabusa Yoshitada 花房義質
Hong Kyǒng-nae 洪景來
Hong Pong-ju 洪鳳周
Hong Sun-mok 洪淳穆
Hong Tae-yong 洪大溶
hose 戶稅
hǔkp'ae 黑牌
hundo 訓導
hundo pyǒlch'a 訓導別差
hǔngni waein 興利倭人
Hǔngsǒn Taewǒn'gun 興宣大院君
Hwang In-jǒm 黃仁點
Hwang Sa-yǒng 黃嗣永
Hwang Sim 黃沁
Hwasǒ 華西
hyanggyo 鄉校

Ijǒngch'ǒng 釐整廳
Iksǒng kun 翼成君
Im Paek-kyǒng 任白經
Inp'yǒng taegun 麟平大君
iyong husaeng 利用厚生

ka hundo 假訓導
Kang No 姜㳛
kanji saiban 幹事裁判
Kiboyǒnhae sunmuyǒng 畿輔沒海巡撫營
Kim Chǒng-hǔi 金正喜

Kim Chwa-gŭn	金左根		nanggwan	郎官
Kim Hŭng-gŭn	金興根		Noron	老論
Kim Mun-gŭn	金汶根			
Kim Pyŏng-hak	金炳學		Ŏ Chae-yŏn	魚在淵
Kim Se-ho	金世鎬		Ŏyŏngch'ŏng	御營廳
Kim Tae-gŏn	金大建			
Kim Yun-sik	金允植		Pak Mun-su	朴文秀
kŏmsang	檢詳		Pibyŏnsa	備邊司
kongsagwan	公事官		pokchuch'on	福酒村
kongsin	功臣		pop'o	保布
kongsinjŏn	功臣田		p'ori	逋吏
kosin	告身		p'oryangmi	砲粮米
Kŭmwiyŏng	禁衛營		p'osu	砲手
kungbangjŏn	宮房田		Pugin	北人
kunp'o	軍布		pujejo	副提調
kwajŏn	科田		pukhak	北學
kyŏl	結		p'um	品
kyŏlchŏn	結錢		puma	駙馬
kyŏlmi	結米		Pumabu	府
kyŏng	頃		puwi	副尉
kyori	校理		Pyŏkp'a	僻派
Kyujanggak	奎章閣		pyŏlsajŏn	別賜田
kyunyŏkpŏp	均役法			
			saaek sŏwŏn	賜額書院
Mandongmyo	萬東廟		saiban shokei	裁判書契
Min Ch'i-sang	閔致庠		sain	舍人
Min Pi	閔妃		Samgun toch'ongjebu	
mukwa	武科		三軍都摠制府	
munin	文引		sangp'yŏng t'ongbo	常平通寶
munkwa	文科		sarok	司錄
Myŏnam	勉菴		segyŏnsŏn	歲遣船
			silsa kusi	實事求是
Nam Chong-sam	南鍾三		Sin Kwan-ho	申觀浩
Namin	南人		Sip'a	時派

Sirhak	實學
sŏban	西班
soch'asa	小差使
sŏgyŏng	小經
sŏhak	西學
sŏjanggwan	書狀官
Song Si-yŏl	宋時烈
Sŏnggyun'gwan	成均館
sŏnghŏn	成憲
sŏnjŏn'gwan	宣傳官
sŏnmu kun'gwan	選武軍官
Soron	小論
sŏsa	小署事
sot'ongsa	小通事
sŏwŏn	書院
sujigin	受職人
sŭngji	承旨
Sungjŏngwŏn	承政院
Sŭngmunwŏn	承文院
taech'asa	大差使
taegwan (taikan in Jap.)	代官
Taewŏn'gun	大院君
taishū taisashi	大大差使
tangbaekchŏn	當百錢
t'oho	土豪
tojang	導掌
tojejo	都提調
Tollyŏngbu	敦寧府
tongban	東班
Tonghak	東學
tosŏ	圖書
Ŭibinbu	儀賓府

Ŭihŭng samgunbu	義興三軍府
Ŭijŏngbu	議政府
ŭimang	擬望
ŭmban	陰班
Up'och'ŏng	右捕廳
Wang Chŏng-yang	王庭揚
wŏnnapchŏn	願納錢
Yabe Junshuku	八戶順叔
Yang Hŏn-su	梁憲洙
yangban	兩班
yangyŏk	良役
Yi Ch'oe-ŭng	李最應
Yi Ha-ŭng	李昰應
Yi Hang-no	李恒老
Yi Kyŏng-ha	李景夏
Yi Kyŏng-jae	李景在
Yi Myŏng-bok	李命福
Yi Sŏng-gye	李成桂
Yi Sŭng-hun	李承薰
Yi Tong-uk	李東郁
Yi Wŏn-hŭi	李元熙
Yi Yong-hŭi	李容熙
Yi Yu-wŏn	李裕元
Yŏgakchuin	旅閣主人
Yu Hu-jo	柳厚祚
Yu Sŏng-nyong	柳成龍
yuhyŏn	儒賢
yurim	儒林
yusa	有司
yusa tangsang	有司堂上

INDEX

clan), 67
Chŏn'gye, Grand Prince, 181n1
Chŏnho, 2
Chonhwap'a, 167
Chŏnjo (rent), 2-4
Chŏnse (tax), 2-4, 6
Chŏrilche (examination given four times
   a year), 78, 79
Ch'oryang, 138, 141, 148, 155, 157, 159,
   161, 163
Chōsen shuppei ("dispatch of troops to
   Korea"), 164
Chou Wen-mo (P. Jacques Tsiou), 93
Chu Se-bung, 70, 211n1
Ch'uksŏngsa, 45
Chungch'ubu, 45, 200n18
Chungch'uwŏn, 42, 44, 119n11,
   200n18
Chungjong, King, 7, 43
Ch'un'gwan t'onggo, 80
Chwap'och'ŏng, 48
Cowles, John P., Jr., 127, 128

Dajōkan, 145, 154, 156, 164, 165
Daveluy, Marie-Antoine-Nicolas, 94f.
Departments, the six, 42, 43, 46
Drew, Edward B., 127, 131, 133

Etō Shimpei, 165

Factionalism, xvi, xvii, 9, 19, 65, 92,
   166, 205n2
Febinger, Capt. John C., 119, 121, 125
Féron, Stanislas, 96, 112, 120
Ferréol, Jean-Joseph, 94
Fish, Hamilton, 122, 123, 130, 131
Fukami Rokurō (Masakage), 159, 161-
   163
Furuga Chikugo-no-kami 140

General Sherman, 50, 114, 115, 117-120,
   123-125, 143
Goldsborough, Commodore J.R., 118
Gotō Shojirō, 165
Govéa, Bishop, 93
Gramon, Father de, 92

Haeng chisa (first assistant president of
   the re-established Military Council),
   49
Han Kye-wŏn, 55, 57, 171, 174, 175
Han River, 99-103, 107, 128, 129
Hanabusa Yoshitada, 162, 163
Hanjŏn (limitation of landholding), 16
Hermit nation, 82
Hideyoshi invasions (Japanese invasions),
   5, 7, 38, 56, 74, 83, 136, 144, 218n4
Higuchi Tetsusaburō, 147-149, 157, 159
Hirayama Keichū, 140, 141
Hirose Naoyuki, 157, 159, 161-163
Hirotsu Hironobu, 155, 156, 159-161
Hŏ Kyun, 91
Hŏ Mok, 71
Hojo pyŏlbi hyŏllok, 36
Hong Chae-hak, 167
Hong Kyŏng-nae, uprising of, 60
Hong Man-sŏp, 175
Hong Pong-ju, 95, 96
Hong Si-hyŏng, 172
Hong Sun-mok, 55, 57, 171, 174, 175
Hong Tae-yong, 13, 19
Hong Yŏng-sik, 63
Hongmun'gwan (Academy of Literature),
   62
Hongmun'gwan chi, 62, 214n43
Hŏnjong, King, 56, 60
Hop'o (household tax), 35, 40, 172,
   196n23
Hose, 40
Hundo (language officer), 138
[Hundo] pyŏlch'a (assistant language
   officer), 138, 148
Hŭngni waein (speculator), 134
Hwang Sa-yŏng, 93
Hwang Sim, 93
Hwanja (gathering and distributing of
   grain), 6
Hwayang Academy, 72
Hyanggyo (local Confucian shrines), 3,
   9, 76
Hyanggyojŏn, 3
Hyangsa ("shrine"), 70
Hyŏn P'ung-sŏ, 162, 163

HARVARD EAST ASIAN MONOGRAPHS

18. Frank H. H. King (ed.) and Prescott Clarke, *A Research Guide to China-Coast Newspapers, 1822-1911*

19. Ellis Joffe, *Party and Army: Professionalism and Political Control in the Chinese Officer Corps, 1949-1964*

20. Toshio G. Tsukahira, *Feudal Control in Tokugawa Japan: The Sankin Kōtai System*

21. Kwang-Ching Liu, ed., *American Missionaries in China: Papers from Harvard Seminars*

22. George Moseley, *A Sino-Soviet Cultural Frontier: The Ili Kazakh Autonomous Chou*

23. Carl F. Nathan, *Plague Prevention and Politics in Manchuria, 1910-1931*

24. Adrian Arthur Bennett, *John Fryer: The Introduction of Western Science and Technology into Nineteenth-Century China*

25. Donald J. Friedman, *The Road from Isolation: The Campaign of the American Committee for Non-Participation in Japanese Aggression, 1938-1941*

26. Edward Le Fevour, *Western Enterprise in Late Ch'ing China: A Selective Survey of Jardine, Matheson and Company's Operations, 1842-1895*

27. Charles Neuhauser, *Third World Politics: China and the Afro-Asian People's Solidarity Organization, 1957-1967*

28. Kungtu C. Sun, assisted by Ralph W. Huenemann, *The Economic Development of Manchuria in the First Half of the Twentieth Century*

29. Shahid Javed Burki, *A Study of Chinese Communes, 1965*

30. John Carter Vincent, *The Extraterritorial System in China: Final Phase*

31. Madeleine Chi, *China Diplomacy, 1914-1918*

32. Clifton Jackson Phillips, *Protestant America and the Pagan World: The First Half Century of the American Board of Commissioners for Foreign Missions, 1810-1860*

33. James Pusey, *Wu Han: Attacking the Present through the Past*